Chelsea FC
PLAYERS
Who's Who

by Scott Cheshire
photographs Ron Hockings

By the same authors
Chelsea F.C. The full statistical story 1905-1986

© S Cheshire   R Hockings 1987

1st Edition August 1987

All rights reserved. No part of this publication may be
reproduced, stored in a retrieval system, or transmitted
in any form or by any means, electronic, mechanical,
photocopying, recording or otherwise, without the
prior permission of the copyright owners.

Published by Scott Cheshire, Lane End, Barlaston, Stoke-on-Trent,
Staffordshire ST12 9AU

Designed and Typeset by Articulate Studios, Emsworth, Hampshire
Printed and Bound by Redwood Burn, Trowbridge, Wiltshire

Forewords by Ken Bates & Ron Greenwood

On behalf of Scott and Ron I am very pleased to welcome their latest tome on Chelsea.

It is a remarkable achievement to chronicle the history of every player who has ever worn a Chelsea shirt. Unfortunately this, together with their sister book, has effectively killed off all future arguments because the facts are there in black and white.

However, apart from instant reference, it will give many happy hours of pouring over little-known facts and turn us all into Chelsea "Masterminds".

With eager anticipation I await their next project.

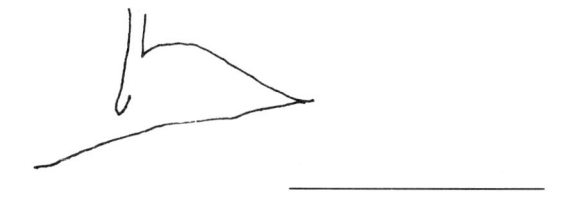

I am delighted to write a foreword for a Chelsea "Who's Who", for I know personally what happy memories spring to mind regarding my association with the Club, and one can imagine what the real Chelsea fans will gain from such a book, and it will no doubt help to settle many a dispute about 'who' and 'when' etc.

Chelsea Football Club is an institution in English football history, and the many players who have worn the coveted blue shirt are part of that history.

To the players of yesterday and to the players of today this book is a tribute to their loyal service.

Abbreviations

FL	=	Football League
FAC	=	F.A. Cup
LC	=	Football League Cup
FC	=	Inter Cities Fairs' Cup
ECWC	=	European Cup Winners' Cup
FMC	=	Full Members' Cup

Players The details of every player who has played League and Cup football in a recognised 1st team competition have been included, excluding those who appeared only in any of the three games at the start of the abandoned 1939-40 season, and which have never been recognised as "official" by the Football League. The seasons covered therefore are: 1905-06 to 1914-15; 1919-20 to 1938-39; 1945-46 (F.A. Cup only); and 1946-47 to 1986-87.

Personal details It has been decided to include heights and weights of players, where known, although it is realised that, especially in the latter, these may vary considerably throughout a playing career. Transfers have been included, with dates and fees involving Chelsea Football Club added, but it is pointed out that quoted fees are in many cases "estimates" obtained from press reports which can also be the subject of surprising variation. The date given for a player joining Chelsea is that of signing professional forms and registered with the Football League.

Positions The terms adopted to describe positions on the field are those normally used at the time of the player's career. For example, the role adopted by a wing-half, or inside-forward, in the 1930s may well have closely corresponded to that of a midfield performer in the 1980s.

LAURENCE ABRAMS

WANTED
If anyone has
a photograph
of
DAVID
It would be appreciated if you
would allow us to copy it.
Please forward it to Ron at
36 Lockier Walk,
Wembley, Middx.
It will be returned safely

DAVID B. ALEXANDER

ABRAMS, Laurence (1914–1920) Wing-half

Born Southport Height 5ft 9½in Weight 12st 12lb. Career Southport Central, Stockport County, Heart of Midlothian, Chelsea (June 1914), Cardiff City (June 1920).
Chelsea details Debut 5.9.14. 49 Appearances 7 Goals.

	Appearances		Goals	
	FL	FAC	FL	FAC
1914–15	31	5	5	–
1919–20	13	–	2	–
Total	44	5	7	–

One of the many players whose career was mutilated by World War I. He established himself in the first-team soon after his arrival at Stamford Bridge, in the left-half position, but after a few games at outside left following the resumption of normal football five years later, he was unable to hold his place. Powerfully built, he was noted for his strong tackling qualities and was most unlucky not to be selected to play for Chelsea in the 1915 FA Cup Final against Sheffield United at Old Trafford.

ALEXANDER, David B. (1939–1945) Wing-half

Born Glasgow. Career Chelsea (1939–45).
Chelsea details Debut 7.4.39. 1 Appearance.

	Appearances		Goals	
	FL	FAC	FL	FAC
1938–39	1	–	–	–
Total	1	–	–	–

A signing from Lancastrian football in the early months of 1939. After making his first-team debut on Good Friday 1939 against Charlton Athletic at The Valley he became a regular member of the side in the first season of war-time "regional" football. An athletically built, skilful player his promising career was ended prematurely by a motor-cycle accident during his Army service and he was invalided out the forces.

ALLEN, Leslie (1954–1959) Forward

Born Dagenham 4.9.37 Height 5ft 8in Weight 10st. Career Briggs Sports, Chelsea (September 1954), Tottenham Hotspur (December 1959, part-exchange Johnny Brooks), Queens Park Rangers.
Honours England U-23 (1 cap), Football League Championship Medal 1961, FA Cup Winner's Medal 1961.
Chelsea details Debut 1.9.56. 49 Appearances 11 Goals

	Appearances			Goals		
	FL	FAC	LC	FL	FAC	LC
1956–57	19	1	–	4	–	–
1957–58	9	1	–	3	–	–
1958–59	11	–	3	3	–	–
1959–60	5	–	–	1	–	–
Total	44	2	3	11	–	–

One of manager Ted Drake's many young signings, his opportunities at Stamford Bridge were reduced by the keen competition for first-team places at that time and he was allowed to move on to Tottenham Hotspur (in part-exchange for Johnny Brooks), where he became an integral part of the famous Spurs 1960–61 League and FA Cup "double" team, playing in every League game and scoring 23 goals. A neat, ball-playing inside, or centre, forward. Father of English international Clive Allen, he was also manager of Swindon Town for a spell.

ALLISTER, John G. (1949–1952) Wing-half

Born Edinburgh 30.6.27 Height 5ft 9in Weight 11st 2lb. Career Tranent Juniors, Chelsea (July 1949), Aberdeen (July 1952), Chesterfield.
Chelsea details Debut 12.3.52. 4 Appearances 1 Goal

	Appearances		Goals	
	FL	FAC	FL	FAC
1951–52	3	–	1	–
1952–53	1	–	–	–
Total	4	–	1	–

A strong, forceful, attacking wing-half who could also perform adequately at centre-forward, he was unable to establish a first-team place at Chelsea but, on returning north of the border, was a member of Aberdeen's Scottish first division team for some six seasons.

LESLIE ALLEN

JOHN G. ALLISTER

LEONARD ALLUM | SYLVAN ANDERTON

ALLUM, Leonard (1932–1939) Wing-half

Born Reading Height 5ft 9in Weight 9st. 12lb. Career Maidenhead United, Chelsea (May 1932), Clapton Orient (May 1939).
Chelsea details Debut 29.10.32. 102 Appearances 2 Goals

	Appearances		Goals	
	FL	FAC	FL	FAC
1932–33	13	1	–	–
1933–34	14	4	–	–
1934–35	22	1	–	–
1935–36	12	2	1	–
1936–37	4	–	–	–
1937–38	15	1	–	–
1938–39	13	–	1	–
Total	93	9	2	–

A slim, light-weight, wing-half with considerable skill on the ball, he proved himself a most dependable reserve player for the seven seasons leading up to the outbreak of World War II. Having won amateur representative honours with Maidenhead United, he was unable to establish himself fully at Stamford Bridge. Moving to Clapton Orient, he played many games for the East London club in regional football throughout the period of hostilities.

ANDERTON, Sylvan (1959–1962) Wing-half

Born Reading 23.11.34 Height 5ft 9in Weight 12st. Career Reading, Chelsea (March 1959, £10,000), QPR (January 1962, £5,000).
Chelsea details Debut 28.3.59. 82 Appearances 2 Goals

	Appearances				Goals			
	FL	FAC	LC	FC	FL	FAC	LC	FC
1958–59	8	–	–	2	–	–	–	–
1959–60	40	2	–	–	1	–	–	–
1960–61	22	1	1	–	1	–	–	–
1961–62	6	–	–	–	–	–	–	–
Total	76	3	1	2	2	–	–	–

After nearly 200 first-team games with Reading, he spent more than three years at Chelsea, mostly in the senior side. A strongly-built, hard-tackling and constructive wing-half, the arrival of Andy Malcolm from West Ham United signalled the end of his days at The Bridge.

ANDERSON, George R. (1927–1929) Centre-Forward

Born Glasgow. Career Airdrieonians, Brentford, Chelsea (May 1927), Norwich City (Summer 1929).
Chelsea details Debut 4.2.28. 9 Appearances

	Appearances		Goals	
	FL	FAC	FL	FAC
1927–28	5	–	–	–
1928–29	4	–	–	–
Total	9	–	–	–

He began his career at Airdrie where he was deputy to Hughie Gallacher, the famous Scottish international centre-forward. At Chelsea he was given several opportunities to establish himself in the first-team but was unable to adapt himself to the faster pace of English first division football.

ARGUE, James (1933–1947) Inside-forward

Born Glasgow 27.11.17 Height 5ft 11in Weight 11st 11lb. Died August 1978. Career St. Roch's Juniors (Glasgow), Birmingham, Chelsea (December 1933, free transfer), Shrewsbury Town (Summer 1947).
Chelsea details Debut 9.12.33. 125 Appearances 35 Goals

	Appearances		Goals	
	FL	FAC	FL	FAC
1933–34	1	–	–	–
1934–35	27	2	5	1
1935–36	9	–	2	–
1936–37	32	2	6	1
1937–38	21	–	9	–
1938–39	27	3	7	3
1946–47	1	–	1	–
Total	118	7	30	5

Jimmy was manager Leslie Knighton's first signing after his appointment in 1933, rejoining his boss from Birmingham. A strongly-built, tough and aggressive inside-forward with a flair for scoring vital goals, he was easily identified by his shock of red hair. He became an integral member of the team in the immediate pre-war period despite missing many games through injury. He was captain of the reserve team in 1946–47 before moving, briefly, to Shrewsbury Town. His son played for St. Johnstone in Scottish League football.

GEORGE R. ANDERSON

JAMES ARGUE

JAMES W. ARMSTRONG

JAMES W. ASHFORD

ARMSTRONG, James W. (1922–1928) Forward

Born Newcastle-on-Tyne Height 5ft 8in Weight 10st. Career Chelsea.
Chelsea details Debut 23.12.22. 31 Appearances 10 Goals

	Appearances		Goals	
	FL	FAC	FL	FAC
1922–23	14	2	7	1
1923–24	13	–	2	–
1924–25	1	–	–	–
1925–26	1	–	–	–
Total	29	2	9	1

After a promising start to his Chelsea career, scoring on his debut against Tottenham Hotspur at White Hart Lane, he never fulfilled his potential, largely because of a somewhat frail physique.

ASHFORD, James W. (1920–1925) Full-back

Born Barlborough (Derbyshire) Height 5ft 8in. Weight 9st 7lb. Career Ebbw Vale, Chelsea (March 1920)
Chelsea details Debut 23.4.21. 8 Appearances

	Appearances		Goals	
	FL	FAC	FL	FAC
1920–21	4	–	–	–
1921–22	2	–	–	–
1922–23	1	–	–	–
1924–25	1	–	–	–
Total	8	–	–	–

A light-weight full/back who made occasional first-team appearances during his five seasons on the staff, deputising for Walter Bettridge, Jack Harrow or George Smith.

ARMSTRONG, Ken (1946–1957) Wing-half

Born Bradford 3.6.24 Died June 1984. Height 5ft 8in Weight 11st. Career Bradford Rovers, Chelsea (December 1946). Retired May 1957.
Honours England International (1 cap), 'B' International (3), Football League XI. Football League Championship Medal 1955.
Chelsea details Debut 23.8.47. 402 Appearances 30 Goals

	Appearances		Goals	
	FL	FAC	FL	FAC
1947–48	42	2	11	2
1948–49	25	3	1	–
1949–50	41	7	–	–
1950–51	40	5	4	–
1951–52	37	9	2	2
1952–53	41	7	1	1
1953–54	40	1	2	–
1954–55	39	3	1	–
1955–56	24	–	–	–
1956–57	33	2	3	–
Total	362	39	25	5

(Also 1 Charity Shield appearance in 1955–56)

One of Chelsea's most popular, and most consistent players. He joined the club from Army football in December 1946 and acclimatised easily to the demands of professional football. For ten seasons he was a permanent fixture in the first-team, usually at right-half but, on occasions, in the forward line. Indeed, in 1947–48 he was top scorer after he had temporarily taken over the centre-forward spot from Tommy Lawton. A polished and artistic performer, he deserved more than the one full international cap which came his way, against Scotland at Wembley in 1955, when England won by a decisive 7–2 margin. He held Chelsea's all-time record of League appearances until Peter Bonetti overtook his total in 1969. Having been granted a testimonial, he retired from football and went to live in New Zealand where he became National Coach. After his death his ashes were strewn on the Stamford Bridge pitch.

KEN ARMSTRONG

TREVOR AYLOTT   JAMES A. BAIN

AYLOTT, Trevor (1975–1979) Striker

Born Bermondsey 26.11.57 Height 6ft 1in Weight 13st 10lb. Career Chelsea (November 1975), Barnsley (November 1979 £50,000), Millwall, Luton Town, Crystal Palace, Barnsley (loan), AFC Bournemouth.
Chelsea details Debut 22.10.77. 29(3) Appearances 2 Goals

	Appearances			Goals		
	FL	FAC	LC	FL	FAC	LC
1977–78	10(1)	1	–	2	–	–
1978–79	13(2)	–	–	–	–	–
1979–80	3	–	–	2	–	–
Total	26(3)	1	–	2	–	–

A heavily-built striker who graduated to full professional status from the Chelsea Juniors without ever establishing himself in the first-team, lacking the finesse to break down first division defences.

BAIN, James A. (1945–1947) Outside-left

Born Blairgowrie 14.12.19 Height 5ft 8in Weight 10st. Career Gillingham, Chelsea (May 1945), Swindon Town (May 1947).
Chelsea details Debut 5.1.46. 14 Appearances 1 Goal

	Appearances		Goals	
	FL	FAC	FL	FAC
1945–46	–	5	–	–
1946–47	9	–	1	–
Total	9	–	1	–

Jimmy had the distinction of being Chelsea's first full-time professional after the end of World War II. Lightly-built, he was unable to establish a regular first-team place but went on to play more than 250 first team games for Swindon Town before retiring in 1953.

BAKER, B. Howard (1921–1926) Goalkeeper

Born Liverpool. Career Corinthians, Northern Nomads, Everton (amateur), Preston North End (amateur), Liverpool (amateur), Chelsea (amateur) (1921–26).
Honours England (2 caps), Football League XI, England amateur international.
Chelsea details Debut 15.10.21. 93 Appearances 1 Goal

	Appearances		Goals	
	FL	FAC	FL	FAC
1921–22	23	1	1	–
1922–23	17	–	–	–
1923–24	11	–	–	–
1924–25	28	–	–	–
1925–26	13	–	–	–
Total	92	1	1	–

One of football's legendary names. One-time British high-jump champion, he was a distinguished and colourful personality who retained his amateur status throughout his playing career. A famous Corinthian footballer who was their goalkeeper at a time when they consistently challenged the best professional teams in the land in the FA Cup competition, he played for Chelsea whenever available for five seasons. His unorthodox methods made him a star attraction wherever he played. The length of his goalkicking, his dashes into midfield and his taking of penalty-kicks were all part of his remarkable repertoire.

B. HOWARD BAKER

TOMMY BALDWIN

BALDWIN, Tommy (1966–1974) Striker

Born Gateshead 10.6.45 Height 5ft 9½in Weight 12st. Career Wrekenton, Arsenal, Chelsea (September 1966, part-exchange George Graham), Gravesend & Northfleet, Millwall, Brentford.
Honours England Under-23 (2 caps), FA Cup winners' medal 1970, loser's medal 1967.
Chelsea details Debut 1.10.66. 227 Appearances 92 Goals

	Appearances					Goals				
	FL	FAC	LC	FC	ECWC	FL	FAC	LC	FC	ECWC
1966–67	30(2)	7	–	–	–	16	1	–	–	–
1967–68	39	4	1	–	–	15	1	–	–	–
1968–69	25	–	2	4	–	16	–	–	1	–
1969–70	17(2)	5	1	–	–	5	1	–	–	–
1970–71	18	2	2	–	4(3)	2	2	1	–	2
1971–72	20	–	5(2)	–	3	10	–	4	–	4
1972–73	11	1	2	–	–	1	–	–	–	–
1973–74	18(1)	2	–	–	–	9	–	–	–	–
1974–75	4	–	0(1)	–	–	–	–	1	–	–
Total	182(5)	21	13(3)	4	7(3)	74	5	6	1	6

Known as the 'sponge' for his ability to retain the ball under pressure and skilfully shield it from opponents while seeking an opening to set up an attack, he was a regular scorer of goals, especially in his early days at The Bridge. While lacking the flair of some of his colleagues he was, nevertheless, a vital cog in the team which made four cup final appearances between 1967 and 1972. He was Coach at Brentford for a period after his playing career ended.

BAMBRICK, Joseph (1934–1938) Centre-forward

Born Belfast. Died 1983. Height 5ft 11in Weight 11st 2lb. Career Linfield, Chelsea (December 1934), Walsall (March 1938).
Honours Ireland (11 caps)
Chelsea details Debut 25.12.34 66 Appearances 37 Goals

	Appearances		Goals	
	FL	FAC	FL	FAC
1934–35	21	2	15	–
1935–36	25	5	15	4
1936–37	10	–	2	–
1937–38	3	–	1	–
Total	59	7	33	4

A prolific scorer of goals whose 6 for Ireland v Wales at Celtic Park, Belfast in February 1930 is still a record. At Linfield he once scored 94 goals in a season. In English football he found the competition a good deal more intense and at Chelsea he contested the centre-forward spot with George Mills. Strongly built, he was a highly intelligent player, a powerful header of the ball and with clever control on the ground.

BANNON, Eamonn (1979) Midfield

Born Edinburgh 18.4.58. Height 5ft 10in Weight 11st 7lb. Career Heart of Midlothian, Chelsea (January 1979, £200,000), Dundee United (November 1979, £170,000).
Honours Scotland (10 caps), Scotland Under 21 (7 caps), Schoolboy International, Scottish League XI (1 appearance), Scottish FA Cup losers' medals 1981, 1985, Scottish League Cup winners' medals 1980, 1981, losers' medals 1982, 1985, Scottish League Championship medal 1983.
Chelsea details Debut 3.2.79 27 Appearances 1 Goal

	Appearances			Goals		
	FL	FAC	LC	FL	FAC	LC
1978–79	19	–	–	1	–	–
1979–80	6	–	2	–	–	–
Total	25	–	2	1	–	–

Manager Danny Blanchflower's first signing for Chelsea. A most talented midfield player who was unable to settle into English football at a time when Chelsea were in the throes of relegation from Division 1 and in dire financial straits. On his return north of the border he rapidly developed into one of his country's outstanding players.

JOSEPH BAMBRICK

EAMONN BANNON

GEORGE F. BARBER

BARBER George F. (1930–1941) Full-back

Born West Ham 1909. Height 6ft 1in Weight 10st 13lb. Career Redhill, Luton Town, Chelsea (May 1930, free-transfer). Retired September 1941.
Chelsea details Debut 26.12.30. 294 Appearances 1 Goal

	Appearances		Goals	
	FL	FAC	FL	FAC
1930–31	11	5	–	–
1931–32	33	6	–	–
1932–33	24	1	–	1
1933–34	31	5	–	–
1934–35	39	2	–	–
1935–36	27	5	–	–
1936–37	41	2	–	–
1937–38	29	1	–	–
1938–39	27	5	–	–
Total	262	32	–	1

One of the best bargain signings ever made by Chelsea. At a time when the club was shelling out large sums of money for star players of proven reputation, he was obtained on a free-transfer and went on to become a reliable pillar of the defence for a decade. Tutored by Scottish international Tommy Law, he was surprisingly light on his feet for such a big man. At home on either right or left, he is perhaps best recalled for his sliding tackle which dispossessed many a startled opponent.

BARKAS, Edward (1937–1939) Full-back

Born Wardley Colliery. Height 5ft 7½in Weight 12st 12lb. Career Bedlington, South Shields, Hebburn Colliery, Huddersfield Town, Birmingham, Chelsea (May 1937), Free transfer May 1939.
Honours Football League Championship medals 1925, 1926, FA Cup losers' medal 1931.
Chelsea details Debut 1.1.38 28 Appearances

	Appearances		Goals	
	FL	FAC	FL	FAC
1937–38	18	1	–	–
1938–39	9	–	–	–
Total	27	1	–	–

Signed by manager Leslie Knighton, under whom he had played at Birmingham, in the twilight of his distinguished career. After sixteen years as a League player, he was, not surprisingly, lacking in pace, but played regularly during the second half of the 1937–38 campaign.

BARRACLOUGH, William (1934–1937) Outside-left

Born Hull 3.1.09. Died August 1969. Height 5ft 4in Weight 9st 10lb. Career Bridlington Town, Hull City (amateur), Wolverhampton Wanderers, Chelsea (October 1934), Colchester United, Doncaster Rovers.
Honours Second Division Championship medal 1932.
Chelsea details Debut 3.11.34 81 Appearances 11 Goals

	Appearances		Goals	
	FL	FAC	FL	FAC
1934–35	29	1	6	–
1935–36	30	5	2	3
1936–37	15	1	–	–
Total	74	7	8	3

A clever winger whose intricate ball skills were sometimes displayed at the cost of directness, a fact which did not make him popular with the Stamford Bridge fans and he became a target for barracking from a section of the crowd.

EDWARD BARKAS

WILLIAM BARARCLOUGH

FRED BARRETT   JAMES BARRON

BARRETT, Fred (1920–27) Full-back

Born Woodford (Essex).
Honours Irish League XI.
Chelsea details Debut 18.9.20 70 Appearances 6 Goals

	Appearances		Goals	
	FL	FAC	FL	FAC
1920–21	10	2	–	–
1921–22	9	1	–	–
1923–24	4	–	–	–
1924–25	7	1	–	–
1925–26	28	2	5	–
1926–27	6	–	1	–
Total	64	6	6	–

Already had six seasons of first-team experience with Belfast Celtic before he signed for Chelsea. Apart from one season, his time at Stamford Bridge was spent mainly in the reserve team. Noted for his long kicking, most of his goals came from set-pieces – he once scored two against Darlington, both from free-kicks.

BARRON, James (1965–66) Goalkeeper

Born Tantobie, Co. Durham 19.10.43 Height 5ft 11in Weight 11st 12lb. Career Newcastle WE, Wolverhampton Wanderers, Chelsea (April 1965, £5,000), Oxford United (March 1966), Nottingham Forest, Swindon Town, Peterborough United.
Chelsea details Debut 1.9.65 1 Appearance

	Appearances			Goals		
	FL	FAC	LC	FL	FAC	LC
1965–66	1	–	–	–	–	–
Total	1	–	–	–	–	–

One of several 'keepers who had the thankless task of understudying Peter Bonetti, he later went on to make some 400 League appearances, most of them at Oxford and Forest, and was also Assistant Manager at Wolverhampton for a time.

BASON, Brian (1972–77) Midfield

Born Epsom 3.9.55. Height 5ft 9in Weight 11st 1lb. Career Chelsea (September 1972), Plymouth Argyle (September 1977 £30,000), Crystal Palace, Portsmouth (Loan), Reading.
Honours England Schoolboy International.
Chelsea details Debut 16.9.72 20(2) Appearances 1 Goal

	Appearances			Goals		
	FL	FAC	LC	FL	FAC	LC
1972–73	4	–	–	–	–	–
1975–76	8(1)	–	0(1)	1	–	–
1976–77	6	–	2	–	–	–
Total	18(1)	–	2(1)	1	–	–

Making his first-team debut while still an apprentice, he was converted from striker to midfield player. Strong in the tackle and ever-willing to move forward on to attack, his Chelsea career was retarded by a double fracture of the right shin in a League cup tie at Arsenal just when he seemed likely to establish a regular place in the senior side.

BATHGATE, Sidney (1946–1953) Full-back

Born Aberdeen 20.12.19 Died 1963 Height 5ft 8in Weight 11st 6lb. Career Parkvale Juniors (Aberdeen), Chelsea (September 1946), Hamilton Academicals (1953).
Chelsea details Debut 4.1.47 147 Appearances

	Appearances		Goals	
	FL	FAC	FL	FAC
1946–47	7	1	–	–
1947–48	32	2	–	–
1948–49	17	–	–	–
1949–50	10	–	–	–
1950–51	34	3	–	–
1951–52	32	6	–	–
1952–53	3	–	–	–
Total	135	12	–	–

Having lost important seasons of his playing career during the Second World War, he joined Chelsea on demobilisation from the R.A.F. Stockily built, he gave loyal service to the club, often unsure of a regular first-team spot with competition from Welsh internationals Billy Hughes and Danny Winter. A good tackler with a sound positional sense, if a little short of pace, he was a defender of the old school.

BRIAN BASON

SIDNEY BATHGATE

THOMAS J. BAXTER

Dr. JOHN B. BELL

BAXTER, Thomas J. (1919–1920) Wing-half

Born London Height 5ft 9½in Weight 12st.
Career Army football with the Salonika Expeditionary Force, Chelsea (September 1919), Free transfer May 1920.
Chelsea details Debut 27.9.19 1 Appearance

	Appearances		Goals	
	FL	FAC	FL	FAC
1919–20	1	–	–	–
Total	1	–	–	–

Although he was a regular member of the Combination side in the first season after World War I, he was unable to break through into the first-team.

BELL, Dr. John B. (1920–23) Winger

Born Barrow-in-Furness Height 5ft 8½in Weight 11st 10lb. Career Queen's Park, Chelsea (amateur) August 1920, Professional July 1921.
Chelsea details Debut 11.9.20 44 Appearances 10 Goals

	Appearances		Goals	
	FL	FAC	FL	FAC
1920–21	6	–	2	–
1921–22	24	1	5	1
1922–23	12	1	2	–
Total	42	2	9	1

Arrived at Chelsea with the reputation of being the fastest player in the Scottish League. After one season he signed professional forms, but he was never a great favourite with the Stamford Bridge crowd, although he continued his association with the club and signed professional while still fulfilling his medical duties.

BELLETT, Walter R. (1954–1958) Full-back

Born Stratford 14.11.33 Height 5ft 9in Weight 11st 10lb. Career Barking, Chelsea (September 1954), Plymouth Argyle (December 1958, £12,000 with Len Casey), Leyton Orient, Chester, Wrexham, Tranmere Rovers.
Honours England Youth International.
Chelsea details Debut 11.3.56 35 Appearances 1 Goal

	Appearances		Goals	
	FL	FAC	FL	FAC
1955–56	2	–	–	–
1956–57	10	–	–	–
1957–58	20	–	1	–
1958–59	3	–	–	–
Total	35	–	1	–

Hard tackling and quick off the mark, this rugged defender was a contemporary of the brothers Sillett and, apart from one extended run in the first-team, was unable to claim a regular place.

BENNETT, Walter (1922–1924) Wing-half

Career Chelsea (October 1922), Not retained May 1924.
Chelsea details Debut 18.11.22 5 Appearances

	Appearances		Goals	
	FL	FAC	FL	FAC
1922–23	1	–	–	–
1923–24	4	–	–	–
Total	5	–	–	–

A wing-half who was on the staff for almost two seasons, playing mostly in the reserve team at a time when Jack Priestley, Tommy Meehan and Harold Wilding were the recognised choices for the half-back positions.

WALTER R. BENNETT

WALTER BENNETT

ROY F.T. BENTLEY

BENTLEY, Roy F.T. (1948–56) Inside/Centre-forward

Born Bristol 17.5.24 Height 5ft 10in Weight 12st. Career Bristol City, Newcastle United, Chelsea (January 1948, £11,000), Fulham (August 1956), Queen's Park Rangers.
Honours England (12 caps), England 'B' (1 cap), Football League XI (3 appearances), Football League Championship medal 1955
Chelsea details Debut 17.1.48 367 Appearances 150 Goals

	Appearances		Goals	
	FL	FAC	FL	FAC
1947–48	14	1	3	–
1948–49	40	3	20	2
1949–50	39	6	17	5
1950–51	38	5	8	3
1951–52	32	9	12	5
1952–53	37	7	12	5
1953–54	41	1	21	–
1954–55	41	3	21	–
1955–56	38	7	14	1
1956–57	4	–	–	–
Total	324	42	128	21

(also: 1 F.A. Charity Shield appearance and 1 goal, 1955-56)

Captain of the 1955 Football League Championship team, and one of the outstanding players in Chelsea's history. Signed as an inside-forward, he was soon converted into a goalscoring centre-forward of somewhat unorthodox method for those days, employing a degree of mobility which frequently saw him raiding down the flanks. A superb header of the ball, he was Chelsea's leading scorer for eight consecutive seasons. Finishing his career with Fulham and Queen's Park Rangers, for which clubs he played more than 200 first-team games, mostly at centre-half. After retiring as a player he managed Reading and Swansea Town for a spell and subsequently became secretary, first at Reading and later with Aldershot.

BERRY, Paul (1953–1960) Centre-half
Born Chadwell St Mary, Essex 15.11.35 Height 6ft Weight 11st 9lb. Career Chelsea (April 1953), Tonbridge (Summer 1960).
Chelsea details Debut 9.3.57 3 Appearances

	Appearances		Goals	
	FL	FAC	FL	FAC
1956–57	2	–	–	–
1957–58	1	–	–	–
Total	3	–	–	–

A product of the Chelsea Juniors, this tall defender spent nine years on the staff playing almost entirely in the reserve and 'A' teams.

BETTRIDGE, Walter (1909–1922) Full-back
Born Oakthorpe (Leics) Died 1931 Height 5ft 8in Weight 10st 3lb Career Burton United, Chelsea (May 1909), Gillingham (Summer 1922).
Honours F.A. Cup final losers' medal 1915.
Chelsea details Debut 16.10.09 255 Appearances

	Appearances		Goals	
	FL	FAC	FL	FAC
1909–10	18	2	–	–
1910–11	37	6	–	–
1911–12	26	2	–	–
1912–13	33	1	–	–
1913–14	16	1	–	–
1914–15	25	8	–	–
1919–20	41	5	–	–
1920–21	28	6	–	–
Total	224	31	–	–

One of the famous names in Chelsea's history. A stalwart full-back who played regularly in the first-team for 11 seasons (apart from one year during World War I when he was not available). Spotted while playing juniors football in the Burton-on-Trent area, he was one of the first defenders to recognise the advantage of adopting an attacking role. He was also renowned for his consistency and length of kicking. Partnered Jock Cameron in the promotion season of 1911–12 and Jack Harrow in 1914–15, when Chelsea made their first F.A. Cup final appearance.

| PAUL BERRY | WALTER BETTRIDGE |

SIDNEY H. BIDEWELL

HUGH J.R. BILLINGTON

BIDEWELL, Sidney H. (1937–46) Inside/Centre-forward

Born Watford 6.6.18 Career Wealdstone, Chelsea (May 1937), Retired May 1946.
Chelsea details Debut 4.12.37 4 Appearances 2 Goals

	Appearances		Goals	
	FL	FAC	FL	FAC
1937–38	4	–	2	–
Total	4	–	2	–

Any chance this forceful attacker had of establishing himself in the senior side was ruined by the outbreak of World War II. Made a sensational debut against Huddersfield Town by scoring two goals. But the competition for his position was stiff and he could not sustain his success. Served in the Army during the war and after one game in the 1945–46 "transitional" season did not play again.

BILLINGTON, Hugh J.R. (1948–1951) Centre/Inside-forward

Born Ampthill 24.2.16 Height 5ft 8½in Weight 12st 7lb. Career Waterlows, Luton Town, Chelsea (March 1948, £8,000), Worcester City (Summer 1951).
Honours Third Division South Championship medal 1937.
Chelsea details Debut 13.3.48 90 Appearances 32 Goals

	Appearances		Goals	
	FL	FAC	FL	FAC
1947–48	12	–	2	–
1948–49	16	–	3	–
1949–50	35	6	17	3
1950–51	20	1	6	1
Total	83	7	28	4

He came to Chelsea towards the end of a long and honourable career spent, previously, entirely with Luton Town, and at the age of 33 experienced his first complete season of First Division football, ending up joint-leading goalscorer with Roy Bentley. Powerfully built, he possessed a strong shot, from either foot, and many of his goals came from long-range efforts.

BIRCHENHALL, Alan (1967–1970) Striker

Born East Ham Height 5ft 11½in Weight 13st 1lb. Career Sheffield United, Chelsea (November 1967, £100,000), Crystal Palace (June 1970, £100,000), Leicester City, Notts County, Memphis Rogues, Blackburn Rovers, Luton Town, Hereford United.
Honours England Under-23 (4 caps).
Chelsea details Debut 2.12.67 95(1) Appearances 28 Goals

	Appearances				Goals			
	FL	FAC	LC	FC	FL	FAC	LC	FC
1967–68	21	5	–	–	5	2	–	–
1968–69	39	5	3	4	12	1	1	2
1969–70	14(1)	–	4	–	3	–	2	–
Total	74(1)	10	7	4	20	3	3	2

This tall blond striker was manager Dave Sexton's first major signing for Chelsea. Lost his place to Ian Hutchinson early in the 1969–70 season, transferring to Crystal Palace at the end of that campaign to become one of soccer's nomads. After moving into midfield in the later part of his career, he became P.R.O. with Leicester City when his playing days ended.

BIRNIE, Edward L. (1906–1910) Centre-half/Wing-half

Career Newcastle United, Crystal Palace, Chelsea (August 1906), Not retained May 1910.
Chelsea details Debut 8.9.06 108 Appearances 3 Goals

	Appearances		Goals	
	FL	FAC	FL	FAC
1906–07	24	2	1	–
1907–08	36	2	1	–
1908–09	31	3	1	–
1909–10	10	–	–	–
Total	101	7	3	–

A fine commanding defender, Ted played most of his football for Chelsea at left-half where his speed, heading ability, and intelligent reading of the game made him a tremendous asset in the first promotion side of 1906–07. After his playing career ended, he became manager of Southend United and, later, with a German club.

ALAN BIRCHENHALL

EDWARD L. BIRNIE

| SIDNEY M. BISHOP | GEORGE W. BISWELL |

BISHOP, Sidney M. (1928–1933) Wing-half

Born London 1899 Died 1949 Height 6ft 0in Weight 10st 11lb. Career Ilford, West Ham United, Leicester City, Chelsea (June 1928, £4,500), Retired (May 1933).
Honours England (4 caps), F.A. Cup final losers' medal 1923.
Chelsea details Debut 25.8.28 109 Appearances 6 Goals

	Appearances		Goals	
	FL	FAC	FL	FAC
1928–29	21	–	2	–
1929–30	36	1	3	–
1930–31	22	5	–	1
1931–32	17	–	–	–
1932–33	7	–	–	–
Total	103	6	5	1

A cultured and highly skilled half-back who came to Chelsea to finish his days as a respected and fine professional footballer, playing a crucial part in gaining promotion from the Second Division in the spring of 1930. He had first been noticed playing for the R.A.F. and was recruited by West Ham from amateur football. Having left the East enders in November 1926, he spent eighteen months in the Midlands, with Leicester City, but failed to settle there.

BISWELL, George W. (1928–29) Inside-forward/Wing-half

Born Watford Height 5ft 8½in Weight 11st 2lb. Career St Albans City, Watford (amateur), Charlton Athletic, Chelsea (January 1928), Ards Charlton Athletic.
Chelsea details Debut 28.1.28 25 Appearances 10 Goals

	Appearances		Goals	
	FL	FAC	FL	FAC
1927–28	5	–	1	–
1928–29	18	1	9	–
1929–30	1	–	–	–
Total	24	1	10	–

Something of a "utility" player, he played for Chelsea mostly in the forward line, but, especially later in his career, was looked upon mainly as a wing-half. Unable to tie down a regular first-team place at Stamford Bridge he was on the staff for just over a year. Also a fine golfer.

BLOCK, Michael (1957–62) Winger

Born Ipswich 28.1.40 Height 5ft 11in Weight 12st 7lb. Career Chelsea (February 1957), Brentford (January 1962, £5,000), Watford.
Honours England Youth International.
Chelsea details Debut 11.9.57 40 Appearances 6 Goals

	Appearances			Goals		
	FL	FAC	FC	FL	FAC	FC
1957–58	20	–	–	4	–	–
1958–59	13	2	1	1	–	–
1959–60	2	–	–	–	–	–
1960–61	1	–	–	–	–	–
1961–62	1	–	–	1	–	–
Total	37	2	1	6	–	–

A product of the Chelsea Youth Scheme who never quite fulfilled his early promise. Speedy, despite his stocky build, he was unable to displace Peter Brabrook and Frank Blunstone from the wing positions in the first-team but moved on to become a regular in the Brentford side for five seasons.

BOLLAND, Gordon (1960–1962) Inside-forward

Born Boston 12.8.43 Height 5ft 10½in Weight 11st 3lb. Career Boston United (amateur), Chelsea (August 1960), Leyton Orient (March 1962, £8,000), Norwich City, Charlton Athletic, Millwall.
Chelsea details Debut 9.12.61 2 Appearances

	Appearances			Goals		
	FL	FAC	LC	FL	FAC	LC
1961–62	2	–	–	–	–	–
Total	2	–	–	–	–	–

Joined the Chelsea Juniors in February 1959 and turned professional 18 months later. Unable to win a first-team place at Stamford Bridge he, nevertheless, went on to play more than 400 League games with four other clubs, notching up a century of goals.

MICHAEL BLOCK

GORDON BOLLAND

FRANK BLUNSTONE   PETER BONETTI

BLUNSTONE, Frank (1953–1964) Outside-left

Born Crewe 17.10.34 Height 5ft 6in Weight 11st 6lb. Career Crewe Alexandra, Chelsea (February 1953, £7,000), Retired June 1964.
Honours England (5 caps), England Under-23 (5 caps), England Youth International Football League XI (2 appearances), Football League Championship medal 1955.
Chelsea details Debut 14.3.53 347 Appearances 54 Goals

	Appearances				Goals			
	FL	FAC	LC	FC	FL	FAC	LC	FC
1952–53	11	–	–	–	2	–	–	–
1953–54	32	1	–	–	3	–	–	–
1954–55	23	3	–	–	3	1	–	–
1955–56	41	7	–	–	6	1	–	–
1956–57	27	2	–	–	5	–	–	–
1958–59	21	–	–	2	2	–	–	–
1959–60	37	2	–	–	5	1	–	–
1960–61	24	1	2	–	5	1	2	–
1961–62	26	1	–	–	2	–	–	–
1962–63	34	4	–	–	8	–	–	–
1963–64	41	3	1	–	6	–	–	–
Total	317	24	3	2	47	4	2	–

(also: 1 F.A. Charity Shield appearance and 1 Goal)

One of Chelsea's best-ever bargain buys. Despite twice breaking his leg, and being forced to miss the whole of the 1957–58 season, his career was a most distinguished one. A close-dribbling ball player, he was a member of both the 1954–55 Championship team (sharing the outside-left berth with Jim Lewis) and the 1962–63 Second Division promotion team. Injury on the Chelsea Caribbean tour during the summer of 1964 finally forced his premature retirement and he became Youth Team Coach before being appointed Manager of Brentford in December 1969. He was subsequently associated with Manchester United, Derby County and Sheffield Wednesday in either managerial or coaching duties.

BONETTI, Peter (1959–1975 & 1975–1979) Goalkeeper

Born Putney 27.9.41 Height 5ft 10½in Weight 10st 12lb. Career Chelsea (April 1959), Not retained May 1975, Re-signed October 1975, Retired May 1979, Dundee United 1979–80.
Honours England (7 caps), England Under-23 (12 caps), Football League XI (4 appearances),

F.A. Cup winners' medal 1970, losers' medal 1967, Football League Cup winners' medal 1966, losers' medal 1972, European Cup Winners' Cup winners' medal 1971.
Chelsea details Debut 2.4.60 729 Appearances

	Appearances					Goals				
	FL	FAC	LC	FC	ECWC	FL	FAC	LC	FC	ECWC
1959–60	6	–	–	–	–	–	–	–	–	–
1960–61	36	1	3	–	–	–	–	–	–	–
1961–62	33	1	–	–	–	–	–	–	–	–
1962–63	39	4	–	–	–	–	–	–	–	–
1963–64	35	–	1	–	–	–	–	–	–	–
1964–65	41	5	9	–	–	–	–	–	–	–
1965–66	38	6	–	12	–	–	–	–	–	–
1966–67	38	7	3	–	–	–	–	–	–	–
1967–68	40	5	1	–	–	–	–	–	–	–
1968–69	41	5	3	4	–	–	–	–	–	–
1969–70	36	8	4	–	–	–	–	–	–	–
1970–71	28	3	4	–	6	–	–	–	–	–
1971–72	33	3	8	–	4	–	–	–	–	–
1972–73	23	–	5	–	–	–	–	–	–	–
1973–74	20	–	1	–	–	–	–	–	–	–
1974–75	8	–	–	–	–	–	–	–	–	–
1975–76	27	4	–	–	–	–	–	–	–	–
1976–77	31	–	2	–	–	–	–	–	–	–
1977–78	31	4	–	–	–	–	–	–	–	–
1978–79	16	1	1	–	–	–	–	–	–	–
Total	600	57	45	16	10	–	–	–	–	–

(also: 1 F.A. Charity Shield appearance)

Brilliant goalkeeper whose Chelsea career exceeded that of any player in the club's history by extending over 20 seasons. Known as "the Cat", his wonderful agility and safe handling played a vital part in the four Cup winning sides between 1966 and 1971. Contemporary with Gordon Banks, his extraordinary talent never received the recognition due at international level. Having not been retained at the end of the 1974–75 season, he was then hastily summoned back to the colours within weeks of the following campaign starting and went on to add a further century of League appearances to his total. After having moved to the Isle of Mull in 1979, he then returned to London and joined the Stamford Bridge coaching staff to maintain an association lasting over a quarter of a century.

PETAR BOROTA | A.G. BOWER

BOROTA, Petar (1979–1982) Goalkeeper

Born Belgrade 5.3.52 Height 6ft 0in Weight 12st 7lb. Career Partizan Belgrade, Chelsea (March 1979, £70,000), Brentford, Benfica (Portugal), FC Porto (Portugal).
Honours Yugoslavia (14 caps).
Chelsea details Debut 3.3.79 114 Appearances

	Appearances			Goals		
	FL	FAC	LC	FL	FAC	LC
1978–79	12	–	–	–	–	–
1979–80	41	1	2	–	–	–
1980–81	42	1	2	–	–	–
1981–82	12	–	1	–	–	–
Total	107	2	5	–	–	–

Eccentric goalkeeper who endeared himself to Chelsea supporters through his flamboyant and spectacular style. His 'keeping alternated between brilliance and uncertainty – but was never predictable. Never one to be restricted to the confines of his own penalty area, his excursions upfield delighted spectators, and opponents, if not his own colleagues.

BOWER, A.G. ("Baishe") (1923–1925) Full-back

Born Bromley. Career Corinthians, Chelsea (1923–25).
Honours England (5 caps), England Amateur International.
Chelsea details Debut 1.3.24 9 Appearances

	Appearances		Goals	
	FL	FAC	FL	FAC
1923–24	3	–	–	–
1924–25	6	–	–	–
Total	9	–	–	–

One of several fine players from the famous amateur team, Corinthians, who played for Chelsea. A fine, stylish defender, it was a matter of regret that he was not more regularly available.

BOWIE, James D. (1944–1951) Inside-forward

Born Aberdeen 9.8.24 Height 5ft 6in Weight 10st 5lb. Career Park Vale Juniors, Chelsea (January 1944, £25), Fulham (January 1951, £20,000), Watford.
Chelsea details Debut 17.9.47 84 appearances 22 Goals

	Appearances		Goals	
	FL	FAC	FL	FAC
1947–48	22	1	5	1
1948–49	22	3	7	1
1949–50	16	4	4	2
1950–51	16	–	2	–
Total	76	8	18	4

First came to Chelsea's notice as a naval rating during World War II in 1944 and played at Wembley in the War-time Cup final of that year against Charlton Athletic. A ball-playing inside-forward with clever skills and close control, he was also a strong finisher.

BOWMAN, Andrew (1951–1955) Wing-half

Born Pittenweem (Fifeshire) 7.3.34 Height 5ft 8in Weight 11st. Career Chelsea (June 1951), Heart of Midlothian (Summer 1955), Newport County.
Honours Scotland Schoolboy International.
Chelsea details Debut 17.10.53 1 appearance

	Appearances		Goals	
	FL	FAC	FL	FAC
1953–54	1	–	–	–
Total	1	–	–	–

One of the earliest products of the Chelsea Youth Scheme, he signed professional after two years on the groundstaff. An auburn-haired wing-half who was unable to win a first-team place from Ken Armstrong or Derek Saunders, the regular wing-half backs at the time.

ANDREW BOWMAN

JAMES D. BOWIE

JOHN BOYLE

BOYLE, John (1964–1973) Midfield/Defender

Born Motherwell 25.12.46 Height 5ft 8in Weight 11st 10lb. Career Chelsea (August 1964), Brighton & Hove Albion (September 1973, "nominal"), Orient (December 1973).
Honours European Cup Winners' Cup winners' medal 1971, F.A. Cup losers' medal 1967, Football League Cup winners' medal 1966.
Chelsea details Debut 20.1.65 253(13) Appearances 12 Goals

	Appearances					Goals				
	FL	FAC	LC	FC	ECWC	FL	FAC	LC	FC	ECWC
1964–65	6	2	4	–	–	–	–	1	–	–
1965–66	27(3)	5	–	8	–	–	–	–	–	–
1966–67	36	6	3	–	–	5	–	–	–	–
1967–68	31(1)	4	–	–	–	4	–	–	–	–
1968–69	33(1)	4(1)	2	3	–	1	–	–	1	–
1969–70	6(1)	–	3	–	–	–	–	–	–	–
1970–71	19(1)	3	1	–	5(2)	–	–	–	–	–
1971–72	24	–	6	–	4	–	–	–	–	–
1972–73	5(3)	–	2	–	–	–	–	–	–	–
1973–74	1	–	–	–	–	–	–	–	–	–
Total	188(10)	24(1)	21	11	9(2)	10	–	1	1	–

A hard-tackling, tenacious midfield player (or defender) who was in, or on the verge of, the first-team for ten seasons, playing in all three of the cup winning teams of that period. First signed for the club after walking into the Stamford Bridge ground, unannounced, while in London on holiday at the age of 15.

BRABROOK, Peter (1955–1962) Winger

Born Greenwich 8.11.37 Height 5ft 8in Weight 10st 4lb. Career Chelsea (March 1955), West Ham United (October 1962, £35,000), Orient.
Honours England (3 caps), England Under-23 (9 caps), Football League XI (3 appearances), England Youth International, F.A. Cup winners' medal 1964. *Chelsea details* Debut 29.3.55 271 Appearances 57 Goals Also one F.A. Charity Shield appearance 1955-56.

	Appearances				Goals			
	FL	FAC	LC	FC	FL	FAC	LC	FC
1954–55	3	–	–	–	–	–	–	–
1955–56	18	1	–	–	3	–	–	–
1956–57	38	2	–	–	6	1	–	–
1957–58	41	3	–	–	8	–	–	–
1958–59	39	2	–	3	7	1	–	2
1959–60	39	2	–	–	7	2	–	–
1960–61	36	1	4	–	8	–	4	–
1961–62	37	1	–	–	8	–	–	–
Total	251	12	4	3	47	4	4	2

A fast and most skilful winger who joined the Chelsea groundstaff at Easter 1953, signing professional forms two years later. Played three games in the 1954–55 Championship winning team and went on to become a permanent fixture on the right-wing for the next seven seasons. Possessing intricate footwork he was also extremely fast and liked to move direct towards goal.

BRADBURY, Terry E. (1957–1962) Wing-half

Born London 15.11.39 Height 5ft 11in Weight 11st 6lb. Career Chelsea (July 1957), Southend United (September 1962, £4,500), Leyton Orient, Wrexham, Chester.
Honours England Schoolboy International.
Chelsea details Debut 20.8.60 29 Appearances 1 Goal

	Appearances			Goals		
	FL	FAC	LC	FL	FAC	LC
1960–61	15	–	–	1	–	–
1961–62	14	–	–	–	–	–
Total	29	–	–	1	–	–

A strongly-built wing-half who was on the verge of the first-team for two seasons at a time when the club were very much in a transition stage. The emergence of Terry Venables and the signing of Frank Upton effectively ended his chances of becoming a regular.

PETER BRABROOK

TERRY E. BRADBURY

| JAMES BRADSHAW | WILLIAM F. BRAWN |

BRADSHAW, James (1909–1910) Inside-forward
Born Burnely Height 5ft 7in Weight 10st 6lb. Career Woolwich Polytechnic, Arsenal (amateur), West Norwood, Fulham, Chelsea (May 1909).
Chelsea details Debut 4.12.09 6 Appearances 3 Goals

	Appearances			Goals		
	FL	FAC	FC	FL	FAC	FC
1909–10	6	–	–	3	–	–
Total	6	–	–	3	–	–

One of Chelsea's more mysterious players. He burst on to the scene by scoring a fine goal on his debut for the club and followed this up with two more in the next two games, attracting much favourable comment in the process. Then, after three more outings he disappeared from the scene and never played for the club again. Later he became manager of Southend United, Swansea Town and Bristol City. His father was at one time manager of Fulham.

BRAWN, William F. (1907–1911) Outside-right
Born Wellingborough Died 1931 Height 6ft 2½in Weight 13st 5lb. Career Wellingborough, Northampton Town, Sheffield United, Aston Villa, Middlesbrough, Chelsea (November 1907), Brentford (1911).
Honours England (2 caps).
Chelsea details Debut 23.11.07 99 Appearances 11 Goals

	Appearances		Goals	
	FL	FAC	FL	FAC
1907–08	26	2	4	–
1908–09	32	2	3	–
1909–10	23	2	3	1
1910–11	12	–	–	–
Total	93	6	10	1

Described as "one of the most dangerous outside-rights in the kingdom", Billy was renowned for his speed and, for three seasons, lived up to this reputation and was a prominent member of the side which established itself in the First Division for the first time.

BREBNER, Ronald G. (1906–1907 & 1912–1913) Goalkeeper

Born Darlington Died 1914 Height 5ft 11in Weight 11st 7lb. Career Edinburgh University, Sunderland (amateur), Queen's Park, London Caledonians, Northern Nomads, Wanderers, Darlington (amateur), Stockton (amateur), Huddersfield Town (amateur), Chelsea (amateur, 1906–1907 and 1912–13).
Honours England Amateur International (23 caps), Great Britain Olympic football cup-winners' medal.
Chelsea details Debut 27.10.06 19 Appearances

	Appearances		Goals	
	FL	FAC	FL	FAC
1906–07	1	–	–	–
1912–13	17	1	–	–
Total	18	1	–	–

A true amateur throughout his career, he was a dental surgeon by profession and widely recognised as one of the finest 'keepers of his day. He played for a large number of clubs and for the first part of the 1912–13 season was undisputed first choice at Chelsea, gaining preference ahead of both Jim Molineux and Jack Whitley. His death occurred as a result of an injury sustained while playing football.

BRIDGEMAN, William (1906–1919) Winger/Inside-forward

Born Bromley Height 5ft 7in Weight 12st 1lb. Career West Ham United, Chelsea (November 1906), Southend United.
Chelsea details Debut 1.12.06 160 Appearances 22 Goals

	Appearances		Goals	
	FL	FAC	FL	FAC
1906–07	23	2	4	–
1907–08	18	2	1	1
1908–09	16	1	3	–
1909–10	2	–	–	–
1910–11	15	4	2	1
1911–12	26	2	6	–
1912–13	17	1	2	–
1913–14	29	1	2	–
1914–15	1	–	–	–
Total	147	13	20	2

RONALD G. BREBNER

WILLIAM BRIDGEMAN

BARRY BRIDGES

A fast, dashing winger who had learnt his football in the East End of London as a schoolboy. After beginning his Chelsea career at inside-right, thereafter he played almost entirely at outside-left. Fearless, and with the reputation for being a hard worker, he laid on many scoring opportunities for others. He received a joint-benefit (with George Hilsdon) on Easter Monday 1912 (receipts £180). Despite often not being an automatic choice, he played first-team football for thirteen consecutive seasons (including war-time years).

BRIDGES, Barry (1958–1966) Striker

Born Horsford (Nr Norwich) 29.4.41 Height 5ft 10in Weight 11st 13lb. Career Chelsea (May 1958), Birmingham City (May 1966, £55,000), Queen's Park Rangers, Millwall, Brighton & Hove Albion.
Honours England (4 caps), England Youth International, England Schoolboy International, Football League XI, Football League Cup winners' medal 1966.
Chelsea details Debut 7.2.59 203(2) Appearances 93 Goals

	Appearances				Goals			
	FL	FAC	LC	FC	FL	FAC	LC	FC
1958–59	2	–	–	–	1	–	–	–
1959–60	1	–	–	–	–	–	–	–
1960–61	2	–	–	–	1	–	–	–
1961–62	32	1	–	–	19	1	–	–
1962–63	36	2	–	–	15	2	–	–
1963–64	33	3	–	–	15	–	–	–
1964–65	41	5	5	–	20	4	3	–
1965–66	27(2)	6	–	7	9	2	–	1
Total	174(2)	17	5	7	80	9	3	1

One of the earliest of the products of the Chelsea Youth Scheme to play for England. Made a sensational debut while still a junior, at the age of 16, with Bobby Tambling (also 16), each of them scoring in the 3–2 home win over West Ham United. A striking forward, either in the centre or down the flanks, with a devastating burst of speed, he left Chelsea after the arrival of Peter Osgood and went on to score over 200 League goals in his career with five clubs over 14 years.

BRITTAN, Harold P. (1913–1920) Inside/Centre-forward
Born Nottingham Height 5ft 8ins Weight 11st 3lb. Career Ilkeston United, Chelsea (December 1913), Free-Transfer May 1920.
Chelsea details Debut 18.4.14 24 Appearances 7 Goals

	Appearances		Goals	
	FL	FAC	FL	FAC
1913–14	2	–	2	–
1914–15	9	–	2	–
1919–20	13	–	3	–
Total	24	–	7	–

His career, so promising at the outset, was marred by illness and the outbreak of the First World War. Failing to establish himself as a first-team regular he left Stamford Bridge in the summer of 1920 to play in the U.S.A.

BRITTON, Ian (1971–1982) Midfield
Born Dundee 19.5.54 Height 5ft 5in Weight 9st 7lb. Career Chelsea (July 1971), Dundee United (August 1982), Blackpool, Burnley.
Chelsea details Debut 30.12.72 279(10) Appearances 34 Goals

	Appearances			Goals		
	FL	FAC	LC	FL	FAC	LC
1972–73	11(3)	–	–	–	–	–
1973–74	17	2	–	2	–	–
1974–75	14(1)	–	2	1	–	1
1975–76	40	4	1	8	–	–
1976–77	37	2	1	10	–	–
1977–78	40	4	1	1	–	–
1978–79	9(4)	1	–	–	–	–
1979–80	41	1	2	10	–	–
1980–81	27(1)	1	2	1	–	–
1981–82	17(1)	–	2	–	–	–
Total	253(10)	15	11	33	–	1

Dynamic non-stop runner whose enthusiasm and skill with the ball kept him in, or on the fringe of, the first-team for more than ten years, although his lack of physical strength prevented him from becoming a controlling force in midfield. Sadly his Chelsea days coincided with a barren period for the club but he never failed to make a whole-hearted contribution, however depressing the circumstances.

HAROLD BRITTAN

IAN BRITTON

MICHAEL BROLLY   JOHN BROOKS

BROLLY, Michael (1971–74) Midfield

Born Kilmarnock 6.10.54 Height 5ft 8in Weight 10st 12lb. Career Chelsea (November 1971), Bristol City (June 1974), Grimsby Town, Derby County, Scunthorpe United.
Honours Scottish Schoolboy International.
Chelsea details Debut 3.4.73 8(1) Appearances 1 Goal

	Appearances			Goals		
	FL	FAC	LC	FL	FAC	LC
1972–73	6(1)	–	–	1	–	–
1973–74	1	1	–	–	–	–
Total	7(1)	1	–	1	–	–

Signed professional after graduating from the Juniors. Opportunities were limited for him at Stamford Bridge but he went on to a fruitful career comprising some 500 senior games for his five clubs, developing into a skilful and highly respected midfield player.

BROOKS, John (1959–1961) Inside-forward

Born Reading 23.12.31 Height 5ft 9½in Weight 11st 10lb. Career Reading, Tottenham Hotspur, Chelsea (December 1959, part-exchange Les Allen), Brentford (September 1961), Crystal Palace.
Honours England (3 caps).
Chelsea details Debut 12.12.59 52 Appearances 7 Goals

	Appearances			Goals		
	FL	FAC	LC	FL	FAC	LC
1959–60	20	2	–	5	–	–
1960–61	26	–	4	1	–	1
Total	46	2	4	6	–	1

Arrived from Tottenham with a big reputation and high hopes but never did himself justice at Chelsea. Well-built, forceful inside-forward, his son, Shaun, also played professional football for Crystal Palace and Orient.

BROWN, Dennis (1962–1964) Inside-forward

Born Reading Height 5ft 7½ins Weight 10st 10lb. Career Chelsea (June 1962), Swindon (November 1964, £17,000), Northampton Town, Aldershot.
Chelsea details Debut 7.9.63 13 Appearances 2 Goals

	Appearances			Goals		
	FL	FAC	LC	FL	FAC	LC
1963–64	10	1	1	1	–	–
1964–65	–	–	1	–	–	1
Total	10	1	2	1	–	1

Another of those who reached professional ranks via the Chelsea Juniors. Possessing a powerful shot (hence his nickname "Bullets"), he failed to oust such as Bobby Tambling and George Graham from the senior side and moved into a lower division to further his career which ended with nearly 400 League games and over a century of goals.

BROWN, John A. (1912–1915) Winger

Born Dysart Height 5ft 11in Weight 12st 3lb. Career Glasgow Celtic, Chelsea (December 1912).
Chelsea details Debut 26.12.12 16 Appearances 4 Goals

	Appearances		Goals	
	FL	FAC	FL	FAC
1912–13	11	–	3	–
1913–14	3	–	–	–
1914–15	2	–	1	–
Total	16	–	4	–

After having a spell in the first-team shortly after coming to England from Scottish football, he played mostly for the reserves and did not resume his career after the First World War ended.

DENNIS BROWN

JOHN BROWN

| WILLIAM BROWN | WILLIAM Y. BROWN |

BROWN, William (1924–29) Inside-forward

Born Fence Houses (Co. Durham) Height 5ft 7½in Weight 11st 6lb. Career Hetton (Co. Durham), West Ham United, Chelsea (February 1924), Fulham (Summer 1929).
Honours F.A. Cup losers' medal 1923.
Chelsea details Debut 1.3.24 57 Appearances 21 Goals

	Appearances		Goals	
	FL	FAC	FL	FAC
1923–24	11	–	4	–
1924–25	18	1	7	–
1925–26	12	1	1	–
1926–27	11	–	7	–
1927–28	2	1	1	1
Total	54	3	20	1

Signed in an unsuccessful attempt to stave off relegation from Division II, this thrustful inside-forward never succeeded in establishing a regular first-team place – this despite an impressive "striking ratio". Previously he had scored two goals for West Ham against Derby County in an F.A. Cup semi-final at Stamford Bridge and had gone on to play in the first Wembley final.

BROWN, William Y. (1911–1913) Inside-forward

Born Wellingborough. Career Chelsea (July 1911), Bristol City (November 1913), Swansea Town.
Chelsea details Debut 9.9.11 10 Appearances 2 Goals

	Appearances		Goals	
	FL	FAC	FL	FAC
1911–12	3	–	1	–
1960–61	6	1	1	–
Total	9	1	2	–

A Scottish inside-forward who was a regular scorer of goals in the Combination team but failed to establish himself in the first-team and became the butt for much barracking from the terraces. He later played for Swansea Town and was wounded in World War I.

BROWNING, John (1919–1920) Outside-left

Born Dumbarton 29.1.88 Height 5ft 6½ins Weight 11st 8lb. Career Vale of Leven, Dumbarton Harp. Glasgow Celtic, Chelsea (June 1919), Vale of Leven, Dumbarton.
Honours Scotland (1 cap), Scottish League (2 appearances), Scottish Cup winner's medal 1914.
Chelsea details Debut 20.8.19 6 Appearances 2 Goals

	Appearances		Goals	
	FL.	FAC	FL	FAC
1919–20	5	1	1	1
Total	5	1	1	1

Arrived with a reputation of being one of the best players in Scottish football but failed to justify this assertion and was soon replaced in the first-time by Bobby McNeil.

BUCHANAN, Peter S. (1936–1946) Winger

Born Glasgow 13.10.15. Career Wishaw Juniors, Chelsea (February 1936), Fulham (1946), Brentford, Headington United.
Honours Scotland (1 cap).
Chelsea details Debut 13.2.37 40 Appearances 6 Goals

	Appearances		Goals	
	FL	FAC	FL	FAC
1936–37	1	–	–	–
1937–38	33	1	6	–
1938–39	5	–	–	–
Total	39	1	6	–

A highly talented, if rather unpredictable and mercurial, performer. After first coming to Chelsea in 1933 as an apprentice on the groundstaff, but failing to settle down in London, he was signed on a permanent basis three years later and went on to win an international cap within months of making his first-team debut. Vying with Dick Spence for the outside-right position he had only one full season as first choice before his promising career was further hampered by the outbreak of war.

WANTED

If anyone has a photograph of **JOHN**

It would be appreciated if you would allow us to copy it. Please forward it to Ron at 36 Lockier Walk, Wembley, Middx.
It will be returned safely

JOHN BROWNING

PETER S. BUCHANAN

ROBERT BUCHANAN | JOHN BUMSTEAD

BUCHANAN, Robert (1911–13) Full-back

Career Leyton, Chelsea (May 1911), Southend United (Summer 1913).
Chelsea details Debut 21.10.11 3 Appearances

	Appearances		Goals	
	FL	FAC	FL	FAC
1911–12	3	–	–	–
Total	3	–	–	–

Was on the Chelsea staff for two seasons, playing regularly in the Combination team as deputy to Walter Bettridge.

BUMSTEAD, John (1976–) Midfield

Born Rotherhithe 27.11.58 Height 5ft 7in Weight 10st 5lb. Career Chelsea (December 1976). Honours Second Division Championship medal 1984, Full Members' Cup winners' medal 1986. *Chelsea details* Debut 22.11.78. 285 (13) Appearances 37 Goals

	Appearances				Goals			
	FL	FAC	LC	FC	FL	FAC	LC	FC
1978–79	6(2)	–	–	–	1	–	–	–
1979–80	27(1)	–	1(1)	–	3	–	–	–
1980–81	40(1)	1	2	–	1	–	–	–
1981–82	21	6	2	–	4	1	1	–
1982–83	35(1)	3	3	–	4	1	–	–
1983–84	30(1)	–	4	–	7	–	–	–
1984–85	21(4)	0(1)	5(1)	–	3	–	–	–
1985–86	32	1	5	4	1	–	–	1
1986–87	29	3	3	1	8	1	–	–
Total	241(10)	14(1)	25(2)	5	32	3	1	1

Strong-running and hard-tackling midfield player who made the step-up from reserve football in 1978–79, having first joined Chelsea as a 13-year-old schoolboy. He signed apprentice forms in July 1975 and turned professional eighteen months later. A powerful defender and forceful attacker with good shooting ability, he played a notable part in the 1983–84 Second Division promotion team, several of his 7 goals coming from direct free-kicks.

BURGESS, Harry (1935–1945) Inside-forward

Born Alderly Edge Height 5ft 8in Weight 11st 10lb. Career: Stockport County, Sandbach Ramblers (loan), Sheffield Wednesday, Chelsea (March 1935), Retired 1945.
Honours England (4 caps), Football League Championship medal 1930.
Chelsea details Debut 16.3.35. 155 Appearances 37 Goals

	Appearances		Goals	
	FL	FAC	FL	FAC
1934–35	10	–	3	–
1935–36	31	5	11	1
1936–37	29	1	4	–
1937–38	36	1	7	–
1938–39	36	6	8	3
Total	142	13	33	4

Long-striding, forceful inside-forward who came to Chelsea after an already distinguished career during which he had played for England four times. For the five seasons leading up to the outbreak of the Second World War he was a vital pillar of a team, often struggling to find consistency, and scoring crucial goals, some of them from the penalty spot. He moved back north after the outbreak of hostilities and continued to make "guest" appearances for several clubs.

BUSH, Robert (1906–07) Wing-half

Career West Ham United, Chelsea (Summer 1906).
Chelsea details Debut 10.11.06. 4 Appearances 1 Goal

	Appearances		Goals	
	FL	FAC	FL	FAC
1906–07	4	–	1	1
Total	4	–	1	1

A half-back who spent one season only at Stamford Bridge. Apart from four consecutive first-team games in November and December he played entirely in the reserve team.

HARRY BURGESS

WANTED
If anyone has a photograph of
ROBERT
It would be appreciated if you would allow us to copy it. Please forward it to Ron at 36 Lockier Walk, Wembley, Middx.
It will be returned safely.

ROBERT BUSH

DENNIS M. BUTTLER

GEOFFREY BUTLER

BUTLER, Dennis M. (1960–1963) Full-back

Born Fulham 7.3.43 Height 5ft 9in Weight 11st 10lb. Career Chelsea (May 1960), Hull City (June 1963, £10,000), Reading.
Honours Third Division Championship medal 1966.
Chelsea details Debut 18.11.61. 18 Appearances

	Appearances			Goals		
	FL	FAC	LC	FL	FAC	LC
1961–62	16	–	–	–	–	–
1962–63	2	–	–	–	–	–
Total	18	–	–	–	–	–

Signed professional after two years as a Chelsea Junior. A strong defender who made a promising start but was unable to win a regular first-team place against the challenge of Ken Shellito and Eddie McCreadie. Subsequently made over 400 appearances in his League career.

BUTLER, Geoffrey (1967–1968) Full-back

Born Middlesbrough 29.9.46 Height 5ft 9in Weight 11st 2lb. Career Middlesbrough, Chelsea (September 1967, £57,000), Sunderland (January 1968, £65,000), Norwich City, Bournemouth & Boscombe Athletic.
Chelsea details Debut 23.9.67. 8(1) Appearances

	Appearances			Goals		
	FL	FAC	LC	FL	FAC	LC
1967–68	8(1)	–	–	–	–	–
Total	8(1)	–	–	–	–	–

His stay at Stamford Bridge was limited to four months despite an obvious first-team vacancy at right-back. Made a promising start but never settled in London, although he subsequently made some 300 senior appearances for Norwich City and Bournemouth.

BYRNE, Michael T. G. (1905–1906) Goalkeeper

Career Bristol Rovers, Southampton, Chelsea (August 1905) Contract cancelled September 1906.
Chelsea details Debut 28.10.05. 5 Appearances

	Appearances		Goals	
	FL	FAC	FL	FAC
1905–06	3	1	–	–
1906–07	1	–	–	–
Total	4	1	–	–

Popular Irishman who was signed as deputy for Willie Foulke and who began the 1906–07 as first choice 'keeper, following the "big man's" departure. Lost his place through dislocating his shoulder in the first game of that season and never played in the first team again. A fearless and most dependable goalkeeper.

CALDERHEAD, David (Junior) (1907–1914) Centre-half

Career Lincoln City, Chelsea (September 1907), Leicester Fosse (1914).
Chelsea details Debut 21.1.11. 43 Appearances 1 Goal

	Appearances		Goals	
	FL	FAC	FL	FAC
1910–11	10	6	–	–
1911–12	1	–	–	–
1912–13	16	3	–	–
1913–14	7	–	1	–
Total	34	9	1	–

The son of the Chelsea manager, David Calderhead (Senior), at one time he looked like becoming Chelsea's regular centre-half. But the signings of Andy Ormiston and Tom Logan in an endeavour to establish the club in the first division restricted his opportunities.

BYRNE, Michael T.G.

DAVID CALDERHEAD (Junior)

DAVID F. CAMERON   JOHN ("JOCK") CAMERON

CAMERON, David F. (1920–1926) Full-back or Wing-half

Born Partick 5ft 11in Weight 12st. Career Queen's Park, Chelsea (June 1920), Helensburgh (December 1926).
Chelsea details Debut 28.8.20 81. Appearances 2 Goals

	Appearances		Goals	
	FL	FAC	FL	FAC
1920–21	13	5	2	–
1921–22	13	–	–	–
1922–23	25	3	–	–
1923–24	11	–	–	–
1924–25	11	–	–	–
Total	73	8	2	–

A tall, commanding defender, whose promising career was marred by injury almost as soon as he arrived at Chelsea. He had served with the Cameron Highlanders, appropriately, during World War I, and had played for two seasons with Queen's Park in the Scottish League after demobilisation. "There is no better defender in Scottish football today", wrote one expert. After his initial setback at Stamford Bridge, he found it difficult to hold his place in a side that was struggling to maintain its first division status.

CAMERON, John ("Jock") (1907–1913) Full-back

Born Kirkwoodin (Lanarkshire). Career Kirkwood Thistle, St. Mirren, Blackburn Rovers, Chelsea (October 1907). Port Vale (1913).
Honours Scotland (2 caps), Scottish League (3 appearances)
Chelsea details Debut 12.10.07. 194 Appearances

	Appearances		Goals	
	FL	FAC	FL	FAC
1907–08	32	2	–	–
1908–09	35	3	–	–
1909–10	26	–	–	–
1910–11	34	6	–	–
1911–12	36	2	–	–
1912–13	16	2	–	–
Total	179	15	–	–

One of the outstanding full-backs in Chelsea's history. For six seasons he was an automatic choice in the first-team, partnering Walter Bettridge in what was often considered to be the strongest full-back pairing in the country in those days. He captained the Chelsea team for much of his time with the club and was renowned for his sound defensive qualities, being a particularly fearsome tackler. He had won a Scottish international cap early in his career, with St. Mirren, and added to this when he represented his country against England at Crystal Palace in 1908–09.

CAMPBELL, Robert I. (1947–1954) Outside-right

Born Glasgow 28.6.22 Height 5ft 9in Weight 11st 7lb. Career Falkirk, Chelsea (May 1947), Reading (August 1954).
Honours Scotland (5 caps)
Chelsea details Debut 4.1.10.47. 213 Appearances 40 Goals

	Appearances		Goals	
	FL	FAC	FL	FAC
1947–48	32	2	11	1
1948–49	36	3	7	–
1949–50	35	6	4	2
1950–51	33	4	6	–
1951–52	32	4	5	–
1952–53	18	6	3	1
1953–54	2	–	–	–
Total	188	25	36	4

Signing for Falkirk in 1941, he lost some of the best years of his career to war-time football, but his talents were quickly realised when the game returned to normal and he was soon recognised by the national selectors. His arrival in London to take over the right-wing berth from long-serving Dick Spence was an immediate success as Bobby scored twice on his debut, and for six seasons he was first-choice for his position. Fast and direct, he had spells on the left and also at inside-forward. His goal in a memorable cup-tie against Newcastle United in 1950 is often considered one of the best ever seen at Stamford Bridge. Running from the half-way line he outpaced all defenders on a treacherous surface, before drawing the goalkeeper to put the ball into the net. After spells as both Coach and Trainer to Bristol Rovers, he managed the Gloucestershire club for a period.

ROBERT I. CAMPBELL

PAUL K. CANOVILLE JOHN J. CARR

CANOVILLE, Paul K. (1981–1986) Forward

Born Hillingdon 4.3.62 Height 5ft 10in Weight 11st 5lb. Career Hillingdon Borough, Chelsea (December 1981), Reading (August 1986, £50,000).
Chelsea details Debut 12.4.82. 67(36) Appearances 15 Goals

	Appearances				Goals			
	FL	FAC	LC	FMC	FL	FAC	LC	FMC
1981–82	1 (2)	–	–	–	–	–	–	–
1982–83	16 (3)	–	2	–	3	–	–	–
1983–84	17 (3)	1	4	–	6	–	1	–
1984–85	15 (9)	1(1)	5(4)	–	1	1	2	–
1985–86	4 (9)	0(2)	1(2)	0(1)	1	–	–	–
Total	53(26)	2(3)	12(6)	0(1)	11	1	3	–

The first coloured player to play first-team football for Chelsea. Fast-running striker with a flair for scoring spectacular goals, operated mainly down the flanks. Despite great ability, his inconsistency limited his chances and he was allowed to leave, moving on to Reading after his provisional transfer to Brentford had been cancelled.

CARR, John J. (1928–1931) Full-back

Born Gateshead Height 5ft 9in Weight 9st 1lb. Career Chelsea (October 1928), Chester (Summer 1931).
Chelsea details Debut 17.4.29. 1 Appearance

	Appearances		Goals	
	FL	FAC	FL	FAC
1928–29	1	–	–	–
Total	1	–	–	–

Signed early in the 1928–29 season, this light-weight full-back was a regular in the Combination side for three seasons, but was unable to break through to first-team football at a time when "big-name stars" were being signed for large fees.

CARTER, Robert (1929–1933) Wing-half

Born Bolton Height 5ft 7½in Weight 11st 1lb. Career Chelsea (September 1929), Plymouth Argyle (May 1933).
Chelsea details Debut 7.4.31. 18 Appearances

	Appearances		Goals	
	FL	FAC	FL	FAC
1930–31	1	–	–	–
1931–32	16	–	–	–
1932–33	1	–	–	–
Total	18	–	–	–

Discovered while playing football in the Army. Injury problems gave him an extended run in the first-team early in the 1931–32 season, but the arrival of Peter O'Dowd and Allan Craig limited his opportunities and he moved on to Plymouth Argyle, where he played mainly at centre-half.

CARTWRIGHT, William (1908–1913) Full-back

Career Gainsborough Trinity, Chelsea (May 1908), Tottenham Hotspur (Summer 1913), Swansea Town.
Chelsea details Debut 12.9.08. 46 Appearances

	Appearances		Goals	
	FL	FAC	FL	FAC
1908–09	12	–	–	–
1909–10	24	2	–	–
1910–11	5	–	–	–
1911–12	1	–	–	–
1912–13	2	–	–	–
Total	44	2	–	–

A full-back who played most of his football with Chelsea in the reserve team during a stay of five years. He then moved on to Tottenham Hotspur, but is perhaps better remembered at Southend where he gave the Essex club long and devoted service on their training staff before being granted a testimonial.

ROBERT CARTER	WILLIAM CARTWRIGHT

LEN CASEY

SIDNEY R. CASTLE

CASEY, Len (1954–1958) Wing-half

Born Hackney 24.5.31 Height 5ft 8in Weight 11st 7lb. Career Leyton, Chelsea (February 1954), Plymouth Argyle (December 1958, £12,000 with Wally Bellett).
Chelsea details Debut 24.3.56. 37 Appearances

	Appearances			Goals		
	FL	FAC	LC	FL	FAC	LC
1955–56	7	–	–	–	–	–
1956–57	3	–	–	–	–	–
1957–58	21	3	–	–	–	–
1958–59	3	–	–	–	–	–
Total	34	3	–	–	–	–

Having won an FA Amateur Cup medal with Leyton at Wembley in 1952, he was one of several amateurs to be recruited to Chelsea by manager Ted Drake at that time. He found the transition to the professional game difficult to make, however, and he failed to tie down a regular first-team place.

CASTLE, Sidney R. (1923–1926) Winger

Born Guildford Height 5ft 8in Weight 10st. 8lb. Career Crystal Palace, Tottenham Hotspur, Charlton Athletic, Chelsea (May 1923).
Chelsea details Debut 27.8.23. 32 Appearances 2 Goals

	Appearances		Goals	
	FL	FAC	FL	FAC
1923–24	24	–	2	–
1924–25	8	–	–	–
Total	32	–	2	–

A clever winger who looked as if he had established himself in the 1923–24 campaign, but it was a traumatic time for the club with relegation occurring at the end of the season and soon Jackie Crawford had arrived to take over the right-wing position. After that he remained a pillar of the reserve side for a time but was never given a further chance to develop his undoubted potential.

CHEYNE, Alexander G. (1930–1931 & 1934–1936) Inside-forward

Born Glasgow 28.4.07, Died 5.8.83 Height 5ft 8in Weight 10st. 6lb. Career Shettleston Juniors, Aberdeen, Chelsea (June 1930, £6,000). Nimes (1932), Chelsea (1934), Colchester United (1936).
Honours Scotland (5 caps), Scottish League XI (1 appearance)
Chelsea details Debut 30.8.30. 69 Appearances 13 Goals

	Appearances		Goals	
	FL	FAC	FL	FAC
1930–31	34	5	9	1
1931–32	19	2	1	–
1934–35	3	–	1	–
1935–36	6	–	1	–
Total	62	7	12	1

A versatile forward who played on the wing during the earlier part of his career but entirely as an inside-forward for Chelsea. After five years with Aberdeen, where he won his five Scottish international caps, he found it difficult to adjust to the greater speed of English football and rarely produced his best form south of the border. Along with others he became unsettled in London and went to France for two years where he had been enticed by a most attractive financial offer before coming back to Stamford Bridge where, again, he failed to do his great ability the justice it deserved. Sadly he drifted into the Southern League with Colchester United, and later managed Arbroath in the Scottish League for a time.

ALEXANDER G. CHEYNE

WILFRED S. CHITTY GARY P.S. CHIVERS

CHITTY, Wilfred S. (1930–1938) Winger/Full-back
Born Walton-on-Thames 10.7.12 Height 5ft 10in Weight 10st. 6lb. Career Woking, Chelsea (March 1930), Plymouth Argyle (December 1938), Reading.
Chelsea details Debut 6.4.32. 46 Appearances 16 Goals

	Appearances		Goals	
	FL	FAC	FL	FAC
1931–32	6	–	1	–
1932–33	6	–	2	–
1933–34	5	–	1	–
1935–36	1	–	–	–
1936–37	8	–	1	–
1937–38	19	1	11	–
Total	45	1	16	–

A loyal servant of Chelsea during most of the 1930s, spending the majority of his time at Stamford Bridge in reserve-team football. A speedy winger with a powerful shot, he perhaps lacked the necessary determination to win himself a permanent place in the senior side. For one season, too, he showed himself to be a competent full-back. After moving to Plymouth Argyle, he returned to play for Reading throughout the war and, indeed, in the first post-war season, after which he retired.

CHIVERS, Gary P. S. (1978–1983) Defender
Born Stockwell 15.5.60 Height 5ft 11in Weight 11st. 7lb. Career Chelsea (July 1978), Swansea City (Summer 1983), Queens Park Rangers.
Chelsea details Debut 21.4.79. 143(5) Appearances 4 Goals

	Appearances			Goals		
	FL	FAC	LC	FL	FAC	LC
1978–79	5	–	–	–	–	–
1979–80	27(2)	1	1	2	–	–
1980–81	39(1)	1	2	2	–	–
1981–82	28(1)	3	3	–	–	–
1982–83	29(1)	2	2	–	–	–
Total	128(5)	7	8	4	–	–

Joined Chelsea as a schoolboy and made his debut, against Middlesbrough, within nine months of becoming a professional. Almost his entire career at Stamford Bridge was played in the second division, often with the threat of further relegation looming and, partially as a result of this, he failed to do justice to his undoubted ability.

CLARKE, Stephen, (1987–   ) Defender

Career St. Mirren, Chelsea (January 1987, £400,000)
Honours Scotland Under-21 International (9 caps)
Chelsea details Debut 24.1.87 17(1) Appearances.

	Appearances			Goals		
	FL	FAC	FMC	FL	FAC	FMC
1986–87	15(1)	1	1	–	–	–
Total	15(1)	1	1	–	–	–

Talented defender, either at full-back or in the middle of the back-four. He was signed in the face of stiff competition, on both sides of the border, and comes from a family with a strong football tradition. A sound defensive player and good in the tackle, one of his greatest assets is his speed and acceleration which snuffs out many a dangerous situation and takes him away from opponents.

CLARE, James E. (1977–1981) Midfield

Born Islington 6.11.59 Height 5ft 8in Weight 9st. 9lb. Career Chelsea (November 1977). Not retained 1981–82.
Chelsea details Debut 4.10.80. 0(1) Appearances

	Appearances		Goals	
	FL	FAC	FL	FAC
1980–81	0(1)	–	–	–
Total	0(1)	–	–	–

Graduated to the ranks of professional via the Chelsea Youth Scheme as an apprentice, but failed to bridge the gap between reserve and first-team football.

STEPHEN CLARKE

JAMES E. CLARE

DAVID CLISS   JOHN COADY

CLISS, David (1956–1962) Inside-forward

Born Enfield 15.11.39 Height 5ft 6in Weight 9st. Career Chelsea (November 1956), Guildford City (Summer 1962).
Honours England Youth.
Chelsea details Debut 8.2.58. 24 Appearances 1 Goal

	Appearances			Goals		
	FL	FAC	LC	FL	FAC	LC
1957–58	9	–	–	1	–	–
1958–59	3	–	–	–	–	–
1959–60	4	–	–	–	–	–
1961–62	8	–	–	–	–	–
Total	24	–	–	1	–	–

A clever, intricate, ball-playing inside-forward whose skills delighted onlookers. His frail physique was something of a handicap but his Chelsea career was virtually ended when he broke his leg at the beginning of the 1960–61 season.

COADY, John (1986–   ) Full-back/Midfield

Born Dublin 25.5.60
Career Shamrock Rovers, Chelsea (December 1986, £25,000).
Chelsea details Debut 3.3.87. 5(2) Appearances 1 Goal

	Appearances		Goals	
	FL	FMC	FL	FMC
1986–87	5(1)	0(1)	1	–
Total	5(1)	0(1)	1	–

Had his first taste of full-time professional football at the age of 26 when he crossed the Irish Sea after several years experience with the Dublin club, Shamrock Rovers, with whom he had appeared in the European Cup. An ex-postman he had played in midfield, as well as in his usual position of left-back.

COCK, Jack G. (1919–1923) Centre-forward

Born Brentford 1895. Died April 1966. Height 5ft 11in Weight 12st. 5lb. Career Old Kingstonians, Brentford, Huddersfield Town, Chelsea (October 1919, £2,500), Everton (February 1923), Millwall.
Honours England International (2 caps).
Chelsea details Debut 1.11.19. 110 Appearances 53 Goals

	Appearances		Goals	
	FL	FAC	FL	FAC
1919–20	25	5	21	3
1920–21	32	6	12	3
1921–22	31	–	13	–
1922–23	11	–	1	–
Total	99	11	47	6

One of the many famous centre-forwards in Chelsea's history. A beautifully built natural athlete, he possessed a strong shot in either foot and was a particularly fine header of the ball. But for the outbreak of World War I he would have made an even bigger impact on the game and, undoubtedly, added to his scant reward of two international caps. His move from Chelsea to Everton came at a time when his powers seemed to be in decline but his form with the Merseysiders proved this to be a totally false assumption. His long career extended into the 1930s and ended at Millwall, the club where he subsequently became manager.

COLLINS, R. Michael (1951–1957) Goalkeeper

Born Redcar 8.6.33 Height 5ft 11in Weight 11st. 6lb. Career Redcar Albion, Chelsea (November 1951), Watford (Summer 1957).
Chelsea details Debut 6.3.54. 1 Appearance

	Appearances		Goals	
	FL	FAC	FL	FAC
1953–54	1	–	–	–
Total	1	–	–	–

A goalkeeper whose opportunities were restricted by the presence of Harry Medhurst, Bill Robertson and Charlie Thomson who were all on the Chelsea staff at the time. After five years in the Combination team he moved to Watford where he played in the first-team for two seasons.

JACK G. COCK

R. MICHAEL COLLINS

JOHN F. COMPTON | DAVID C. COPELAND

COMPTON, John F. (1955–1960) Wing-half

Born Poplar 27.8.37 Height 5ft 9in Weight 10st. Career Chelsea (February 1955), Ipswich Town (Summer 1960), Bournemouth & BA.
Honours First Division Championship medal 1962, Second Division Championship medal 1961.
Chelsea details Debut 28.4.56. 12 Appearances

	Appearances			Goals		
	FL	FAC	FC	FL	FAC	FC
1955–56	1	–	–	–		
1957–58	3	–	–	–		
1959–60	8	–	–	–		
Total	12	–	–			

A member of the Chelsea Youth Scheme for two years before signing professional, he was offered few first-team opportunities. At Ipswich, however, his career took off and he played more than a century of league games in their Championship years.

COPELAND, David C. (1905–1907) Inside and Centre-forward

Born Ayr 2.4.75 Died 16.11.31. Career Ayr Parkhouse, Walsall, Bedminster, Tottenham Hotspur, Chelsea (August 1905). (Retired through injury 1907)
Honours FA Cup Winners medal 1901.
Chelsea details Debut 2.9.05. 26 Appearances 9 Goals

	Appearances		Goals	
	FL	FAC	FL	FAC
1905–06	20	–	5	–
1906–07	6	–	4	–
Total	26	–	9	–

One of two players (Johnny Kirwan was the other) signed from Tottenham Hotspur in time for the first Chelsea season. A strong, aggressive forward, who could play either centre, or inside, forward, he was appointed club captain in September 1906 but was injured in the sixth match of the season and never played League football again.

COOKE, Charles (1966–1972 & 1973–1978) Winger/Midfield

Born St. Monace, Fife, 14.10.42 Height 5ft 8in Weight 12st 2lb. Career Renfrew Juniors, Aberdeen, Dundee, Chelsea (April 1966, £72,000), Crystal Palace (September 1972, £85,000), Chelsea (January 1974, £17,000), Memphis Rogues, California Surf.
Honours Scotland (16 caps), Scotland U-23 (4 caps), Scottish League (4 caps), FA Cup winners' medal 1970 losers' medal 1967; European Cup Winners' medal 1971, Football League Cup losers' medal 1972.
Chelsea details Debut 11.5.66. 360(13) Appearances, 30 Goals

	Appearances					Goals				
	FL	FAC	LC	FC	ECWC	FL	FAC	LC	FC	ECWC
1965–66	–	–	–	2	–	–	–	–	–	–
1966–67	33	6(1)	3	–	–	3	–	–	–	–
1967–68	41	5	1	–	–	3	1	1	–	–
1968–69	25 (1)	5	2	3	–	–	1	–	1	–
1969–70	35	6	2(1)	–	–	4	–	1	–	–
1970–71	28 (3)	3	3	–	8	1	–	–	–	–
1971–72	35 (3)	3	7	–	4	2	1	1	–	–
1972–73	7 (1)	–	–	–	–	2	–	–	–	–
1973–74	17	–	–	–	–	1	–	–	–	–
1974–75	38 (1)	1	4	–	–	5	–	1	–	–
1975–76	16 (1)	2(1)	–	–	–	1	–	–	–	–
1976–77	8	–	–	–	–	–	–	–	–	–
1977–78	6	1	–	–	–	–	–	–	–	–
Total	289(10)	32(2)	22(1)	5	12	22	3	4	1	–

One of the greatest entertainers of his time and one of the most highly skilled players to play for Chelsea – as well as one of the most popular. A true ball artist, he had begun his career in Scotland almost entirely as an "old-fashioned" winger, but the changing tactics within the game dictated that he widened his scope to become a midfield player. He was a wonderful dribbler, often leaving a series of bemused opponents in his wake. Perhaps his goal tally was disappointing for one of his type, but he was essentially a creator of chances for others. His Chelsea career was in two parts, punctuated by a 16-month sojourn at Crystal Palace. On his return he found the club fortunes in decline but, nevertheless, proceeded to play some of the most effective football of his Stamford Bridge career. After finally leaving the club he continued to play in American football.

CHARLES COOKE

JAMES L. COPELAND

PETER A. CORTHINE

COPELAND, James L. (1932–1937) Centre-forward
Career Park Royal, Chelsea (May 1932).
Chelsea details Debut 9.9.33. 2 Appearances 1 Goal

	Appearances		Goals	
	FL	FAC	FL	FAC
1933–34	1	–	1	–
1934–35	1	–	–	–
Total	2	–	1	–

A prolific goalscorer in Combination football throughout most of his five seasons at Chelsea, he found it impossible to break through into the first-team ahead of three international centre-forwards, Hughie Gallacher, Joe Bambrick and George Mills.

CORTHINE, Peter A. (1957–1960) Winger
Born Highbury 19.7.37 Height 5ft 6in, Weight 9st 12lb. Career Leytonstone, Chelsea (December 1957), Southend United (March 1960).
Chelsea details Debut 31.10.59. 2 Appearances

	Appearances			Goals		
	FL	FAC	LC	FL	FAC	LC
1959–60	2	–	–	–	–	–
Total	2	–	–	–	–	–

Chelsea was his first professional club after he had been spotted playing in Army football. Reserve to Peter Brabrook in his two years on the Stamford Bridge staff, he subsequently played 73 League games (21 goals) for Southend United.

COURT, Colin (1954–1959) Winger

Born Ebbw Vale 3.9.37 Height 5ft 7½in Weight 10st 8lb. Career Chelsea (September 1954), Torquay United (May 1959).
Honours Welsh Schoolboy international.
Chelsea details Debut 30.9.58. 1 Appearance.

	Appearances			Goals		
	FL	FAC	FC	FL	FAC	FC
1958–59	–	–	1	–	–	–
Total	–	–	1	–	–	–

Graduated to professional status via the Chelsea Juniors, but was unable to force his way into the first-team with Eric Parsons and Peter Brabrook on the staff at that time.

CRAIG, Allan (1933–1939) Centre-half

Born Paisley 7.2.04 Height 5ft 10½in Weight 11st 10lb. Career Celtic Victoria (Paisley Juniors), Motherwell, Chelsea (January 1933). Not retained May 1939.
Honours Scotland (1 cap), Scottish League XI (3 appearances), Scottish Championship medal 1932, Scottish Cup losers' medal 1931
Chelsea details Debut 7.1.33. 211 Appearances.

	Appearances		Goals	
	FL	FAC	FL	FAC
1932–33	19	–	–	–
1933–34	30	5	–	–
1934–35	42	2	–	–
1935–36	41	5	–	–
1936–37	41	2	–	–
1937–38	7	–	–	–
1938–39	16	1	–	–
Total	196	15	–	–

A tall, stylish centre-half who was a pillar of the Chelsea defence for seven seasons in the period leading up to the outbreak of World War II and, indeed, captained the team for much of that time. Strangely, he played no football at school. He had spent nine years at Motherwell before coming south and his long and honourable career ended with the outbreak of World War II.

WANTED
If anyone has a photograph of **COLIN**
It would be appreciated if you would allow us to copy it.
Please forward it to Ron at 36 Lockier Walk, Wembley, Middx.
It will be returned safely

COLIN COURT

ALLAN CRAIG

JAMES CRAIGIE | JOHN E. CRAWFORD

CRAIGIE, James (1905–1907) Half-back

Career Chelsea (August 1905).
Chelsea details Debut 7.10.05. 2 Appearances.

	Appearances		Goals	
	FL	FAC	FL	FAC
1905–06	–	2	–	–
Total	–	2	–	–

Signed during the summer of 1905, he was one of a large pool of players who was on the staff at the beginning of Chelsea's first-ever season. In fact, his FA Cup debut was made when the recognised first-team were fulfilling a Football League fixture, and he only received one further opportunity, also in an FA Cup tie.

CRAWFORD, John E. (1923–1934) Winger

Born Jarrow 26.9.96. Died 1975. Height 5ft 2in Weight 10st. Career Palmer's Works (Jarrow), Naval Service (World War I), Hull City, Chelsea (May 1923 £3,000), Queens Park Rangers (May 1934).
Honours England (1 cap).
Chelsea details Debut 17.11.23. 308 Appearances 27 Goals.

	Appearances		Goals	
	FL	FAC	FL	FAC
1923–24	21	1	3	–
1924–25	26	–	1	–
1925–26	36	2	3	–
1926–27	39	5	3	–
1927–28	39	1	6	–
1928–29	27	4	2	–
1929–30	32	1	4	–
1930–31	32	5	4	1
1931–32	21	–	–	–
1932–33	15	1	–	–
Total	288	20	26	1

Jackie was one of Chelsea's greatest-ever wingers, operating on either flank with equal facility. With intricate footwork, a good crosser of the ball, and a strong shot in either foot he was the complete player for his position, even if his goal tally was, perhaps, modest for one of such talent. In the dressing-room he was, also, a first-class influence, having the reputation of being a born optimist who expected to win every match. Altogether a most likeable personality who coached at Queens Park Rangers and, later, Malden Town after his playing career ended.

CROAL, James A. (1914–1922) Inside-forward

Born Glasgow 27.7.85. Died 16.9.39. Height 5ft 8½in Weight 9st 1lb. Career Glasgow Rangers, Falkirk, Chelsea (April 1914 £2,000), Fulham (March 1922).
Honours Scotland (3 caps), Scottish League XI (3 appearances), Scottish Cup winners' medal (1913), FA Cup final losers' medal 1915.
Chelsea details Debut 5.9.14. 130 Appearances 26 Goals.

	Appearances		Goals	
	FL	FAC	FL	FAC
1914–15	27	6	6	1
1919–20	32	4	6	1
1920–21	33	6	7	2
1921–22	21	1	3	–
Total	113	17	22	4

A schoolmaster by profession, he had already won his three Scottish caps before his arrival at Stamford Bridge. Jimmy was renowned for his artistry, if perhaps lacking something in aggression, especially inside the opposition's penalty area. He was a most popular player and a great entertainer who, partnered by Bobby McNeil, played a major part in steering Chelsea to their first-ever FA Cup Final.

JAMES A. CROAL

STANLEY CROWTHER

GEORGE H. DALE

CROWTHER, Stanley (1958–1961) Wing-half

Born Bilston 3.9.35 Height 6ft 1½in Weight 13st 6lb. Career Aston Villa, Manchester United, Chelsea (December 1958, £10,000), Brighton & Hove Albion (March 1961).
Honours FA Cup final Winners medals 1957, losers' medal 1958.
Chelsea details Debut 20.12.58. 58 Appearances.

	Appearances				Goals			
	FL	FAC	LC	FC	FL	FAC	LC	FC
1958–59	21	2	–	2	–	–	–	–
1959–60	30	2	–	–	–	–	–	–
1960–61	–	–	1	–	–	–	–	–
Total	51	4	1	2	–	–	–	–

A powerfully built, hard-tackling wing-half who had already appeared in two FA Cup finals before his arrival at Stamford Bridge. His time at Chelsea was during a transitional phase and he never fitted into Tommy Docherty's rebuilding plans.

DALE, George H. (1919–1922) Inside-forward

Born Nottingham Height 5ft 6in Weight 10st 4lb. Career Queens Park Rangers (World War I), Notts County, Chelsea (May 1919).
Chelsea details Debut 20.8.19. 52 Appearances 1 Goal.

	Appearances		Goals	
	FL	FAC	FL	FAC
1919–20	36	3	1	–
1920–21	8	–	–	–
1921–22	5	–	–	–
Total	49	3	1	–

A skilful dribbler who helped the club re-establish themselves in the first division during the first season after normal football was resumed at the end of World War I. It was felt, however, that he did not have the necessary finishing power and never again commanded a regular place in the first-team.

D'ARCY, Seamus D. (1951–1952) Forward

Born Newry 14.12.21. Died February 1985. Height 6ft Weight 12st. Career Charlton Athletic, Chelsea (October 1951, £6,000), Brentford (October 1952).
Honours Northern Ireland (5 caps).
Chelsea details Debut 27.10.51. 31 Appearances 14 Goals.

	Appearances		Goals	
	FL	FAC	FL	FAC
1951–52	21	8	13	1
1952–53	2	–	–	–
Total	23	8	13	1

"Jimmy" proved a good investment in the short-term, being joint leading goalscorer with Roy Bentley in his first season at Stamford Bridge. But he did not fit into manager Ted Drake's plans for building a championship winning team. A tall, somewhat awkwardly built man, on his day he was an accurate finisher. His transfer to Brentford was in part-exchange for Ron Greenwood.

DAVIDSON, Alexander M. (1946–1948) Inside-forward

Born Langholm 6.6.20 Height 5ft 7in Weight 11st. Career Hibernian, Chelsea (August 1946), Crystal Palace (August 1948).
Chelsea details Debut 30.11.46. 2 Appearances.

	Appearances		Goals	
	FL	FAC	FL	FAC
1946–47	2	–	–	–
Total	2	–	–	–

A fair-haired forward whose two years at Stamford Bridge were spent almost entirely in the Combination side. He played 10 further League games after moving to Crystal Palace.

SEAMUS D. D'ARCY

ALEXANDER M. DAVIDSON

GORDON J. DAVIES | JOHN DEMPSEY

DAVIES, Gordon J. (1984–1985) Striker

Born Merthyr Tydfil 3.8.55 Height 5ft 7in Weight 10st 12lb. Career Merthyr Tydfil, Fulham, Chelsea (November 1984, £90,000), Manchester City (October 1985, £100,000), Fulham.
Honours Wales (18 caps).
Chelsea details Debut 8.12.84. 13(2) Appearances 6 Goals.

	Appearances		Goals	
	FL	FAC	FL	FAC
1984–85	10(2)	2	6	–
1985–86	1	–	–	–
Total	11(2)	2	6	–

Having scored over 100 League goals for Fulham he moved to Stamford Bridge in an attempt to establish himself in First Division football. However, the consistency of Kerry Dixon and David Speedie limited his chances and, understandably impatient at the age of 30, he moved to Manchester City after 11 months with Chelsea. Small and determined, with the eye for a half-chance, he will be remembered at The Bridge chiefly for his hat-trick against Everton in a League match at Goodison.

DEMPSEY, John (1969–1978) Centre-half

Born Hampstead 15.3.46 Height 6ft 1in Weight 11st 3lb. Career Fulham, Chelsea (January 1969, £70,000), Philadelphia Furies (March 1978).
Honours Republic of Ireland (19 caps), FA Cup winners' medal 1970, European Cup Winners Cup winners' medal 1971.
Chelsea details Debut 1.2.69 200(7) Appearances 7 Goals

	Appearances				Goals			
	FL	FAC	LC	ECWC	FL	FAC	LC	ECW
1968–69	15	1	–	–	–	–	–	–
1969–70	37	8	3	–	2	1	–	–
1970–71	29(2)	0(1)	2	7	1	–	–	1
1971–72	35	2	5(2)	2	1	1	–	–
1972–73	10(1)	4	1	–	–	–	–	–
1973–74	11(1)	–	3	–	–	–	–	–
1974–75	24	–	1	–	–	–	–	–
Total	161(4)	15(1)	15(2)	9	4	2	–	1

Dominant, uncompromising centre-half who was a pillar of Chelsea's defence in the most successful period of the club's history. His height enabled him to control the majority of opponents in the air and he will also be remembered for scoring the vital goal in the replayed final of the European Cup Winners' Cup final in Athens.

DICKIE, Murdock M. (1945–1946) Outside-right

Career Guildford City, Chelsea (April 1945), Bournemouth & Boscombe Athletic (February 1947).
Chelsea details Debut 7.9.46. 1 Appearance

	Appearances		Goals	
	FL	FAC	FL	FAC
1946–47	1	–	–	–
Total	1	–	–	–

Although he played a handful of first-team games in the final season of regional war-time football, he was unable to win a place in the senior side thereafter, but later played intermittently, for Bournemouth's third division side for two seasons.

DICKIE, William C. (1919–1921) Half-back

Born Kilmarnock Height 5ft 7½in Weight 10st. Career Kilmarnock, Chelsea (June 1919), Stoke City (April 1921), Sittingbourne.
Chelsea details Debut 20.8.19. 40 Appearances

	Appearances		Goals	
	FL	FAC	FL	FAC
1919–20	28	2	–	–
1920–21	7	3	–	–
Total	35	5	–	–

Although he was only a registered Chelsea player for two seasons, his association with the club began in September 1917 when he made guest appearances in the unofficial regional war-time competitions. Further, he was a member of the Chelsea London "Victory" Cup-winning side which beat Fulham, 3–0, in the final of that competition. Noted for his fitness and hard work, he was unable to hold a first-team place after his initial season in the League side.

MURDOCK M. DICKIE

WILLIAM C. DICKIE

| ALAN V. DICKS | WILLIAM DICKSON |

DICKS, Alan V. (1951–1958) Half-back

Born Kennington 29.8.34 Height 5ft 10in, Weight 11st 7lb. Career Dulwich Hamlet, Rainham Town, Millwall (amateur), Chelsea (August 1951), Southend United (November 1958, £12,000 – combined fee with Les Stubbs), Coventry City.
Chelsea details Debut 13.12.52. 38 Appearances 1 Goal

	Appearances		Goals	
	FL	FAC	FL	FAC
1952–1953	1	–	–	–
1953–1954	2	–	–	–
1954–1955	1	–	–	–
1955–1956	4	4	1	–
1956–1957	19	1	–	–
1957–1958	6	–	–	–
Total	33	5	1	–

Tall and athletically built, his only prolonged spell in the first-team was in the latter part of the 1956–57 season. Otherwise he remained a pillar of the Combination team for six seasons. After three years of first-team football at Southend, he moved to Coventry where he became Assistant Manager to Jimmy Hill before managing Bristol City for several years. His brother, Ronnie, was a full-back with Middlesbrough from 1947–58.

DICKSON, William (1947–1953) Half-back

Born Lurgan, Co. Armagh 15.4.23 Height 5ft 10ins, Weight 12st 11lb. Career Notts County, Chelsea (November 1947 – part exchange for Tommy Lawton), Arsenal (October 1953, £15,000), Mansfield Town.
Honours Northern Ireland (12 caps)
Chelsea details Debut 1.1.48. 119 Appearances 4 Goals

	Appearances		Goals	
	FL	FAC	FL	FAC
1947–48	1	–	–	–
1948–49	2	–	–	–
1949–50	3	–	–	–
1950–51	20	4	1	–
1951–52	37	7	–	–
1952–53	38	7	3	–
Total	101	18	4	–

A powerfully built attacking wing-half (or useful centre-half), he turned out to be much more than a "make-weight" in the £20,000 (a then record) deal which took Tommy Lawton to Notts County. For three seasons he was outstanding in the first-team, then in the process of being rebuilt, and it was surprising that he did not figure in manager Ted Drake's plans when he assembled the side that went on to win the championship in 1954–55. Eagerly snapped up by Arsenal, his career there was affected by injuries.

DIXON, Kerry M. (1983–   ) Striker

Born Luton 24.7.61 Height 6ft 0in Weight 13st 0lb. Career Dunstable Town, Reading, Chelsea (August 1983, £175,000).
Chelsea details Debut 27.8.83. 193(1) Appearances 105 Goals

	Appearances				Goals			
	FL	FAC	LC	FMC	FL	FAC	LC	FMC
1983–84	42	1	5	–	28	–	6	–
1984–85	41	2	10	–	24	4	8	–
1985–86	38	2	7	4	14	–	5	4
1986–87	35(1)	2	3	1	10	–	1	1
Total	156(1)	7	25	5	76	4	20	5

He had already made his reputation as a goalscorer with Reading in the fourth and third divisions (55 goals in 116 League games) before arriving at Stamford Bridge. He then proceeded to head the second division's list (as Chelsea surged to promotion) and followed this up by topping the first division's scorers to complete a unique quartet. A well-built natural athlete whose strength is his finishing ability, he was a member of the 1986 World Cup squad.

KERRY M. DIXON

JAMES DOCHERTY | THOMAS H. DOCHERTY

DOCHERTY, James (1979) Striker

Born Broxburn 8.11.56 Height 5ft 10in, Weight 10st 5lb. Career East Stirling, Chelsea (February 1979, £50,000), Dundee United (November 1979).
Chelsea details 2(1) Appearances

	Appearances			Goals		
	FL	FAC	LC	FL	FAC	LC
1978–1979	2(1)	–	–	–	–	–
Total	2(1)	–	–	–	–	–

Failing to adjust to the demands of English football, he was on the staff for ten months at a time when the club was going through a difficult period, both on the field and behind the scenes.

DOCHERTY, Thomas H. (1961–1962) Wing-half

Born Glasgow 24.8.28 Height 5ft 9ins, Weight 11st 8lb. Career Shettleston Juniors, Glasgow Celtic, Preston North End, Arsenal, Chelsea (September 1961).
Honours Scotland (25 caps), Scotland 'B' (2 appearances), Second Division championship medal 1951, F.A. Cup losers' medal 1954.
Chelsea details 4 Appearances

	Appearances			Goals		
	FL	FAC	LC	FL	FAC	LC
1961–62	4	–	–	–	–	–
Total	4	–	–	–	–	–

His move from Arsenal to Chelsea in the twilight of his playing days enabled him to launch forth on his "second" career as a manager. It was in fact as "player-coach" that he was signed and he was promoted manager in January 1962, when he succeeded Ted Drake. He then went on to build a promotion team (1962–63), win the Football League Cup (1965), and take Chelsea to their first Wembley F.A. Cup final (1967) – after two unsuccessful semi-final appearances in the same competition – before leaving in controversial circumstances in October 1967.

DODD, George (1911–1913) Inside-forward

Born Stockport County, Notts County, Chelsea (October 1911), Millwall (February 1913), Luton Town.
Chelsea details Debut 14.10.11. 31 Appearances 9 Goals

	Appearances		Goals	
	FL	FAC	FL	FAC
1911–12	18	2	8	1
1912–13	11	–	–	–
Total	29	2	8	1

A regular first-team player for only his first year at Stamford Bridge, when he was succeeded by the legendary amateur Corinthian, V.J. Woodward. His main claim to a spot in Chelsea's history is the fact that he scored the first-ever goal recorded against the club in League football when he notched the only goal of the game at Stockport on September 2nd, 1905. After his playing career ended he managed both Catford and Southend United.

DODDS, William (1986–   ) Striker

Born New Cumnock Height 5ft 7in, Weight 10st
Career Chelsea
Chelsea details Debut 3.3.87 0(2) Appearances

	Appearances		Goals	
	FL	FMC	FL	FMC
1986–87	0(1)	0(1)	–	–
Total	0(1)	0(1)	–	–

Joined Chelsea as a Apprentice at the start of the 1985–86 season during which he was top scorer for the Juniors (27 goals in 30 games in League and Cup competitions), as well as playing in several matches for the reserve team. A fast, nippy attacker with a keen eye for an opening and a strong finisher.

GEORGE DODD

WILLIAM DODDS

HUGH R. DOLBY   D. LEONARD DOLDING

DOLBY, Hugh R. (1909–1912) Winger

Born Agra (India). Career Nunhead, Chelsea (Summer 1909), Brentford.
Chelsea details Debut 11.12.09 2 Appearances

	Appearances		Goals	
	FL	FAC	FL	FAC
1909–10	1	–	–	–
1910–11	1	–	–	–
Total	2	–	–	–

A dependable reserve player who in three years on the staff could not force his way into the first-team ahead of Billy Brawn and Angus Douglas.

DOLDING, D. Leonard (1945–1948) Winger

Born Oeregaum 13.12.22 Died 23.11.54 (Car crash) Height 5ft 9ins, Weight 10st 7lb. Career Wealdstone, Chelsea (July 1945), Norwich City (July 1948).
Chelsea details Debut 12.2.46 27 Appearances 2 Goals

	Appearances		Goals	
	FL	FAC	FL	FAC
1945–46	–	1	1	–
1946–47	17	–	1	–
1947–48	9	–	1	–
Total	26	1	2	–

After a brief spell with Wealdstone, he joined Chelsea at the end of World War II in which he had served as a member of an air-crew with the R.A.F. He never fully established a first-team place and the arrival of "expensive" signings such as Bobby Campbell, Johnny Paton and John McInnes limited the chances which came his way. A member of the M.C.C. cricket groundstaff, he played one game for Middlesex in 1951.

DONAGHY, Charles (1905–1907) Winger

Born India. Career Chelsea (September 1905), contract cancelled (September 1906).
Chelsea details Debut 18.11.05. 3 Appearances 1 Goal

	Appearances		Goals	
	FL	FAC	FL	FAC
1905–06	1	1	1	–
1906–07	1	–	–	–
Total	2	1	1	–

A member of the hastily assembled squad of players starting Chelsea's first-ever season in football, he played most of his career at Stamford Bridge in the reserve team.

DONALD, Alexander (1930–1932) Full-back

Born Kirkintilloch. Height 5ft 9in, Weight 10st 11lb. Career Partick Thistle, New York Nationals, Chelsea (July 1930), Bristol Rovers (Summer 1932).
Chelsea details Debut 8.11.30 24 Appearances 1 Goal

	Appearances		Goals	
	FL	FAC	FL	FAC
1930–31	12	–	1	–
1931–32	12	–	–	–
Total	24	–	1	–

His arrival at Stamford Bridge from U.S.A. coincided with the club's promotion from Division II. Two spells in the first-team, when he deputised for Scottish international Tommy Law, were insufficient to win him a more permanent place.

CHARLES DONAGHY

ALEXANDER DONALD

ANGUS DOUGLAS

DOUGLAS, Angus (1908–1913) Outside-right

Born Dumfries 1.1.89, Died 14.12.18. Career Dumfries, Glasgow Rangers, Chelsea (May 1908), Newcastle United (November 1913).
Honours Scotland (1 cap).
Chelsea details Debut 1.9.08. 103 Appearances 11 Goals

	Appearances		Goals	
	FL	FAC	FL	FAC
1908–09	7	–	1	–
1909–10	14	–	2	–
1910–11	24	6	6	–
1911–12	35	1	2	–
1912–13	16	–	–	–
Total	96	7	11	–

Chelsea had to compete with Everton for the signature of the Scot and he at once became a great favourite with the Stamford Bridge crowd. Fast and clever, with all the traditional Scottish ball skills, he shared the outside-right position with Billy Brawn in his early years on the staff, but had established himself when he was, surprisingly, transferred to Newcastle United – not a popular move with the Bridge regulars Died of influenza shortly after serving in World War I.

DOWNING, Sam (1909–1914) Wing-half

Born Willesden 1883, Died March 1974. Height 5ft 10ins, Weight 13st. Career West Hampstead, Willesden Town, Queens Park Rangers, Chelsea (April 1909), Croydon Common.
Chelsea details Debut 9.4.09. 144 Appearances 10 Goals

	Appearances		Goals	
	FL	FAC	FL	FAC
1908–09	6	–	–	–
1909–10	37	2	5	–
1910–11	34	6	2	1
1911–12	28	2	1	–
1912–13	25	–	1	–
1913–14	4	–	–	–
Total	134	10	9	1

An artistic, constructive wing-half whose lack of pace probably cost him more widespread recognition. A most popular player who was given a benefit match to mark his retirement. Captain of the side for a period, he was noted for his accurate and powerful long-range shooting and for his scrupulously fair play. Continued to live in North London until the time of his death.

DRIVER, Philip A. (1980–1983) Winger

Born Huddersfield 10.8.59. Height 5ft 10in, Weight 10st 12lb. Career Bedford Town, Wimbledon, Chelsea (September 1980, £20,000), Wimbledon (Summer 1983), St Alban's City.
Chelsea details Debut 8.10.80 25(21) Appearances 4 Goals

	Appearances			Goals		
	FL	FAC	LC	FL	FAC	LC
1980–81	12(11)	0(1)	–	1	–	–
1981–82	4(4)	–	–	3	–	–
1982–83	9(4)	–	0(1)	–	–	–
Total	25(19)	0(1)	0(1)	4	–	–

His speed on the wing combined with intricate footwork and the ability to cross the ball accurately made him, potentially, a fine player. Yet his comparatively short League career was hampered by injuries and he never did himself full justice.

SAM DOWNING

PHILIP A. DRIVER

MICKY DROY

DROY, Micky (1970–1985) Central Defender

Born Highbury 7.5.51. Height 6ft 4in Weight 15st 2lb. Career Slough Town, Chelsea (October 1970), Crystal Palace (free), Brentford.
Chelsea details Debut 13.2.71. 302(11) Appearances, 19 Goals

	Appearances				Goals			
	FL	FAC	LC	ECWC	FL	FAC	LC	ECWC
1970–71	3(1)	–	–	1	–	–	–	–
1971–72	1	–	–	–	–	–	–	–
1972–73	14(1)	–	1	–	–	–	–	–
1973–74	29(1)	2	1	–	1	–	–	–
1974–75	26	2	4	–	2	2	–	–
1975–76	25	3	1	–	1	–	–	–
1976–77	8	2	1	–	1	–	–	–
1977–78	35	3	1	–	1	1	–	–
1978–79	14	1	1	–	–	–	–	–
1979–80	26(2)	–	2	–	1	–	1	–
1980–81	30	1	2	–	1	–	1	–
1981–82	20(3)	4	0(2)	–	2	1	–	–
1982–83	31	3	3	–	3	–	–	–
1984–85	1(1)	–	–	–	–	–	–	–
Total	263(9)	21	17(2)	1	13	4	2	–

It was his misfortune that his career coincided with one of the most difficult phases in Chelsea's history. As a result his lot was usually to shore up a defence lacking in experience and confidence under a succession of different managers with financial, and other, worries never far away. Nevertheless he remained the pillar of the defence for a dozen or so seasons. Powerful in the air, he frequently displayed deft skills at ground level for such a big man, his telescopic left foot dispossessing many a startled opponent with its immense range.

DUBLIN, Keith B. L. (1984–   ) Full-back

Born Wycombe 29.1.66 Height 5ft 11in Weight 11st 10lb. Career Chelsea (January 1984).
Honours England Youth International
Chelsea details Debut 7.5.84. 66(2) Appearances

	Appearances				Goals			
	FL	FAC	LC	FMC	FL	FAC	LC	FMC
1983–84	1	–	–	–	–	–	–	–
1984–85	10(1)	–	–	–	–	–	–	–
1985–86	11	2	5	3(1)	–	–	–	–
1986–87	28	3	1	2	–	–	–	–
Total	50(1)	5	6	5(1)	–	–	–	–

Well-built full-back who came to Chelsea as an Apprentice in July 1982 after Watford (where he had also signed apprentice forms), West Ham United and Crystal Palace had also shown interest. Speedy and a strong tackler, his debut came in the final home fixture of the 1983–84 season when Chelsea were celebrating their promotion back to Division One.

DUDLEY, Samuel (1932–1934) Outside-left

Born Tipton Height 5ft 7½in Weight 10st 2lb. Career Clapton Orient, Chelsea (June 1932).
Chelsea details Debut 4.2.33. 1 Appearance

	Appearances		Goals	
	FL	FAC	FL	FAC
1932–33	1	–	–	–
Total	1	–	–	–

His arrival at Stamford Bridge coincided with a time when famous names were being signed in an endeavour to bring instant success for Chelsea and he was unable to displace such stars.

KEITH B.L. DUBLIN

SAMUEL DUDLEY

BERNARD DUFFY   JOHN A. DUNN

DUFFY, Bernard (1923–27) Wing-half

Born Glasgow Height 5ft 9in Weight 11st 8lb. Career Bellshill Athletic (Glasgow), Chelsea (June 1923), Clapton Orient (March 1927).
Chelsea details Debut 27.10.23. 3 Appearances

	Appearances		Goals	
	FL	FAC	FL	FAC
1923–24	1	–	–	–
1924–25	1	–	–	–
1925–26	1	–	–	–
Total	3	–	–	–

Coming to Chelsea direct from junior football in the Glasgow area, he failed to make his mark in English football, although he was a dependable member of the reserve team.

DUNN, John A. (1962–66) Goalkeeper

Born Barking 21.6.44 Height 5ft 11in Weight 12st 6lb. Career Chelsea (February 1962), Torquay United (October 1966), Aston Villa, Charlton Athletic, Tooting & Mitcham.
Chelsea details Debut 27.30.63. 16 Appearances

	Appearances			Goals		
	FL	FAC	LC	FL	FAC	LC
1962–63	3	–	–	–	–	–
1963–64	6	3	–	–	–	–
1964–65	1	–	–	–	–	–
1965–66	3	–	–	–	–	–
Total	13	3	–	–	–	–

One of several talented 'keepers whose lot was to deputise for Peter Bonetti. Signed professional after joining Chelsea as an apprentice, he was a reliable and sound performer who went on to make more than a century of League appearances with both Aston Villa and Charlton.

DURIE, Gordon (1986–   ) Striker

Born Paisley 6.11.65 Height 6ft 0in Weight 11st 6lb. Career East Fife, Hibernian, Chelsea (April 1986, £380,000).
Honours
Chelsea details Debut 5.5.86. 22(7) Appearances 6 Goals

	Appearances		Goals	
	FL	FAC	FL	FAC
1985–86	1	–	–	–
1986–87	18(7)	3	5	1
Total	19(7)	3	5	1

A fast, well-built and brave striker who moved from Scottish football where he had scored 41 goals (121 games) with his previous clubs. At Hibernian he had become something of a "folk hero" amongst the fans. Operating either in the middle or down the flanks, he won recognition from the Scottish selectors in his first season at Stamford Bridge, being called up for the Under-21 squad.

DYKE, Charlie H. (1947–1951) Outside-right

Born Caerphilly 23.9.26 Height 5ft 6in Weight 10st 12lb. Career Troedyrhiw, Chelsea (November 1947), Barry Town (Summer 1951).
Chelsea details Debut 21.2.48. 25 Appearances 2 Goals

	Appearances		Goals	
	FL	FAC	FL	FAC
1947–48	13	–	1	–
1948–49	2	–	–	–
1950–51	9	1	1	–
Total	24	1	2	–

A cheerful, slightly-built, ginger-haired winger who was a great trier as a thrustful winger. But, having failed to oust Bobby Campbell from the League team, he returned to his native South Wales after four seasons at The Bridge.

GORDON DURIE

CHARLIE H. DYKE

ROBERT H. EDWARDS	SIDNEY ELLIOT

EDWARDS, Robert H. (1951–55) Inside-forward

Born Guildford 22.5.31 Height 5ft 11in Weight 12st. Career Woking, Chelsea (November 1951), Swindon Town (July 1955), Norwich City, Northampton Town.
Chelsea details Debut 26.12.52. 13 Appearances 2 Goals

	Appearances		Goals	
	FL	FAC	FL	FAC
1952–53	12	–	2	–
1954–55	1	–	–	–
Total	13	–	2	–

Signed professional forms immediately after demobilisation from the RAF. An elegant player who understudied John McNichol for some four years and made one appearance in the League Championship season. Later, he played nearly 200 games in his four-year stay with Swindon Town.

ELLIOT, Sidney (1928–1930) Centre-forward

Born Sunderland Career Arcade Mission, Durham City, Fulham, Chelsea (May 1928, £3,000), Bristol City (July 1930), Notts County.
Chelsea details Debut 25.8.28. 30 Appearances 9 Goals

	Appearances		Goals	
	FL	FAC	FL	FAC
1928–29	14	–	3	–
1929–30	16	–	6	–
Total	30	–	9	–

Having scored more than 100 goals in a season for Arcade Mission in his native Sunderland, he was snapped up by Durham City at the age of 16, and arrived at Stamford Bridge after one season at Craven Cottage. At the time Chelsea were desperate to end their stay in the Second Division but did not consider his output of goals sufficient to give him extended opportunities.

ELMES, Timothy (1980–1982) Midfield

Born Thornton Heath 28.9.62 Height 5ft 10in Weight 12st Career Chelsea (July 1980), Orient.
Chelsea details Debut 26.12.80. 2(2) Appearances

	Appearances			Goals		
	FL	FAC	LC	FL	FAC	LC
1980–81	2(2)	–	–	–	–	–
Total	2(2)	–	–	–	–	–

Signed professional after a year as an apprentice. A sturdily-built, combative midfield player, sadly, he failed to fulfill his undoubted potential and, after a brief spell with Orient, drifted out of League football altogether.

EVANS, Robert (1960–1961) Half-back

Born Glasgow 16.7.27 Height 5ft 8½in Weight 12st Career St. Anthony (Glasgow), Glasgow Celtic, **Chelsea (May 1960, £12,000)**, Newport County (free transfer), Morton.
Honours Scotland (48 caps), Scottish League XI (24 appearances), Scottish League championship medal 1954, Scottish Cup winners' medals 1951, 1954, losers' medals 1955, 1956, Scottish League cup winners' medals 1957, 1958.
Chelsea details Debut 20.8.60. 37 Appearances 1 Goal

	Appearances			Goals		
	FL	FAC	LC	FL	FAC	LC
1960–61	32	1	4	–	–	1
Total	32	1	4	–	–	1

His move to Chelsea as his long and distinguished career was drawing to its close was scarcely a success. At 33 he had lost his edge and being asked to operate at centre-half, having spent the majority of his career as a wing-half, also presented its problems. As a result the young, emerging players around him never fully felt the benefit of his experience. **Earlier he had had a magnificent and highly successful career with Celtic, having been virtually a permanent fixture in the Scottish side for ten years from 1949.** On leaving Chelsea he was appointed Player-Manager of Newport County.

TIMOTHY ELMES

ROBERT EVANS

NORMAN FAIRGRAY | MARK P. FALCO

FAIRGRAY, Norman (1907–1914) Outside-left

Born Dumfries. Career Maxwelltown Volunteers, Lincoln City, Chelsea (September 1907).
Chelsea details Debut 14.9.07. 84 Appearances 6 Goals

	Appearances		Goals	
	FL	FAC	FL	FAC
1907–08	28	–	2	–
1908–09	18	2	–	–
1909–10	6	–	2	–
1910–11	2	–	–	–
1911–12	10	–	–	–
1912–13	9	2	2	–
1913–14	6	1	–	–
Total	79	5	6	–

In retrospect, it is surprising that "Norrie" did not play more frequently in the first-team during his seven years on the staff. On his day he was a brilliant winger of the orthodox type, exhibiting tricky footwork and an extensive repertoire of ball-skills. Certainly he was most popular with the Stamford Bridge regulars, but his slight physique was against him at a time when most full-backs were selected for their strength of tackle and ability to win the ball.

FALCO, Mark P. (1982) Striker

Born Hackney 22.10.60 Height 6ft, Weight 12st. Career Tottenham Hotspur, Chelsea (November 1982 on loan), Tottenham Hotspur, Watford.
Honours England Youth.
Chelsea details Debut 27.11.82. 3 Appearances

	Appearances			Goals		
	FL	FAC	LC	FL	FAC	LC
1982–83	3	–	–	–	–	–
Total	3	–	–	–	–	–

Joined Chelsea on a month's loan in November 1982. A tall, well-built striker, he then returned to Tottenham where he had a long run in the first-team before being transferred to Watford in October 1986.

FASCIONE, Joe (1962–1969) Winger

Born Coatbridge 5.2.45 Height 5ft 4½in Weight 9st 12lb. Career Kirkintilloch Rob Roy, Chelsea (September 1962), Durham City (Summer 1969), Romford, Barking.
Chelsea details Debut 23.9.64. 27(7) Appearances 1 Goal

	Appearances				Goals			
	FL	FAC	LC	FC	FL	FAC	LC	FC
1964–65	–	–	3	–	–	–	–	–
1965–66	12(3)	–	–	2	1	–	–	–
1966–67	4(1)	–	–	–	–	–	–	–
1967–68	6(2)	–	–	–	–	–	–	–
1968–69	0(1)	–	–	–	–	–	–	–
Total	22(7)	–	3	2	1	–	–	–

A small, tricky winger whose time at Chelsea was largely spent in the reserve team. However he was "on-call" for first team duty for six seasons and gave some excellent displays on the rare opportunities to show his true ability.

FEELY, Peter (1970–1973) Striker

Born City of London 3.1.50 Height 5ft 11in Weight 12st 10lb. Career Enfield, Chelsea (April 1970), Bournemouth & Boscombe (February 1973, £1,000), Fulham, Gillingham, Sheffield Wednesday, Stockport County.
Honours England Amateur, England Youth
Chelsea details Debut 24.4.71. 4(1) Appearances 2 Goals

	Appearances			Goals		
	FL	FAC	LC	FL	FAC	LC
1970–71	2	–	–	1	–	–
1971–72	0(1)	–	–	–	–	–
1972–73	2	–	–	1	–	–
Total	4(1)	–	–	2	–	–

After scoring on his first-team League debut against Coventry City, he found it impossible to win a permanent place in the senior side in the era of Peter Osgood, Ian Hutchinson and Tommy Baldwin. One of soccer's nomads, his most successful spell was at Gillingham where he averaged more than a goal in every two games.

JOE FASCIONE

PETER FEELY

WANTED
If anyone has a photograph of **CHRISTOPHER** It would be appreciated if you would allow us to copy it. Please forward it to Ron at 36 Lockier Walk, Wembley, Middx. It will be returned safely

CHRISTOPHER FERGUSON

EDWARD FERGUSON

FERGUSON, Christopher (1927–1930) Forward

Born Kirkonnel Height 5ft 6in Weight 10st 2lb. Career Chelsea (October 1927), Queens Park Rangers (Summer 1930).
Chelsea details Debut 28.4.28. 1 Appearance

	Appearances		Goals	
	FL	FAC	FL	FAC
1927–28	1	–	–	–
Total	1	–	–	–

Younger brother of Willie Ferguson, Chelsea was his first professional club and he remained on the Stamford Bridge staff for three seasons, playing at inside, or centre forward in the reserve team.

FERGUSON, Edward (1920–1923) Full-back

Born Dunfermline. Career Chelsea (March 1920–Summer 1923).
Chelsea details Debut 7.5.21. 2 Appearances

	Appearances		Goals	
	FL	FAC	FL	FAC
1920–21	1	–	–	–
1922–23	1	–	–	–
Total	2	–	–	–

His opportunities were strictly limited by the consistency of Jack Harrow, who was firmly installed at full-back in partnership with either Walter Bettridge or George Smith at this time.

FERGUSON, William (1921–1933) Inside-forward/Wing-half

Born Muirkirk Height 5ft 6ins Weight 9st 13lb. Career Kelso Rovers, Queen of the South Wanderers, Chelsea (October 1921), Queen of the South (Summer 1933).
Chelsea details Debut 30.3.23. 294 Appearances 11 Goals

	Appearances		Goals	
	FL	FAC	FL	FAC
1922–23	9	–	–	–
1923–24	27	2	1	–
1924–25	30	1	2	–
1925–26	27	2	–	–
1926–27	42	5	3	–
1927–28	41	1	1	–
1928–29	22	4	–	–
1929–30	11	–	2	–
1930–31	25	–	–	–
1931–32	21	7	2	–
1932–33	17	–	–	–
Total	272	22	11	–

Willie was one of the best-liked and most loyal players in Chelsea's history. He began his Stamford Bridge career in the forward line, but soon moved back to wing-half where he was undisputed first choice for nine seasons in good times and bad. The disappointment of relegation in April 1924 was more than compensated for him by the return to Division I six years later. A terrier-type and most consistent player, he overcame his lack of height and was noted both for his firm tackling and accurate distribution of the ball. After returning to his native land, he was appointed manager of Queen of the South in 1937 at the conclusion of his long and honourable playing career.

WILLIAM FERGUSON

JAMES FERRIS

MICHAEL FILLERY

FERRIS, James (1920–1922) Inside-forward

Born Belfast Height 5ft 7in Weight 9st 7lb Career Distillery, Belfast Celtic, Chelsea (September 1920), Preston North End (March 1922), Belfast Celtic.
Honours Northern Ireland (5 caps), Irish League
Chelsea details Debut 6.9.20. 39 Appearances 9 Goals

	Appearances		Goals	
	FL	FAC	FL	FAC
1920–21	27	6	8	1
1921–22	6	–	–	–
Total	33	6	8	1

Arrived at Chelsea with a big reputation but, although winning a further two international caps during his time at Stamford Bridge, he never settled in London. A forceful inside-forward, after one season he unaccountably lost form, moved to Preston North End, before finishing his playing career in his native land.

FILLERY, Michael (1978–1983) Midfield

Born Mitcham 19.9.60 Height 5ft 10ins Weight 13st. Career Chelsea (August 1978), Queens Park Rangers (August 1983, £200,000).
Honours England Schoolboy and Youth international.
Chelsea details Debut 4.4.79. 176(5) Appearances 41 Goals

	Appearances			Goals		
	FL	FAC	LC	FL	FAC	LC
1978–79	6(1)	–	–	–	–	–
1979–80	40(1)	1	1	11	–	2
1980–81	35(1)	1	2	6	–	–
1981–82	39(1)	6	3	6	1	3
1982–83	36(1)	3	3	9	2	1
Total	156(5)	11	9	32	3	6

Signed after being an apprentice on the Stamford Bridge staff. A highly talented and stylish midfield player who, at times, lacked the consistency and application to do his ability justice. His time in the first-team was spent almost wholly in the Second Division and at a time of general instability both on and off the field which, perhaps, hindered his development and shaped an attitude which appeared casual and disinterested on occasions.

FINLAYSON, William (1920–1923) Centre-forward

Born Thornliebank (Renfrewshire) Height 5ft 7in Weight 9st 7lb Career Ashfield (Glasgow), Thornliebank, Chelsea (June 1920), Clapton Orient (1923), Brentford.
Chelsea details Debut 21.1.22. 5 Appearances 1 Goal

	Appearances		Goals	
	FL	FAC	FL	FAC
1921–22	1	–	1	–
1923–24	4	–	1	–
Total	5	–	1	–

A junior player from Scotland who spent most of his four years at Stamford Bridge in the reserve team at a time when Jack Cock and Andy Wilson were recognised centre-forwards on the staff.

FINNIESTON, Steve (1971–1978) Striker

Born Edinburgh 30.11.54 Height 5ft 11in Weight 11st 3lb Career Chelsea (December 1971), Cardiff City (loan), Sheffield United (June 1978 £90,000), Addlestone, Hartney Wintney.
Honours Scotland Youth
Chelsea details Debut 1.2.75. 86(4) Appearances 37 Goals

	Appearances			Goals		
	FL	FAC	LC	FL	FAC	LC
1974–75	9	–	–	2	–	–
1975–76	12	–	–	5	–	–
1976–77	39	2	3	24	–	2
1977–78	18(2)	2(2)	1	3	1	–
Total	78(2)	4(2)	4	34	1	2

Joined Chelsea as an apprentice from school at Weybridge and became a prolific goalscorer in junior and reserve football. Established himself in the senior side on the 1974 club tour of Australia. However, at a time of instability within the club, his career was adversely affected by a series of injuries and he was unable to do full justice to his undoubted ability. After a spell at Sheffield United he was forced to give up full-time football, as a result of another injury.

WILLIAM FINLAYSON

STEVE FINNIESTON

WANTED
If anyone has
a photograph
of
JAMES
It would be appreciated if you
would allow us to copy it.
Please forward it to Ron at
36 Lockier Walk,
Wembley, Middx.
It will be returned safely

JAMES FLETCHER

HARRY FORD

FLETCHER, James (1905–1906) Full-back
Career Chelsea (1905–06).
Chelsea details Debut 17.2.06. 1 Appearance

	Appearances			Goals		
	FL	FAC	LC	FL	FAC	LC
1905–06	1	–	–	–	–	–
Total	1	–	–	–	–	–

A somewhat mysterious character who played one League game as an amateur in Chelsea's first-ever season – without, apparently, being registered with the Football League.

FORD, Harry (1912–1924) Winger
Born Fulham Height 5ft 7½ins Weight 11st 4lb Career Tunbridge Wells Rangers, Chelsea (April 1912), Retired 1924.
Honours FA Cup Final losers' medal (1915).
Chelsea details Debut 7.9.12. 248 Appearances 46 Goals

	Appearances			Goals		
	FL	FAC	LC	FL	FAC	LC
1912–13	29	3	–	9	–	–
1913–14	37	2	–	9	–	–
1914–15	33	8	–	3	2	–
1919–20	30	5	–	3	2	–
1921–21	23	4	–	4	–	–
1921–22	29	1	–	3	1	–
1922–23	37	3	–	10	–	–
1923–24	4	–	–	–	–	–
Total	222	26	–	41	5	–

Spotted playing for Tunbridge Wells Rangers against Chelsea reserves. A versatile performer who was prepared to turn out in any position, on one occasion even playing the role of deputy goalkeeper – and this despite his lack of inches. It was, however, on the right wing where he most usually operated. One of the best in England at that time, he was very fast, could centre the ball with precision and also possessed impressive shooting power – two of his most crucial goals being instrumental in taking Chelsea to their first FA Cup final in 1915. A most popular man, he would probably have established a club record for the number of games played if he had not lost four seasons in World War I.

FOSS, Sidney R. (1936–1952) Inside-forward/Wing-half

Born Barking 28.11.12 Height 5ft 6in Weight 11st 7lb. Career Southall, Chelsea (May 1936). Retired 1952.
Chelsea details Debut 20.2.37. 48 Appearances 3 Goals

	Appearances			Goals		
	FL	FAC	LC	FL	FAC	LC
1936–37	4	–	–	–	–	–
1937–38	11	–	–	3	–	–
1938–39	11	–	–	–	–	–
1945–46	–	5	–	–	–	–
1946–47	12	–	–	–	–	–
1947–48	3	2	–	–	–	–
Total	41	7	–	3	–	–

One of the many professional footballers whose career was wrecked by World War II. The record books do not show that he played nearly 200 first-team games during the hostilities, yet, at the age of 33 when the war ended, was unable to figure very largely in manager Birrell's post-war rebuilding of his playing staff. Having started in the forward line, he became a sound wing-half. A shrewd reader of the game, it was no surprise when he became Manager of the Chelsea Youth Scheme in 1952 after his career as a player ended. For fourteen years he was largely instrumental in producing a regular and distinguished line of young stars who made their mark in international as well as club football. A most likeable man – and a crucial figure in the history of Chelsea F.C.

FOULKE, William H. (1905–1906) Goalkeeper

Born Dawley, Salop. 12.4.74 Died 1.5.16 Height 6ft 2in Weight 22st 3lb. Career Sheffield United, Chelsea (September 1905), Bradford City (April 1906).
Honours England (1 Cap), FA Cup winners' medals 1899, 1902, losers' medal 1901.
Chelsea details Debut 2.9.05. 35 Appearances

	Appearances		Goals	
	FL	FAC	FL	FAC
1905–06	34	1	–	–
Total	34	1	–	–

SIDNEY R. FOSS

WILLIAM H. FOULKE

STEPHEN FRANCIS	CHARLIE FREEMAN

One of football's legendary characters, the stories surrounding him are legion. "Little Willie" was Chelsea's first goalkeeper and was a giant of a man in every sense of the word. Surprisingly agile for a person of such girth, he spent only one season in London before moving back to finish his playing career in Yorkshire. Possibly uniquely, his name at birth was registered as "Foulk", and his death as "Foulkes". He played four matches as a professional cricketer for Derbyshire in 1900 and died from pneumonia contracted on Blackpool Sands where he was earning his living by inviting members of the public to score goals against him.

FRANCIS, Stephen (1982–1987) Goalkeeper

Born Billericay 29.5.64 Height 5ft 11in Weight 11st 5lb. Career Chelsea (May 1982), Reading (February 1987, £15,000).
Honours England Youth International. Full Members Cup winners' medal 1986.
Chelsea details Debut 6.10.81. 88 Appearances

	Appearances				Goals			
	FL	FAC	LC	FMC	FL	FAC	LC	FMC
1981–82	29	7	2	–	–	–	–	–
1982–83	37	3	3	–	–	–	–	–
1984–85	2	–	1	–	–	–	–	–
1985–86	3	–	–	1	–	–	–	–
Total	71	10	6	1	–	–	–	–

Signed apprentice forms in July 1980 and made an impressive debut at Southampton in the League Cup in October 1981, going on to establish himself as the regular first-team 'keeper in the next two seasons. Lost his place after the signing of Eddie Niedzwiecki whose consistency limited further chances and, after an eventual recall, did not display his previous confidence.

FREEMAN, Charlie (1907–1920) Inside-forward

Born Overseal, (Derbyshire) Died March 1956. Career Overseal Swifts, Burton United, Chelsea (1907), Retired 1920.
Chelsea details Debut 13.2.09. 105 Appearances 22 Goals

	Appearances		Goals	
	FL	FAC	FL	FAC
1908–09	4	–	–	–
1909–10	9	–	2	–
1910–11	18	5	2	1
1911–12	15	–	7	–
1912–13	11	–	3	–
1913–14	21	2	5	–
1914–15	15	2	2	–
1919–20	2	1	–	–
Total	95	10	21	1

Having impressed in a trial game, he was signed as a professional and started an association with Chelsea FC which was to endure for 46 years. As a player his career at Stamford Bridge extended over eight seasons (not including the four lost in World War I). Yet, only once did he win selection for more than half the games played. Always on hand to be recalled from the reserve team, he was a grafting and reliable inside-forward, if lacking in flair and originality. Noted for his dependability, it was entirely appropriate that on retiring as a player he became a member of the "backroom staff". Performing a variety of tasks over the years he became trainer to the first-team during the Second World War, as well as groundsman. He finally retired in the summer of 1953.

FREESTONE, Roger (1987–   ) Goalkeeper

Born Newport (Mon.) 19.8.68 Height 6ft 2in, Weight 13st 3lb.
Career Newport County, Chelsea (March 1987, £75,000)
Chelsea details Debut 18.4.87. 6 Appearances

	Appearances		Goals	
	FL	FAC	FL	FAC
1986–87	6	–	–	–
Total	6	–	–	–

Signed towards the end of the 1986–87 season and made his first-team debut within weeks of his arrival at Stamford Bridge, after a handful of senior games with his previous club, Newport County. Magnificently built, with a safe pair of hands, a player of very great potential.

ROGER FREESTONE

JAMES FREW | LESLIE FRIDGE

FREW, James (1922–1926) Centre-half

Born Kilmarnock Height 5ft 6in Weight 11st 2lb. Career Kilmarnock, Nothsdale Wanderers, Chelsea (June 1922), Southend United (Summer 1927), Carlisle United.
Chelsea details Debut 14.2.23. 43 Appearances

	Appearances		Goals	
	FL	FAC	FL	FAC
1922–23	14	–	–	–
1923–24	8	–	–	–
1924–25	18	1	–	–
1925–26	2	–	–	–
Total	42	1	–	–

Most of his five years at Stamford Bridge were spent in the reserve team but, despite his lack of inches, he proved a reliable and able deputy to Harold Wilding and George Rodger, the regular centre-halves of those days.

FRIDGE, Leslie (1985–1987) Goalkeeper

Born Inverness 27.8.68. Height 5ft 10in. Weight 11st 0lb. Career Inverness Thistle, Chelsea (December 1985), St. Mirren (January 1987, £50,000).
Honours Scotland Youth International, Scotland Under-21 International.
Chelsea details Debut 5.5.86. 1 Appearance

	Appearances		Goals	
	FL	FAC	FL	FAC
1985–86	1	–	–	–
Total	1	–	–	–

Highly rated north of the border, his chances at Stamford Bridge were limited by the form of Eddie Niedzwiecki and, latterly, Tony Godden on the staff. Strongly-built, he signed professional forms after a trial period and was the regular Juniors 'keeper for his two full seasons at Chelsea.

FROST, James L. (1906–1907) Outside-right

Born Wolverton, Northampton Town, Chelsea (December 1906), West Ham United, Croydon Common, Clapton Orient.
Chelsea details Debut 15.12.06. 22 Appearances, 4 Goals

	Appearances		Goals	
	FL	FAC	FL	FAC
1906–07	19	–	4	–
1907–08	3	–	–	–
Total	22	–	4	–

A fast and direct winger who came to Chelsea at a time when several other clubs were competing for his services. After seemingly establishing his first-team spot soon after his arrival, he then suffered injury and was unable to displace Billy Brawn, leaving Chelsea soon afterwards.

FROST, Lee A. (1976–1980) Winger

Born Woking 4.12.57 Height 5ft 8½in Weight 10st 7lb. Career Chelsea (July 1976), Brentford (December 1980, £15,000).
Chelsea details Debut 15.4.78. 11(3) Appearances 5 Goals

	Appearances		Goals	
	FL	FAC	FL	FAC
1977–78	1	–	–	–
1978–79	2(1)	–	–	–
1979–80	8(2)	–	5	–
Total	11(3)	–	5	–

Joined Chelsea as a junior and progressed to the first-team via reserve team football. A speedy and potentially dangerous and direct forward, he, nevertheless, failed to develop his early promise – this after scoring a hat-trick in a 7–3 win at Orient in November 1977.

JAMES L. FROST

LEE A. FROST

HUGH K. GALLACHER

GALLACHER, Hugh K. (1930–1934) Centre-forward

Born Bellshill (Lanarkshire) 2.2.03, Died 11.6.57 Height 5ft 5in Weight 10st 10lb. Career Bellshill Academy, Bellshill Athletic, Queen of the South Wanderers, Airdrieonians, Newcastle United, Chelsea (May 1930, £10,000), Derby County (November 1934, £3,000), Notts County, Grimsby Town, Gateshead.
Honours Scotland (20 caps), Scottish League representative XI, Scottish FA Cup final winners' medal 1924, Football League championship medal 1927.
Chelsea details Debut 30.8.30. 144 Appearances 81 Goals

	Appearances		Goals	
	FL	FAC	FL	FAC
1930–31	30	1	14	–
1931–32	36	5	24	6
1932–33	36	1	19	–
1933–34	23	5	13	3
1934–35	7	–	2	–
Total	132	12	72	9

One of the legendary names of football history. Playing in the same school teams as Alex James, he had been a war-time munitions worker and coalminer before starting his professional career with Airdrieonians, for whom he scored 91 goals in 111 League games. Signing for Newcastle United in December 1925, for a £6,500 fee, he became idolised on Tyneside and, indeed, the largest crowd (68,386) ever seen on their ground was for the fixture against Chelsea – less than four months after he came to Stamford Bridge. He was the complete centre-forward. With superb ball control, he loved to leave defenders trailing in his wake after his trickery and acceleration had bewildered them. Indeed he was very fast, both mentally, in sizing up a situation and, physically, in speed over a short distance. And his heading, for such a small man, brought him a good proportion of his goals. But for his fiery temperament, he would have achieved still more glory. Basically a kindly man, he easily lost his temper when provoked and was constantly in trouble with referees, on one occasion invoking a two-month suspension. Yet, at least one manager found him easy to handle and a great club man. After two successful seasons at Derby he moved into the lower divisions and ended his League career in 1938–39 with Gateshead, scoring 18 goals in 31 games. After a handful of matches at the beginning of the war he retired and, in 1957 ended his life when he stepped in front of an express train near his Gateshead home.

GALLON, James (1919–1921) Wing-half

Born Stoke-on-Trent Height 5ft 9in Weight 11st 7lb. Career Hanley, Chelsea (August 1919), Not retained May 1921.
Chelsea details Debut 4.2.20. 2 Appearances

	Appearances		Goals	
	FL	FAC	FL	FAC
1919–20	2	–	–	–
Total	2	–	–	–

Signed after impressing as a trialist, he played in the reserve team regularly for two seasons without being able to force his way into the senior side at a time of post-war rebuilding.

GALLOWAY, John A. (1946–1949) Inside-forward

Born Grangemouth 29.10.18 Height 5ft 10in Weight 11st 10lb. Career Glasgow Rangers, Chelsea (August 1946). Retired 1949.
Honours Scotland Schoolboy international.
Chelsea details Debut 31.8.46. 4 Appearances

	Appearances		Goals	
	FL	FAC	FL	FAC
1946–47	3	–	–	–
1947–48	1	–	–	–
Total	4	–	–	–

Tall, well-built inside forward who "guested" for Chelsea during World War II, in the 1940–41 season. A Captain in the Royal Signals regiment, he had served in the Middle East, being wounded in the Italy campaign, and was a member of the Wanderers (Middle East select) soccer team. A school teacher by profession, he never adjusted to the pace and demands of English football and reverted to amateur status as a "permit" player in October 1949, after which he played little further football.

WANTED
If anyone has a photograph of
JAMES
It would be appreciated if you would allow us to copy it. Please forward it to Ron at 36 Lockier Walk, Wembley, Middx.
It will be returned safely

JAMES GALLON

JOHN A. GALLOWAY

CHRISTOPHER S. GARLAND   WILLIAM GARNER

GARLAND, Christopher S. (1971–1975) Striker
Born Bristol 24.4.498 Height 5ft 9½in Weight 11st 8lb. Career Bristol City, Chelsea (September 1971, £100,000), Leicester City (February 1975, £95,000), Bristol City. Honours England Under-23 (1 cap), Football League Cup final losers' medal 1972.
Chelsea details Debut 4.9.71. 111(3) Appearances 31 Goals

	Appearances			Goals		
	FL	FAC	LC	FL	FAC	LC
1971–72	16(1)	1	5	4	–	2
1972–73	27	3	6	11	–	3
1973–74	26	1	1	3	–	–
1974–75	20(2)	2	3	4	1	3
Total	89(3)	7	15	22	1	8

Signed as a "cover" for strikers Peter Osgood, Tommy Baldwin and Ian Hutchinson, he never did justice to his ability as a thrustful and dangerous attacker. His period at Chelsea coincided with the gradual break-up of the cup-winning sides of 1970 and 1971 and he was rarely certain of his first-team place.

GARNER, William (1972–1978) Striker
Born Leicester 14.12.47 Height 6ft ½in Weight 13st. Career Bedford Town, Notts County, Southend United, Chelsea (September 1972, £80,000), Cambridge United (November 1978, free transfer), Brentford, Whyteleafe.
Chelsea details Debut 9.9.72. 105(14) Appearances 37 Goals

	Appearances			Goals		
	FL	FAC	LC	FL	FAC	LC
1972–73	19 (2)	4	–	7	3	–
1973–74	23	–	–	7	–	–
1974–75	15 (2)	1	1	6	–	–
1975–76	21 (4)	3(1)	1	7	2	–
1977–78	15 (3)	1	0(1)	5	–	–
1978–79	1	–	–	–	–	–
Total	94(11)	9(1)	2(2)	32	5	–

A striker whose build made him a formidable opponent. His height enabled him to win many balls in the air and he was difficult to dispossess. On his day his finishing could be an additional asset, but his game suffered from inconsistency and a temperament which constantly brought him into conflict with referees.

GIBBS, Derek W. (1955–1960) Inside-forward

Born Fulham 22.12.34 Height 5ft 10in Weight 11st 7lb. Career Chelsea (April 1955), Leyton Orient (November 1960), Queens Park Rangers.
Chelsea details Debut 1.1.57. 25 Appearances 6 Goals

	Appearances			Goals		
	FL	FAC	LC	FL	FAC	LC
1956–57	4	–	–	1	–	–
1957–58	4	–	–	1	–	–
1958–59	8	2	–	1	1	–
1959–60	4	–	–	1	–	–
1960–61	3	2	–	1	–	–
Total	23	2	–	5	1	–

Signed professional forms after originally joining Chelsea Juniors. A dependable reserve team player who never succeeded in establishing a first-team spot over such contemporaries as Jimmy Greaves, Tony Nicholas and Johnny Brooks.

GIBSON, George B. (1933–1938) Inside-left

Born Hamilton Height 5ft 9½in Weight 12st 4lb. Career Hamilton Academicals, Dundee, Bolton Wanderers, Chelsea (February 1933), Not retained (May 1938).
Honours FA Cup winners' medal 1929.
Chelsea details Debut 1.3.33. 141 Appearances 24 Goals

	Appearances		Goals	
	FL	FAC	FL	FAC
1932–33	13	–	5	–
1933–34	32	4	9	1
1934–35	23	2	1	–
1935–36	33	5	4	–
1936–37	19	1	3	–
1937–38	9	–	1	–
Total	129	12	23	1

One of Chelsea's many "big-name" signings of the 1930s. He possessed all the brilliant ball skills so often associated with Scottish players, so much so that he was at times likened to the great Alex James. A typical "dribbler" of that period, gaining possession in midfield, he would set out for goal taking on, and beating defenders. A creator and scorer of goals, he was the complete inside-forward.

DEREK W. GIBBS

GEORGE B. GIBSON

RAY GODDARD	ANTHONY GODDEN

GODDARD, Ray (1946–1948) Half-back

Born Ecclesfield (Sheffield) 17.10.20 Height 5ft 8in Weight 11st. Career Red Rovers, Wolverhampton Wanderers, Chelsea (September 1946), Plymouth Argyle (July 1948), Exeter City.
Chelsea details Debut 7.9.46. 15 Appearances 1 Goal

	Appearances		Goals	
	FL	FAC	FL	FAC
1946–47	5	–	–	–
1947–48	9	1	1	–
Total	14	1	1	–

One of the famous pre-World War II "Buckley Babes", military service took him to Burma as one of General Wingate's men. Subsequently he toured India, Burma and Ceylon with the Army Soccer team. At home in any of the half-back positions, he was a tough, hard-tackling defender whose ability suggested he could have made a bigger reputation had he not lost seven of his best years to the war.

GODDEN, Anthony (1986–   ) Goalkeeper

Born Gillingham 2.8.55 Height 6ft ½in Weight 13st. Career Ashford Town, West Bromwich Albion, Chelsea (August 1986, free-transfer).
Chelsea details Debut 5.4.86. 38 Appearances

	Appearances				Goals			
	FL	FAC	LC	FMC	FL	FAC	LC	FMC
1985–86	8	–	–	–	–	–	–	–
1986–87	26	1	2	1	–	–	–	–
Total	34	1	2	1	–	–	–	–

Hurriedly signed on loan to solve Chelsea's goalkeeping problem, following an injury to Eddie Niedzwiecki and Steve Francis' loss of form, he performed with distinction and bravery and was signed on a permanent basis before the start of the following season. He had previously played 267 League games for West Bromwich Albion, as well as having brief periods on loan with Preston North End, Luton Town and Walsall.

GOODWIN, Joe (1905–1906) Outside-left

Career Chelsea (amateur) 1905–06.
Chelsea details Debut 28.10.05 2 Appearances

	Appearances		Goals	
	FL	FAC	FL	FAC
1905–06	–	2	–	–
Total	–	2	–	–

Although playing twice in the FA Cup competition in Chelsea's first season, he never played in a League fixture. Most of his career was spent in amateur football in the London area.

GOULDEN, Leonard A. (1945–1950) Inside-left

Born Plaistow 16.7.12 Height 5ft 8in Weight 10st 12lb. Career Chelmsford, Leyton, West Ham United, Chelsea (August 1945 £4,500). Retired 1950.
Honours England (14 caps), Football League, England Schoolboy International.
Chelsea details Debut 5.1.46 111 Appearances 19 goals

	Appearances		Goals	
	FL	FAC	FL	FAC
1945–46	–	3	–	1
1946–47	38	5	10	–
1947–48	27	2	4	1
1948–49	20	–	1	–
1949–50	14	2	2	–
Total	99	12	17	2

One of the outstanding inside-forwards of the immediate pre-World War II period. Came to Chelsea in the autumn of his career but was still a fine player and good influence on those around him in a team in the process of reconstruction. With his educated left foot he both scored regular goals and carved out scoring opportunities for others. Late in his career he had a successful spell at wing-half before being appointed Chelsea Coach at the end of the 1949–50 season. His professional career had begun at West Ham United in 1933 and, after he left Stamford Bridge, he was appointed manager of Watford in November 1952.

WANTED
If anyone has a photograph of
JOE
It would be appreciated if you would allow us to copy it. Please forward it to Ron at 36 Lockier Walk, Wembley, Middx.
It will be returned safely

JOE GOODWIN

LEONARD A. GOULDEN

GEORGE GRAHAM   WILLIAM P. GRAY

GRAHAM, George (1964–1966) Striker

Born Bargeddie 30.11.44 Height 5ft 10½in Weight 11st 10lb. Career Aston Villa, Chelsea (June 1964, £5,000), Arsenal (September 1966, Exchange Tommy Baldwin), Manchester United, Portsmouth, Crystal Palace.
Honours Scotland (12 caps), Scotland Under-23 (2 caps), Scotland Schoolboy International, FA Cup winners' medal 1971, FA Cup losers' medal 1972, Football League Championship medal 1971, Football League cup losers' medals 1963, 1968, 1969, Inter-Cities Cup winners' medal 1970.
Chelsea details Debut 29.8.64 102 Appearances 46 Goals

	Appearances				Goals			
	FL	FAC	LC	FC	FL	FAC	LC	FC
1964–65	30	5	7	–	17	–	4	–
1965–66	33	6	–	11	17	3	–	3
1966–67	9	–	1	–	1	–	1	–
Total	72	11	8	11	35	3	5	3

During an all-too-short stay at Stamford Bridge he immediately struck up a fruitful partnership with Barry Bridges – over 80 goals coming from their "striker-duo" in the two seasons they were together. A stylish, elegant player of great intelligence, he was appointed manager of Millwall in 1983 and moved to Arsenal in a similar capacity in 1986.

GRAY, William P. (1949–1953) Winger

Born Dinnington, Co. Durham 24.5.27 Height 5ft 6in Weight 10st 1lb. Career Dinnington Colliery, Leyton Orient, Chelsea (March 1949), Burnley (August 1953), Nottingham Forest, Millwall.
Honours England 'B' (1 cap), FA Cup winners' medal 1960.
Chelsea details Debut 30.4.49 172 Appearances 15 Goals

	Appearances		Goals	
	FL	FAC	FL	FAC
1948–49	2	–	–	–
1949–50	39	7	2	–
1950–51	31	5	6	–
1951–52	42	9	1	3
1952–53	32	5	3	–
Total	146	26	12	3

A fast and clever winger who was a first-team regular for four seasons, during which time Chelsea twice reached the semi-final stage of the FA Cup. A most popular player, his move to Burnley was much regretted by supporters and he went on to give the Lancashire club, and Nottingham Forest, years of excellent service, playing over 500 games in his distinguished League career. He later managed both Brentford and Millwall for a time.

GREAVES, James (1957–1961) Inside-forward

Born East Ham 20.2.40 Height 5ft 8in Weight 10st 4lb. Career Chelsea (May 1957), AC Milan (June 1961, £80,000), Tottenham Hotspur, West Ham United, Barnet.
Honours England (57 caps), England Under-23 (12 caps), England Youth International, Football League XI. FA Cup winners' medals 1962, 1967.
Chelsea details Debut 24.8.57 169 Appearances 132 Goals

	Appearances				Goals			
	FL	FAC	LC	FC	FL	FAC	LC	FC
1957–58	35	2	–	–	22	–	–	–
1958–59	42	2	–	3	32	2	–	3
1959–60	40	2	–	–	29	–	–	–
1960–61	40	1	2	–	41	1	2	–
Total	157	7	2	3	124	3	2	3

One of the most lethal goalscorers the game of football has ever known, and certainly the most prolific scorer in Chelsea's history – as measured by goals-per-game. An ex-Chelsea Junior whose feats in finding the back of the net had already won him a reputation, he was soon skating through First Division defences with ridiculous ease. He possessed speed off the mark, the ability to go round opponents, and an uncanny knack of stealing unnoticed into space – especially in the enemy's penalty area. Three times he scored 5 goals in a match for Chelsea, topping the list of scorers in each of his four seasons in the senior side. His transfer to Italy in the summer of 1961 aroused much publicity, and protests from Chelsea fans, and it was a further source of disappointment that, despite strenuous efforts on the part of the Board, he did not return to Stamford Bridge when he came back to England in December 1961.

JAMES GREAVES

RON GREENWOOD | ROBERT E. GREGG

GREENWOOD, Ron (1940–1945 & 1952–1955) Centre-half
Born Burnley 11.11.21 Height 5ft 10in Weight 10st. Career Chelsea (1940–1945), Bradford Park Avenue, Brentford, Chelsea (October 1952), Fulham (February 1955). Honours England "B" (1 cap), Football League Championship medal 1955.
Chelsea details Debut 25.10.52 66 Appearances

	Appearances			Goals		
	FL	FAC	LC	FL	FAC	LC
1952–53	11	–	–	–	–	–
1953–54	33	1	–	–	–	–
1954–55	21	–	–	–	–	–
Total	65	1	–	–	–	–

First came to Chelsea as a boy and played for the club in war-time football. Then, with John Harris installed at centre-half in the first-team, he moved to Bradford where he was assured of regular League football. Next, after nearly four seasons at Brentford he arrived back at Stamford Bridge to play a vital role in bringing the League Championship to Chelsea, sharing the centre-half spot with Stan Wicks. One of the most knowledgeable and respected coaches of his time, he subsequently managed West Ham United and, until the end of the 1982 World Cup campaign, the England national side.

GREGG, Robert E. (1933–1938) Inside-forward
Born Ferryhill Height 5ft 8in Weight 11st 7lb. Career Darlington, Sheffield Wednesday, Birmingham, Chelsea (September 1933), Boston United (Summer 1938). Honours Football League Championship medal 1929, FA Cup Final losers' medal 1931.
Chelsea details Debut 13.9.33. 51 Appearances 6 Goals

	Appearances		Goals	
	FL	FAC	FL	FAC
1933–34	28	2	2	1
1934–35	13	–	3	–
1935–36	3	–	–	–
1936–37	3	–	–	–
1937–38	1	1	–	–
Total	48	3	5	1

After a distinguished career with his two previous clubs, he failed to settle at Stamford Bridge and played the majority of his games in the reserve team. A clever ball player, his failing was an inability to play the early ball and to spot an opening.

GRIFFITHS, Robert (1931–1941) Half-back

Born Chapleton (Scotland) Height 5ft 9in Weight 10st 8lb. Career Pollok Juniors, Chelsea (July 1931), Retired 1941.
Chelsea details Debut 17.9.32. 45 Appearances

	Appearances		Goals	
	FL	FAC	FL	FAC
1932–34	2	1	–	–
1933–34	1	1	–	–
1935–36	1	–	–	–
1936–37	1	–	–	–
1937–38	35	1	–	–
1938–39	2	–	–	–
Total	42	3	–	–

A most loyal club servant for his ten years with the club. Lacking the necessary height to become a dominating centre-half, nevertheless he was a most skilled and resourceful performer. In turn he understudied Peter O'Dowd, Allan Craig and Bob Salmond and, for one season, he not only was the recognised first choice for his position, but also captained the side. He joined the Police War Reserve in 1939 and continued to make occasional appearances in war-time regional football until he retired.

HALES, Kevin P. (1979–1983) Defender/Midfield

Born Dartford 13.1.61 Height 5ft 7in Weight 10st 4lb. Career Chelsea (January 1979), Orient (Summer 1983).
Chelsea details Debut 10.11.79. 25(2) Appearances 2 Goals

	Appearances		Goals	
	FL	FAC	FL	FAC
1979–80	5(2)	1	–	–
1981–82	10	5	2	–
1982–83	3	7	–	–
Total	18(2)	7	2	–

Graduated to professional ranks after joining Chelsea after eighteen months as an apprentice. A versatile player whose Stamford Bridge career was dogged by injuries which prevented him establishing a permanent first-team berth.

ROBERT GRIFFITHS

KEVIN P. HALES

GARETH HALL   HAROLD J. HALSE

HALL, Gareth (1985–) Full-back
Born Croydon 20.3.69. Height 5ft 8in, Weight 10st 7lb
Career Chelsea
Honours England Under-15 International
Chelsea details Debut 5.5.87 0(1) Appearances

	Appearances		Goals	
	FL	FAC	FL	FAC
1986-87	0(1)	–	–	–
Total	0(1)	–	–	–

Strongly-built defender who joined the club as an Apprentice in August 1984 and graduated to the first-team via the juniors and reserve teams. Chelsea Young-Player-of-the-Year in 1984–85, he also played cricket for Surrey Schools.

HALSE, Harold J. (1913–1921) Inside-forward
Born Leytonstone January 1886. Height 5ft 7in, Weight 10st 10lb. Career: Clapton Orient, Southend United, Manchester United, Aston Villa, Chelsea (June 1913), Charlton Athletic (Summer 1921).
Honours: England (1 cap), Football League XI, F.A. Cup winners' medals 1909, 1913, F.A. Cup losers' medal 1915, Football League Championship medal 1911.
Chelsea details: Debut 6.9.13. 111 Appearances, 25 Goals

	Appearances		Goals	
	FL	FAC	FL	FAC
1913–14	30	2	10	–
1914–15	27	8	10	2
1919–20	31	5	3	–
1920–21	8	–	–	–
Total	96	15	23	2

A slightly built inside-forward whose forte was his mastery of the ball. This, allied to deadly shooting power, made him one of the most respected forwards of his day. The first man to play in F.A. Cup finals for three different teams, it was surprising that he was only once recognised by the England selectors, although it must be remembered that he lost four of his potentially best seasons to World War I. After leaving Chelsea he captained Charlton Athletic in their first season in the Football League.

HAMILTON, Ian M. (1968) Forward/Midfield
Born: Streatham 31.10.50. Height 5ft 9½, Weight 10st 6lb.
Career: Chelsea (January 1968), Southend United (August 1968 £5,000), Aston Villa, Sheffield United
Chelsea details: Debut 18.3.67. 3(2) Appearances, 2 Goals

	Appearances		Goals	
	FL	FAC	FL	FAC
1966–67	3(2)	–	2	–
Total	3(2)	–	2	–

His somewhat curious Chelsea career began when, as a junior, he became the youngest player in the club's history to play in a senior competitive game. He was 16 years 4 months and 18 days when he played against Tottenham Hotspur in a League fixture at White Hart Lane, and, indeed scored Chelsea's goal in a 1-1 draw. Yet, ultimately signing professional forms, he remained on the staff only for a further eight months before his transfer to Third Division Southend United. Later he played more than 200 senior games for Aston VIlla.

HAMPTON, Colin (1914–1925) Goalkeeper
Born: Brechin. Height 5ft 11in, Weight 11st 4lb.
Career: Brechin City, Motherwell, Chelsea (April 1914)
Honours: Scottish League XI
Chelsea details: Debut 25.4.14. 82 Appearances

	Appearances		Goals	
	FL	FAC	FL	FAC
1913–14	1	–	–	–
1914–15	1	–	–	–
1919–20	15	–	–	–
1920–21	6	–	–	–
1921–22	9	–	–	–
1922–23	25	3	–	–
1923–24	22	–	–	–
Total	79	3	–	–

Most of his 11 years on the staff was spent understudying such as Jim Molyneux and Benjamin Howard Baker, yet he was an extremely sound and reliable 'keeper. Perhaps more exciting were his exploits in World War I when he was a Machine Gunner in Mesopotamia. After his car was shattered by shells he was taken prisoner, set out on foot to Constantinople but never arrived as armistice was declared soon afterwards! He was awarded the Military Medal for gallantry in that campaign.

IAN M. HAMILTON

COLIN HAMPTON

ALFRED J. HANSON | TOMMY C. HARMER

HANSON, Alfred J. (1938–1946) Outside-left

Born: Bootle. Height 5ft 8½in, Weight 10st 10lb.
Career: Liverpool, Chelsea (Summer 1938), Retired 1946
Chelsea details: Debut 27.8.38. 45 Appearances. 9 Goals

	Appearances		Goals	
	FL	FAC	FL	FAC
1938–39	37	8	8	1
Total	37	8	8	1

Moved to London from Liverpool just before World War II, having scored 50 goals in 166 games during his five seasons at Anfield. A fast and direct left-winger his career was virtually terminated by the outbreak of war, although he continued to play regional football as a "guest" player for various clubs in the north of England. A good cricketer and baseball player, his brother, Stan, kept goal for Bolton Wanderers for several years.

HARMER, Tommy C. (1962–1967) Inside-forward

Born: Hackney 2.2.28. Height 5ft 5in, Weight 10st.
Career: Finchley, Tottenham Hotspur, Watford, Chelsea (September 1962 £3,500), retired 1967.
Honours: England 'B' (1 cap)
Chelsea details Debut 20.10.62. 9 Appearances, 1 Goal.

	Appearances			Goals		
	FL	FAC	LC	FL	FAC	LC
1962–63	5	–	–	1	–	–
1963–64	3	–	1	–	–	–
Total	8	–	1	1	–	–

Signed at the age of 34 with a view mainly to coach the young players, he nevertheless made a handful of appearances in the first-team where he exhibited all his old mastery of the ball for which he was renowned. At Chelsea he will always be remembered for scoring the all-important goal against Sunderland at Roker Park in the penultimate game of the 1962–63 season which was vital in ensuring promotion to the First Division. He stayed at Stamford Bridge as Youth Team Coach until June 1967, still making occasional appearances as a player in the reserve team.

HARDING, Augustus (1906–1913) Full-back

Career: Tottenham Hotspur (amateur), Chelsea (December 1906, amateur forms, professional June 1907), Exeter City
Chelsea details: Debut 14.12.07. 5 Appearances.

	Appearances		Goals	
	FL	FAC	FL	FAC
1907–08	1	1	–	–
1909–10	3	–	–	–
Total	4	1	–	–

For almost all of his seven years on the staff he played reserve team football, yet his loyalty was rewarded with a Testimonial in February 1913. He was renowned as much for his fine sportsmanship as for his ability on the field.

HARRIS, Allan J. (1960–1964 & 1966–1967) Full-back

Born: Hackney 28.12.42. Height 5ft 8in, Weight 10st 7lb.
Career: Chelsea (June 1960), Coventry City (November 1964, £35,000), Chelsea (May 1966, £45,000), Queens Park Rangers (July 1967, £30,000) Plymouth Argyle, Cambridge United
Honours: England Schoolboy and Youth International, FA Cup losers' medal 1967
Chelsea details Debut 24.10.60. 98(4) Appearances, 1 Goal

	Appearances				Goals			
	FL	FAC	LC	FC	FL	FAC	LC	FC
1960–61	17	1	3	–	–	–	–	–
1961–62	27	1	–	–	–	–	–	–
1962–63	15	2	–	–	–	–	–	–
1963–64	10	–	1	–	–	–	–	–
1964–65	1	–	2	–	–	–	1	–
1965–66	–	–	–	2	–	–	–	–
1966–67	12(2)	3(1)	1(1)	–	–	–	–	–
Total	82(2)	7(1)	7(1)	2	–	–	1	–

Originally signed from the Chelsea Juniors. The elder brother of Ron, he was usually on the fringe of the first-team, competing for the full-back spot with Eddie McCreadie, Ken Shellito or Marvin Hinton. Nevertheless, he chalked up some 300 games in his League career. Later Assistant-Manager at Queens Park Rangers and F.C. Barcelona.

AUGUSTUS HARDING

ALLAN J. HARRIS

MICHAEL J. HARRISON   CHARLES HARRIS

HARRISON, Michael J. Outside-left

Born: Ilford 18.4.40. Height 5ft 11½in, Weight 11st 10lb.
Career: Chelsea (April 1957), Blackburn Rovers (September 1962 £18,000), Plymouth Argyle, Luton Town
Honours: England Schoolboy International, England Under-23 International (3 caps)
Chelsea details Debut 15.4.57. 64 Appearances, 9 Goals

	Appearances				Goals			
	FL	FAC	LC	FC	FL	FAC	LC	FC
1956–57	1	–	–	–	–	–	–	–
1957–58	1	–	–	–	–	–	–	–
1958–59	16	–	–	3	2	–	–	1
1959–60	5	–	–	–	2	–	–	–
1960–61	15	–	–	–	1	–	–	–
1961–62	22	–	–	–	3	–	–	–
1962–63	1	–	–	–	–	–	–	–
Total	61	–	–	3	8	–	–	1

One of the many products of Chelsea's Youth Scheme, he had the misfortune to be on the staff at a time when Frank Blunstone was the recognised left-winger. Extremely quick, and a direct attacker, he moved to Blackburn Rovers where, for five years, he was a regular first-team choice and made nearly 200 appearances for the Lancastrians.

HARRIS, Charles (1905–1909) Full-back - Centre-half

Career: Chelsea 1905–1909
Chelsea details Debut 2.9.05, 2 Appearances

	Appearances		Goals	
	FL	FAC	FL	FAC
1905–06	1	1	–	–
Total	1	1	–	–

Strangely, Charlie's only Football League appearance was in the club's first-ever match in the competition, against Stockport County – a fact of which in later years he was immensely proud. For four seasons he was a stalwart of the reserve team and then was appointed Trainer at Swansea Town, after which he returned to Stamford Bridge where he gave more than 30 years loyal service on the training staff.

HARRIS, John (1945–1956) Centre-half - Full-back

Born: Glasgow 30.6.17. Height 5ft 10in, Weight 12st.
Career: Wolverhampton Wanderers, Chelsea (August 1945, £5,000), Chester (April 1956)
Honours: Scottish war-time International, Football League Championship medal 1955
Chelsea details Debut 5.1.46, 364 Appearances, 14 Goals

	Appearances		Goals	
	FL	FAC	FL	FAC
1945–46	–	6	–	–
1946–47	41	4	–	–
1947–48	41	1	2	–
1948–49	41	3	1	–
1949–50	39	6	3	–
1950–51	36	5	5	–
1951–52	26	9	–	–
1952–53	36	3	3	–
1953–54	32	1	–	–
1954–55	31	–	–	–
1955–56	3	–	–	–
Total	326	38	14	–

After "guesting" in war-time football from 1943–45 (109 appearances), he was signed on a permanent basis and went on to give sterling service, first at centre-half and later at full-back, in the immediate post-World War II period. For most of his fourteen seasons he was both a dominant figure on the field and an influential captain. He had led the team in their two war-time Wembley finals (1944 and 1945) and was renowned for his hard tackling and shrewd positional sense. But for his comparative lack of inches he would have undoubtedly achieved more in the international sphere than his one war-time cap. He moved to Chester as player-manager in April 1956, subsequently joining Sheffield United in that capacity, before crossing that city to begin a long association with Sheffield Wednesday.

JOHN HARRIS

RONALD E. HARRIS

HARRIS, Ronald E. (1961–1980) Defender

Born: Hackney 13.11.44. Height 5ft 8in, Weight 11st 5lb.
Career: Chelsea (November 1961), Brentford (May 1980 Free-transfer)
Honours: England Schoolboy and Youth international, Under-23 International (4 caps) F.A. Cup winners' medal 1970, losers' medal 1967, Football League Cup winners' medal 1965, losers' medal 1972, European Cup Winners' Cup winners' medal 1971, F.A. Youth Cup winners' medal 1961.

Chelsea details Debut 24.2.62. 784(11) Appearances, 14 Goals

	Appearances					Goals				
	FL	FAC	LC	FC	ECWC	FL	FAC	LC	FC	ECWC
1961–62	3	–	–	–	–	–	–	–	–	–
1962–63	7	–	–	–	–	–	–	–	–	–
1963–64	41	3	1	–	–	2	–	–	–	–
1964–65	42	5	6	–	–	2	–	–	–	–
1965–66	36	6	–	10	–	2	–	–	–	–
1966–67	42	7	3	–	–	–	–	–	–	–
1967–68	40	5	1	–	–	–	–	–	–	–
1968–69	40	5	3	4	–	–	–	–	–	–
1969–70	30	8	3	–	–	–	–	–	–	–
1970–71	38	3	4	–	9	1	–	–	–	–
1971–72	41	3	9	–	4	–	–	–	–	1
1972–73	42	3	7	–	–	1	–	–	–	–
1973–74	36	2	1	–	–	2	–	–	–	–
1974–75	42	2	4	–	–	–	–	–	–	–
1975–76	38(2)	4	1	–	–	–	–	–	–	–
1976–77	15(4)	2	0(1)	–	–	–	–	–	–	–
1977–78	37	4	1	–	–	1	–	–	–	–
1978–79	38(2)	1	1	–	–	–	–	–	–	–
1979–80	38(1)	1	1(1)	–	–	2	–	–	–	–
Total	646(9)	64	46(2)	14	13	13	–	–	–	1

(also: 1 F.A. Charity Shield appearance in 1970–71)

No player in Chelsea history can equal his service as a first-team player over 19 seasons during which he made more appearances than anyone else has ever done. Throughout this time he was a pillar of the defence, whether at full-back or in middle of the back line. A superbly fit and dedicated athlete, he joined the club as a junior in August 1960. He was a member of the four cup-final sides of his time, having already played in a winning F.A. Youth Cup team. Indeed at Wembley in 1967 he became the youngest-ever captain in an F.A. Cup final. A Chelsea legend, his strength in the tackle made "Chopper" a respected and formidable opponent. He joined Brentford as Player-Coach after eventually leaving Stamford Bridge and later managed Aldershot for a short time.

HARROW, Jack (1911–1926) Full-back

Born: Mitcham 8.10.88. Height 5ft 8½in, Weight 11st 10lb.
Career: Croydon Common, Chelsea (March 1911, £50, Retired 1926).
Honours: England (2 caps), Football League XI (1 appearance), F.A. Cup final losers' medal 1915.
Chelsea details: Debut 9.12.11. 333 Appearances, 5 Goals

	Appearances		Goals	
	FL	FAC	FL	FAC
1911–12	12	1	–	–
1912–13	6	–	–	–
1913–14	20	2	–	–
1914–15	22	7	–	–
1919–20	39	5	2	–
1920–21	40	8	2	–
1921–22	38	1	1	–
1922–23	40	3	–	–
1923–24	38	2	–	–
1924–25	34	–	–	–
1925–26	15	–	–	–
Total	304	29	5	–

One of Chelsea's most famous players who served the club for 27 years, first as a player and then on the training staff from which retired in 1938. His career was at its peak when it was interrupted by World War I, although he was demobilised from the Army in time to appear in the team which won the London Victory Cup in 1919. For eight years he was a pillar of the defence, playing mostly at left-back and, indeed, was acknowledged as one of the best players in this position in the country. His strength lay in his defensive qualities. He was a strong tackler and had a sound positional sense. Originally he was signed as a wing-half but this, and his burning ambition to play at centre-forward, were soon forgotten. Almost certainly his total number of international caps would have been considerably increased but for the outbreak of hostilities.

JACK HARROW

JACK A. HARWOOD | ANTHONY HATELEY

HARWOOD, Jack A. (1912–1913) Wing-half

Born: Somerstown
Career: Southend United, Chelsea (May 1912), Portsmouth (March 1913), Swansea Town, Aberdare Athletic
Chelsea details: Debut 4.1.13. 4 Appearances

	Appearances		Goals	
	FL	FAC	FL	FAC
1912–13	4	–	–	–
Total	4	–	–	–

His short spell at Stamford Bridge included four games as deputy for the injured Sam Downing. After his playing career ended he was Trainer at Fulham for a time.

HATELEY, Anthony (1966–1967) Centre-forward

Born: Derby 13.6.41. Height 6ft 1½in, Weight 12st 7lb.
Career: Career: Notts County, Aston Villa, Chelsea (October 1966, £100,000), Liverpool (July 1967, £95,000), Coventry City, Birmingham City, Notts County, Oldham Athletic
Honours: F.A. Cup losers' medal 1967
Chelsea details: Debut 26.10.66. 32(1) Appearances. 9 Goals

	Appearances		Goals	
	FL	FAC	FL	FAC
1966–67	26(1)	6	6	3
Total	26(1)	6	6	3

Manager Tommy Docherty moved smartly to sign him when Peter Osgood broke his right leg early in the 1966–67 Season. Although he scored the all-important goal in a semi-final tie against Leeds United which took Chelsea to their first Wembley final, he never justified himself at Stamford Bridge. One of the best headers of a ball in the game, he scored over 200 goals in a career which included seven different clubs.

HAY, David (1974–1980) Midfield/Defender

Born: Paisley 29.1.48. Height 5ft 11in, Weight 11st 7lb.
Career: St. Mirin's Boys, Glasgow Celtic, Chelsea (August 1974, £225,000), Retired 1980
Honours: Scotland (27 caps), Scotland Under-23 (3 caps), Scottish League XI (4 appearances), Scottish League Championship medals 1970, 1971, 1972, 1973, 1974, Scottish F.A. Cup winners' medals 1972, 1974, losers' medal 1970, 1973, Scottish League Cup winners' medal 1970, losers' medals 1971, 1972, 1973, 1974.
Chelsea details Debut: 17.8.74. 118(2) Appearances, 3 Goals

	Appearances			Goals		
	FL	FAC	LC	FL	FAC	LC
1974–75	34	2	–	–	–	–
1975–76	27(1)	2(1)	1	1	–	–
1976–77	31	2	3	1	–	1
1977–78	7	–	–	–	–	–
1978–79	8	–	1	–	–	–
Total	107(1)	6(1)	5	2	–	1

After a brilliant career in Scotland during which he won every honour in the game his time at Chelsea was dogged by misfortune. Even before he arrived, he had experienced an eye injury (in an accident off the field) and later he had trouble with a knee which eventually brought about his premature retirement. At his best he was a dominating, aggressive midfield operator who could also play in any defensive position. He will be especially remembered for his outstanding play for Scotland in the 1974 World Cup competition. Later appointed manager of Glasgow Celtic.

HAZARD, Michael (1985–   ) Midfield

Born: Sunderland 5.2.60 Height 5ft 7in, Weight 10st 5lb.
Career: Tottenham Hotspur, Chelsea (September 1985, £300,000)
Chelsea details: Debut 21.9.85. 42(7) Appearances. 10 Goals

	Appearances				Goals			
	FL	FAC	LC	FMC	FL	FAC	LC	FMC
1985–86	17(1)	1	2(2)	3	1	–	1	1
1986–87	16(2)	2(1)	1(1)	–	6	1	–	–
Total	33(3)	3(1)	3(3)	3	7	1	1	1

Creative midfield player with great skill on the ball. A shrewd and accurate distributor who, on his day, can control the game from the middle of the park. Previously the whole of his professional career had been spent at Tottenham where, in his six years on the staff, he made less than 100 League appearances.

DAVID HAY

MICHAEL HAZARD

| WILLIAM HAYWOOD | GEORGE H. HENDERSON |

HAYWOOD, William (1921–1924) Inside-forward
Born: Eckington. Height 5ft 8in, Weight 10st 9lb.
Career: Eckington, Chelsea (March 1921), Halifax Town (Summer 1924), Petters & Yeovil, Portsmouth, Barrow
Chelsea details: Debut 14.4.22. 23 Appearances, 2 Goals

	Appearances		Goals	
	FL	FAC	FL	FAC
1921–22	5	–	1	–
1922–23	16	–	1	–
1923–24	2	–	–	–
Total	23	–	2	–

After a promising start, he failed to live up to his early promise. He began his first full season on the staff as a recognised first-team choice, but lost his place to Buchanan Sharp and never played regularly again.

HENDERSON, George H. (1905–1909) Half-back
Born: Ladhope (Selkirkshire) 2.5.80
Career: Queens Park, Glasgow Rangers, Dundee, Middlesbrough, Chelsea (April 1905)
Honours: Scotland (1 cap)
Chelsea details: Debut 16.4.06. 64 Appearances, 1 Goal

	Appearances		Goals	
	FL	FAC	FL	FAC
1905–06	3	–	–	–
1906–07	37	2	–	–
1907–08	14	1	1	–
1908–09	6	1	–	–
Total	60	4	1	–

One of the first of many Scottish players who have found their way to Stamford Bridge. An artistic, creative player, he was a strong player well-known for his appetite for hard work. His one Scottish international was against Ireland in 1904.

HEWITT, Thomas J. (1911–1913) Full-back

Born: Connah's Quay 1890
Career: Wrexham, Chelsea (March 1911), South Liverpool, Swansea Town
Honours: Wales (8 caps)
Chelsea details: Debut 2.12.11. 8 Appearances

	Appearances		Goals	
	FL	FAC	FL	FAC
1911–12	8	–	–	–
Total	8	–	–	–

Although winning three of his 8 Welsh international caps while at Chelsea, he failed to break through into the senior side, partly as a result of the consistently good form of Walter Bettidge and Jock Cameron, but also through a series of injuries which kept him on the sidelines for much of his time at Stamford Bridge.

HIGGS, Frank (1928–30) Goalkeeper

Born: Willington (Northumberland) Height 6ft.
Career: Chelsea (October 1928), Linfield, Barnsley, Manchester City, Aldershot, Walsall, Carlisle United
Chelsea details: Debut: 28.9.29. 2 Appearances.

	Appearances		Goals	
	FL	FAC	FL	FAC
1929–30	2	–	–	–
Total	2	–	–	–

Signed as "cover" for Sam Millington, he played two first-team games but was unable to win a first-team place on a permanent basis and moved on after only two years on the staff.

THOMAS J. HEWITT

FRANK HIGGS

GEORGE HILSDON

HILSDON, George (1906–1912) Forward

Born: Bow (East London) 10.8.1885. Died: 7.9.41
Career: West Ham United, Chelsea (May 1906), West Ham United (Summer 1912)
Honours: England (8 caps), Football League XI (1 appearance)
Chelsea details: Debut: 1.9.06. 164 Appearances, 107 Goals

	Appearances		Goals	
	FL	FAC	FL	FAC
1906–07	32	2	27	–
1907–08	33	2	24	6
1908–09	34	3	25	2
1909–10	15	2	3	–
1910–11	26	5	18	1
1911–12	10	–	1	–
Total	150	14	98	9

Signed at the age of 21 as an inside-forward, he was soon converted into leading the attack, his powerful shooting winning him the nickname "Gatling Gun" after he had scored five goals in his first League game for Chelsea against Worksop, still a club record. His 27 goals in his first season at Stamford Bridge was instrumental in the team winning promotion to the First Division for the first time. Then, after five successful years, his form deserted him. According to one writer he had "been too sociable, too careless with his strength and vitality." Be that as it may, his return to West Ham revitalised the Upton Park team and his experience was of particular value to the youngsters on their staff. He played for them up to the outbreak of World War I in which he was badly affected by mustard-gas poising. For many years the silhouette of a footballer which adorned the old EastStand at Stamford Bridge was modelled on George, one of the most famous names in the club's history.

HINSHELWOOD, Walter A.A. (1951) Winger

Born: Chapelhall 11.5.35
Career: Fulham, Chelsea (January 1951 part-exchange Jimmie Bowie), Fulham (May 1951), Reading, Bristol City, Millwall, Newport County
Chelsea details: Debut: 3.2.51. 14 Appearances, 1 Goal

	Appearances		Goals	
	FL	FAC	FL	FAC
1950–51	12	2	1	–
Total	12	2	1	–

Signed, in part-exchange for Jimmy Bowie, from Fulham, he returned to the Craven Cottage club after fifteen weeks. Father of Martin, who was appointed Combination Team Coach in 1985 after his playing career with Crystal Palace ended.

HINTON, Marvin (1963–1976) Defender

Born: Norwood 2.2.40. Height 5ft 10¼, Weight 11st 11lb
Career: Charlton Athletic, Chelsea (August 1963 £30,000;, Barnet (Summer 1976)
Honours: England Under-23 (3 caps), F.A. Cup winners' medal 1970, losers' medal 1967, Football League Cup Final winners' medal 1966.
Chelsea details Debut 25.9.63. 328(16) Appearances, 4 Goals

	Appearances					Goals				
	FL	FAC	LC	FC	ECWC	FL	FAC	LC	FC	ECWC
1963–64	21	3	1	–	–	1	–	–	–	–
1964–65	40	5	6	–	–	1	–	–	–	–
1965–66	38	6	–	11	–	–	–	–	–	–
1966–67	38	7	3	–	–	–	–	–	–	–
1967–68	32(1)	2	0(1)	–	–	–	–	–	–	–
1968–69	6(3)	–	1(1)	2	–	–	–	–	–	–
1969–70	28	0(2)	4	–	–	–	–	–	–	–
1970–71	20	3	2	–	3	–	–	–	–	1
1971–72	5(1)	–	4	–	2(2)	–	–	–	–	–
1972–73	15(3)	3(1)	1(1)	–	–	1	–	–	–	–
1973–74	4	1	–	–	–	–	–	–	–	–
1974–75	10	–	–	–	–	–	–	–	–	–
Total	257(8)	30(3)	22(3)	13	5(2)	3	–	–	–	1

(also 1 F.A. Charity Shield appearance 1970–71)

WALTER A.A. HINSHELWOOD

MARVIN HINTON

FRANK HODDINOTT	ARTHUR HOLDEN

Cultured defender who was equally at home as a full-back or in the centre of the defence. A member of Alf Ramsey's original 1966 World Cup squad, he possessed a fine positional sense and "Lou", as he was known, was also a most intelligent "reader" of the game. His long career at Chelsea was in the club's most successful era and he was a vital part of those days. Yet, he might have gone even further had he been rather more ambitious – few contemporaries had more natural ability.

HODDINOTT, Frank (1921–1923) Inside-forward

Born: Brecon, Height 5ft 8in, Weight 10st 8lb.
Career: Watford, Chelsea (June 1921), Crystal Palace (1923), Rhyl
Honours: Wales (2 caps)
Chelsea details Debut 27.8.21. 32 Appearances, 4 Goals

	Appearances		Goals	
	FL	FAC	FL	FAC
1921–22	23	1	3	–
1922–23	8	–	1	–
Total	31	1	4	–

Had already won his two Welsh caps when he came to Chelsea. An inside-forward of direct method, he never fulfilled his reputation as a goalscorer during his short spell with the club, although it is fair to say that he was pitchforked into playing as an emergency centre-forward for most of his spell in the first-team, due to an injury to Jack Cook.

HOLDEN, Arthur (1908–10) Outside-left

Born: Billingshurst. Height 5ft 7in, Weight 11st.
Career: Portsmouth, Southend United, Plymouth Argyle, Chelsea (April 1908), Aberdeen (Player-Manager)
Chelsea details Debut 17.4.09. 20 Appearances, 1 Goal

	Appearances		Goals	
	FL	FAC	FL	FAC
1908–09	4	–	–	–
1909–10	16	–	–	–
Total	20	–	–	–

A speedy winger who was first choice for his position during most of his short stay at Chelsea. But the signing of Marshall McEwan towards the end of the 1909–10 season ended his Football League career here.

HOLLINS, John W., M.B.E. (1963–1975 1983–1984) Midfield/Defender

Born: Guildford 16.7.46. Height 5ft 8in, Weight 11st 7lb.
Career: Chelsea (July 1963), Queens Park Rangers (June 1975, £80,000), Arsenal, Chelsea (June 1983 – Player-Coach)
Honours: England (1 cap), England Under-23 (12 caps), Youth International, Football League XI (3 appearances), F.A. Cup winners' medal 1970, losers' medal 1967, Football League Cup winners' medal 1966, losers' medal 1972, Football League Second Division Championship medal 1984

Chelsea details Debut 25.9.63. 592 Appearances, 64 Goals

	Appearances					Goals				
	FL	FAC	LC	FC	ECWC	FL	FAC	LC	FC	ECWC
1963–64	2	–	1	–	–	–	–	–	–	–
1964–65	41	5	6	–	–	2	1	–	–	–
1965–66	39	5	–	12	–	2	–	–	–	–
1966–67	39	7	3	–	–	2	–	1	–	–
1967–68	36	5	1	–	–	2	–	–	–	–
1968–69	37	5	3	3	–	2	–	–	1	–
1969–70	42	8	4	–	–	6	1	–	–	–
1970–71	40	3	4	–	8	6	–	1	–	2
1971–72	42	3	9	–	4	11	1	4	–	2
1972–73	42	5	7	–	–	3	1	–	–	–
1973–74	42	2	1	–	–	6	–	–	–	–
1974–75	34	2	4	–	–	5	–	1	–	–
1983–84	29	1	5	–	–	1	–	–	–	–
Total	465	51	48	15	12	48	4	7	1	4

One of the great names in Chelsea's history. Signed professional forms after having graduated as a professional and quickly established himself as an outstanding, attacking midfield player whose energetic running, strong tackling and accurate distribution was a key factor in the most successful era of the club. It was a sad blow when he moved to Queens Park Rangers in the summer of 1975, this following Chelsea's relegation to Division Two. Eight years later he was back again, as Player-Coach, where his influence on and off the field made an immediate impact and was a major factor in the winning of the Second Division Championship. Then, after two years in that role of John Neal's right hand man, he was appointed Manager in June 1985. As a player he was one of the outstanding midfield men in the country, a fact never wholly recognised by the national selectors.

JOHN W. HOLLINS, MBE

PAT HOLTON

JAMES HOPE

HOLTON, Pat (1959–1960) Full-back

Born Hamilton 23.12.35. Height 5ft 9ins, Weight 12st. Career Motherwell, Chelsea (March 1959 £6,000), Southend United (August 1960).
Chelsea details Debut 28.3.59. 1 Appearance

	Appearances	Goals
	FL	FL
1958–59	1	—
Total	1	—

He never settled into the pattern of English League football and after his short stay with Chelsea he played a few games for Southend United.

HOPE, James (1930–1932) Wing-half

Born East Wemyss. Career Gateshead, Chelsea (November 1930), Free-Transfer (May 1932).
Chelsea details Debut 24.10.31. 1 Appearance

	Appearances	Goals
	FL	FL
1931–32	1	—
Total	1	—

A regular player in the reserve team for 18 months, he was unable to supplant Sam Irving, Willie Ferguson and Sid Bishop from the wing-half positions in the League side.

HORN, George (1909–1913) Half-back

Born West Ham. Height 5ft 6½in, weight 10st 6lb. Career Tunbridge Wells Rangers, West Ham United, Chelsea (May 1909), Peterborough (Summer 1913, free transfer).
Chelsea details Debut 2.4.10. 2 Appearances

	Appearances	Goals
	FL	FL
1909–10	2	–
Total	2	–

A sound wing-half who was a regular member of the reserve team which twice won the South-East League Championship during his time at Chelsea.

HORTON, Jack (1933–1937) Outside-left

Born Castleford. Height 5ft 6½ins, weight 11st. Career Castleford Town, Charlton Athletic, Chelsea (March 1933), Crystal Palace (Summer 1937). Honours Football League Division Three (South) Championship medal 1929.
Chelsea details Debut 18.3.33. 66 Appearances 15 Goals

	Appearances		Goals	
	FL	FAC	FL	FAC
1932–33	9	–	2	–
1933–34	30	5	8	–
1934–35	13	1	4	–
1935–36	5	–	1	–
1936–37	2	1	–	–
Total	59	7	15	–

This stockily built winger had a reputation as a regular scorer of goals, but he never quite justified this at Chelsea. He was the regular first-team choice for one season, but the signing of Willie Barraclough effectively ended his days in the League side at a time when no money or effort was spared in attempting to bring overdue success to Stamford Bridge.

| GEORGE HORN | JACK HORTON |

PETER HOUSEMAN

HOUSEMAN, Peter (1962–1965) Winger/Midfield/Full-back

Born Battersea 24.12.45 Died 19.3.77. Height 5ft 8½in. Career Chelsea (December 1962), Oxford United (May 1975 £30,000). Honours F.A. Cup Winners' Cup winners' medal 1971.
Chelsea details Debut 21.12.63 325(18) Appearances 39 Goals

	Appearances					Goals				
	FL	FAC	LC	FC	ECWC	FL	FAC	LC	FC	ECWC
1963–64	4	–	–	–	–	1	–	–	–	–
1964–65	9	–	3	–	–	3	–	–	–	–
1965–66	10	–	–	2	–	–	–	–	–	–
1966–67	13(5)	1	2(1)	–	–	1	1	3	–	–
1967–68	19(1)	2	1	–	–	2	–	–	–	–
1968–69	29(3)	2	1	2	–	2	–	–	1	–
1969–70	42	8	4	–	–	3	6	–	–	–
1970–71	36(1)	3	4	–	8	2	1	–	–	1
1971–72	26(1)	3	7	–	3	1	1	1	–	3
1972–73	19(2)	4	6	–	–	2	1	–	–	–
1973–74	25	1	–	–	–	2	–	–	–	–
1974–75	20(4)	1	4	–	–	1	–	–	–	–
Total	252(17)	25	32(1)	4	11	20	10	4	1	4

(also 1 F.A. Charity Shield appearance 1970-71)

Played an integral part in the Chelsea successes of the 1960s and early 1970s. Originally signed professional forms from the Juniors. He was primarily a left-winger whose accurate crosses produced many goals, but he could also operate effectively in midfield or at full-back. He was not a prolific scorer of goals, but had a happy knack of finding the net in important F.A. Cup ties – his equaliser in the 1970 Wembley final being a case in point. With his wife, Sally, he was tragically killed in a car crash hours after playing in a League game for Oxford United.

HOUSTON, Stewart M. (1967–1972) Defender

Born Dunoon 20.8.49. Height 5ft 11in, Weight 12st 12lb. Career Port Glasgow, Chelsea (August 1967), Brentford (March 1972, £15,000), Manchester United, Sheffield United, Colchester United. Honours Scotland (1 cap), Scotland Under-23 (2 caps), Football League Div. II Championship medal, 1975, Div. IV Championship medal 1982, F.A. Cup losers' medal 1976.

Chelsea details Debut 12.2.68. 10(4) Appearances.

	Appearances			Goals		
	FL	FAC	FC	FL	FAC	FC
1967–68	1	–	–	–	–	–
1968–69	2	3	–	–	–	–
1969–70	3(3)	–	1	–	–	–
1970–71	–	–	0(1)	–	–	–
Total	6(3)	3	1(1)	–	–	–

His Chelsea career, which started so promisingly, was marred by a series of injuries. His fortunes improved after he left Stamford Bridge, first at Brentford and then Manchester United, where he made over 200 League appearances and won a Scottish cap. Later, appointed Coach at Plymouth Argyle.

HOWARD, Terry (1984–1987) Defender

Born Hornchurch 26.2.66. Height 6ft 1in, Weight 11st 7lb. Career Chelsea (February 1984), Orient (March 1987).

Chelsea details Debut 16.4.85. 6 Appearances

	Appearances	Goals
	FL	FL
1984–85	4	–
1985–86	1	–
1986–87	1	–
Total	6	–

Tall defender who played either in the centre or on the flanks. A pillar of the reserve team for three seasons, where he was a regular and frequent goalscorer, he had periods of loan with Crystal Palace (1985–86) and Chester (1986–87).

STEWARD M. HOUSTON

TERRY HOWARD

ALAN A. HUDSON

HARRY J. HUGHES

HUDSON, Alan A. (1968–1974 & 1983–84) Midfield

Born Chelsea 21.6.51 Height 5ft 10½in Weight 12st 4lb. Career Chelsea, Stoke City (January 1974, £240,000), Arsenal, Seattle Sounders, Chelsea (August 1983, £23,500), Stoke City (January 1984).
Honours England (2 caps), England Under-23 (10 caps), European Cup Winners' Cup winners' medal 1971, Football League Cup losers' medal 1972.
Chelsea details Debut 1.2.69 188(1) Appearances 14 Goals

	Appearances				Goals			
	FL	FAC	LC	ECWC	FL	FAC	LC	ECWC
1968–69	1	–	–	–	–	–	–	–
1969–70	29	6	2	–	3	–	–	–
1970–71	33(1)	–	1	9	3	–	–	–
1971–72	36	3	9	4	2	–	2	2
1972–73	26	5	3	–	–	–	–	–
1973–74	19	–	1	–	2	–	–	–
Total	144(1)	14	16	13	10	–	2	2

(also 1 F.A. Charity Shield appearance 1970–71)

Born and brought up in the King's Road, Chelsea, he signed professional forms after being on the club's books as an apprentice. A most gifted player with an uncanny ability to pass the ball with pin-point accuracy, his two England caps were scant reward for so much skill. One of the outstanding midfield players in the country in the early 1970s, he was a vital part of the Chelsea F.A. Cup winning side (although missing the final through injury) and then went on to play some of the most effective football of his career at Stoke. Illness and injury prevented him playing his part in restoring Chelsea's fortunes when he returned to Stamford Bridge in 1983.

HUGHES, Harry J. (1951–1952) Centre-half

Born Hinkley 8.10.29. Height 5ft 11½in, Weight 13st. Career Symington, Southport, Chelsea (February 1951), Bournemouth & Boscombe Athletic (June 1952), Gillingham.
Chelsea details Debut 25.8.51. 1 Appearance

	Appearances	Goals
	FL	FL
1951–52	1	–
Total	1	–

Tall centre-half who came to Chelsea after his demobilisation from the Army as cover for John Harris. Unable to displace the Scot, he moved on after 16 months.

HUGHES, Tommy (1965–1971) Goalkeeper

Born Dalmuir 11.7.47. Height 6ft 1in, Weight 12st. Career Clydebank Juniors, Chelsea (July 1965), Aston Villa (May 1971, £12,500), Brighton & Hove Albion, Hereford United.
Honours Scotland Under-23 (2 caps).
Chelsea details Debut 19.11.66. 11 Appearances

	Appearances		Goals	
	FL	FAC	FL	FAC
1966–67	2	–	–	–
1967–68	2	–	–	–
1968–69	1	–	–	–
1969–70	6	–	–	–
Total	11	–	–	–

One of several goalkeepers who had the thankless task of understudying Peter Bonetti, ultimately moving on to seek a regular place in a first-team. A capable 'keeper who subsequently played more than 200 League games for Hereford United.

HUGHES, William M. (1948–1951) Full-back

Born Llanelly 6.3.18. Height 5ft 10in, Weight 12st 12lb. Career Watchers Celtic, Birmingham City, Luton Town, Chelsea (March 1948, £12,000), Hereford United (Summer 1951).
Honours Wales (10 caps).
Chelsea details Debut 13.3.48. 105 Appearances

	Appearances		Goals	
	FL	FAC	FL	FAC
1947–48	8	–	–	–
1948–49	38	–	–	–
1949–50	24	7	–	–
1950–51	23	5	–	–
Total	93	12	–	–

Past his 30th birthday when he signed for Chelsea, this cultured full-back was an important addition to a side in the process of rehabilitation after World War II. His total of international caps would have been infinitely greater but for the war during which he played for his country in many "unofficial" games. A good tackler and excellent distributor of the ball, especially with his educated left foot, he also played for the Great Britain team which beat the Rest of the World, 6–1, at Hampden Park in 1947.

TOMMY HUGHES   WILLIAM M. HUGHES

PERCY HUMPHREYS | GEORGE HUNTER

HUMPHREYS, Percy (1908–1909) Inside-forward

Career Leicester Fosse, Notts County, Chelsea (February 1908), Tottenham Hotspur (December 1909), Leicester Fosse.
Honours England (1 cap).
Chelsea details Debut 29.2.08. 46 Appearances 13 Goals

	Appearances		Goals	
	FL	FAC	FL	FAC
1907–08	11	–	1	–
1908–09	23	1	9	–
1909–10	11	–	3	–
Total	45	1	13	–

A strongly-built inside-forward who was noted for his dash and enthusiasm or, as writers of those days described him, "a great trier". Ironically, he is perhaps best remembered by Chelsea historians as the player who scored the vital goal in the final match of the 1909–10 season for Spurs at White Hart Lane which, while saving his own club from regulation, sent his previous employers back to Division II.

HUNTER, George (1913–1914) Wing-half

Born Peshawur. Died 1934. Height 5ft 7½in, Weight 12st. Career Aston Villa, Oldham Athletic, Chelsea (February 1913), Manchester United (March 1914).
Chelsea details Debut 1.3.13. 32 Appearances 2 Goals

	Appearances		Goals	
	FL	FAC	FL	FAC
1912–13	11	–	1	–
1913–14	19	2	1	–
Total	30	2	2	–

A stocky wing-half who was noted for his tough and vigorous tackling. As a result, although highly popular with his home supporters, he was not loved by players and fans of the opposition. One of the great characters of his day and noted comedian off the field, he burst into print with a light-hearted book about football. His somewhat fiery temperament made him a difficult customer to handle at times and it was this which led to his sudden and unexpected departure from Stamford Bridge.

HUTCHESON, John H.M. (1934–1937) Wing-half

Born Falkirk. Height 5ft 10in, Weight 11st 5lb. Career Falkirk, Chelsea (March 1934).
Chelsea details Debut 7.4.34. 22 Appearances 1 Goal

	Appearances		Goals	
	FL	FAC	FL	FAC
1933–34	6	–	–	–
1934–35	11	–	1	–
1935–36	5	–	–	–
Total	22	–	1	–

A former miner who had learned his football in Scottish junior circles, he was a stalwart of the reserve side for some three seasons, deputising competently for either Billy Mitchell or Harold Miller (both internationals) when the opportunity arose. His career was effectively ended by cartilage trouble.

HUTCHINGS, Chris (1980–1983) Full-back/Midfield

Born Winchester 5.7.57. Height 5ft 10in Weight 11st. Career Harrow Borough, Chelsea (July 1980, £5,000), Brighton & Hove Albion (November 1983, £50,000).
Chelsea details Debut 31.10.80. 97(4) Appearances 3 Goals.

	Appearances			Goals		
	FL	FAC	LC	FL	FAC	LC
1980–81	8(4)	–	–	1	–	–
1981–82	35	7	3	1	–	–
1982–83	36	–	3	–	–	–
1983–84	4	–	1	1	–	–
Total	83(4)	7	7	3	–	–

Former bricklayer and part-time footballer, he was converted to full-back after beginning his professional career as an aggressive midfield player. Among his assets were boundless enthusiasm and a liking for moving forward to attack at every opportunity.

JOHN H.M. HUTCHESON

CHRIS HUTCHINGS

IAN HUTCHINSON | CLIFF HUXFORD

HUTCHINSON, Ian (1968–1976) Striker

Born Derby 4.8.48. Height 6ft 10in Weight 12st 12lb. Career Burton Albion, Cambridge United, Chelsea (July 1968, £2,500), Retired 1976.
Honours England Under-23 (2 caps), F.A. Cup final winners' medal 1970.
Chelsea details Debut 2.10.68 137(7) Appearances 58 Goals

	Appearances				Goals			
	FL	FAC	LC	ECWC	FL	FAC	LC	ECWC
1968–69	14(1)	–	1	–	6	–	–	–
1969–70	26(1)	8	1	–	16	5	1	–
1970–71	20	1	3	3	5	–	1	3
1972–73	3	–	1	–	3	–	–	–
1973–74	10(4)	–	–	–	3	–	–	–
1974–75	21(1)	1	4	–	7	–	2	–
1975–76	18	1	–	–	4	1	–	–
Total	112(7)	11	10	3	44	6	4	3

(also 1 F.A. Charity Shield appearance and 1 goal 1970–71)

A brave, thrustful striker who was always anxious to get into the centre of the action. A potentially great career was marred by a series of injuries which ultimately ended his football and entailed much of it, latterly, being played under severe physical handicap. Unpredictable, especially in the opposition's penalty area, he was a deadly marksman and fine header of the ball. An immensely long throw (once measured at 112 feet) was an added weapon in his armoury. It was his second equalising goal in the 1970 Wembley final which forced the replay against Leeds United.

HUXFORD, Cliff (1955–1959) Wing-half

Born Stroud 8.6.37. Height 5ft 9in Weight 11st 12lb. Career Chelsea (February 1955), Southampton (May 1959, part-exchange Charlie Livesey), Exeter City.
Chelsea details Debut 30.9.58. 7 Appearances.

	Appearances			Goals		
	FL	FAC	FC	FL	FAC	FC
1958–59	6	–	1	–	–	–
Total	6	–	1	–	–	–

Signed professional for Chelsea after two years as a junior. A rugged, hard-tackling wing-half, he was unable to win a first-team place, but moved on to Southampton where he played some 300 first-team games.

ILES, Robert J. (1978–1983) Goalkeeper

Born Leicester 23.6.58. Height 6ft 1in, Weight 12st 7lb. Career AFC Bournemouth, Poole Town, Weymouth, Chelsea (June 1978, £10,000), Wealdstone (Summer 1983).
Chelsea details Debut 7.10.78. 14 Appearances

	Appearances		Goals	
	FL	FAC	FL	FAC
1978–79	7	–	–	–
1979–80	1	–	–	–
1981–82	1	–	–	–
1982–83	5	–	–	–
Total	14	–	–	–

During his five years at Chelsea, he understudied such as Peter Bonetti, John Phillips, Petar Borota and Steve Francis. A tall 'keeper with a safe pair of hands he never received the extended trial in the first-team which many felt that he deserved.

IRVING, Sam J. (1928–1932) Wing-half

Born Belfast 1894. Height 5ft 10in, Weight 12st 1lb. Career Dundee, Cardiff City, Chelsea (March 1928), Bristol Rovers (May 1932).
Honours Northern Ireland (18 caps), F.A. Cup winners' medal 1927.
Chelsea details Debut 3.3.28. 97 Appearances 5 Goals

	Appearances		Goals	
	FL	FAC	FL	FAC
1927–28	11	–	1	–
1928–29	32	3	1	–
1929–30	17	–	1	–
1930–31	20	5	2	–
1931–32	9	–	–	–
Total	89	8	5	–

Already past his 30th birthday when he came to Chelsea, he nevertheless played an important part in helping the club back to the First Division in the spring of 1930, his forceful and attacking flair proving a great asset to a team which had previously lacked these qualities.

ROBERT J. ILES   SAM J. IRVING

ROBERT ISAAC

ALEXANDER S. JACKSON

ISAAC, Robert (1983–1987) Defender

Born Hackney 30.11.65. Career Chelsea (December 1983), Brighton & Hove Albion (February 1987, £35,000).
Chelsea details Debut 16.3.85 13 Appearances

	Appearances				Goals			
	FL	FAC	LC	FMC	FL	FAC	LC	FMC
1984–85	1	–	–	–	–	–	–	–
1985–86	3	–	2	1	–	–	–	–
1986–87	5	–	–	1	–	–	–	–
Total	9	–	2	2	–	–	–	–

Central defender who could also play at full-back. He progressed through the Youth and Reserve teams and performed impressively in the League side whenever called upon to do so.

JACKSON, Alexander S. (1930–1932) Winger

Born Renton 12.5.05, Died in a road accident 15.11.46. Height 5ft 10ins, Weight 10st 7lb. Career Dumbarton Academy, Renton Victoria, Dumbarton, Aberdeen, Huddersfield Town, Chelsea (September 1930, £8,500), Ashton Nationals (1932), Margate, Nice (France). Honours Scotland (17 caps), Football League Championship medal 1926, F.A. Cup losers' medal 1928, 1930.
Chelsea details Debut 15.9.30. 77 Appearances 29 Goals

	Appearances		Goals	
	FL	FAC	FL	FAC
1930–31	29	5	10	3
1931–32	36	7	15	1
Total	65	12	25	4

One of football's legendary figures, the "Gay Cavalier" had already won a string of honours when he arrived at Chelsea – one of the first in a long line of "big money" signings at that time. Primarily a winger, his speed, ball control and directness of approach, allied to powerful shooting, made him a star box-office attraction (51,000 watched his Stamford Bridge debut). Sadly, differences of opinion with the management abbreviated his career in London and he signed for the unknown team, Ashton Nationals, never again to play League football after the age of 28.

JACKSON, John (1933–1942) Goalkeeper

Born Glasgow 29.11.06, Died Nova Scotia 12.6.65. Height 5ft 9ins, Weight 10st 12lb. Career Kirkintilloch Rob Roy, Partick Thistle, Chelsea (June 1933), Retired 1942.
Honours Scotland (8 caps), Scottish League (4 appearances).
Chelsea details Debut 26.8.33. 51 Appearances

	Appearances		Goals	
	FL	FAC	FL	FAC
1933–34	6	–	–	–
1934–35	27	2	–	–
1935–36	10	–	–	–
1936–37	1	–	–	–
1937–38	2	–	–	–
1938–39	3	–	–	–
Total	49	2	–	–

One of the best goalkeepers in Britain of his time. Most of his days at Chelsea were spent in the shadow of the great Vic Woodley, although he added a further four Scottish caps to a similar number won while with Partick Thistle. Along with Harry Hibbs he was one of the smallest players to play international football in his position. But he was, as his manager once said, "brave as a lion, quick, safe, sure". He played a further 74 games for Chelsea in war-time regional football, also "guesting" for Brentford, before retiring. After the war he emigrated to Canada and became a golf professional, after having played in the 1950 British Open Championship.

JACKSON, William (1928–1931) Outside-left

Born Leyland. Height 5ft 9ins, Weight 10st 1lb. Career Sunderland, Leeds United, West Ham United, Chelsea (February 1928), Leicester City (May 1931), Bristol Rovers.
Chelsea details Debut 31.3.28. 26 Appearances 5 Goals

	Appearances		Goals	
	FL	FAC	FL	FAC
1927–28	8	–	2	–
1928–29	9	–	2	–
1929–30	7	–	2	–
1930–31	2	–	–	–
Total	26	–	6	–

One of soccer's nomads, his three years at Chelsea were spent mostly in the reserve team understudying George Pearson. Given rare opportunities, he nevertheless performed creditably.

JOHN JACKSON

WILLIAM JACKSON

DALE W. JASPER   RICHARD G.C. JENKINS

JASPER, Dale W. (1982–1986) Midfield/Defender

Born Croydon 14.1.64. Career Chelsea (January 1982), Brighton & Hove Albion (May 1986, free transfer).
Chelsea details Debut 31.3.84. 13(2) Appearances

	Appearances				Goals			
	FL	FAC	LC	FMC	FL	FAC	LC	FMC
1983–84	3	–	–	–	–	–	–	–
1984–85	7	–	2(1)	–	–	–	–	–
1985–86	–	–	1	0(1)	–	–	–	–
Total	10	–	3(1)	0(1)	–	–	–	–

Signed professional forms after joining Chelsea as a junior. An elegant player in midfield as well as a versatile defender. His Chelsea days were marred by misfortune and injury, although he captained the Combination team to the Championship in 1984–85.

JENKINS, Richard G.C. (1924–1925) Outside-right

Career Amateur football with London University, London Polytechnic, Corinthians, and Chelsea (amateur 1924–25).
Honours England (10 amateur international caps).
Chelsea details Debut 30.8.24. 4 Appearances

	Appearances		Goals	
	FL	FAC	FL	FAC
1924–25	4	–	–	–
Total	4	–	–	–

The famous Corinthian footballer who signed amateur forms for Chelsea at the beginning of the 1924–25 season and assisted the club occasionally. He was a member of the Corinthian side which played Newcastle United in the famous F.A. cup-tie of 1927. He never played the game professionally.

JENKINS, Thomas Frederick (1949–1951) Inside-forward

Born Sunderland 5.12.25. Height 5ft 8in, Weight 10st 8lb. Career Queen of the South, Chelsea (July 1949, £8,000), Barry Town (1951), Leicester City.
Chelsea details Debut 25.2.50. 5 Appearances

	Appearances		Goals	
	FL	FAC	FL	FAC
1949–50	5	–	–	–
Total	5	–	–	–

A slightly-built inside-forward who moved into English football with a big reputation which he never justified. Most of his Chelsea days were spent in the reserve team. After leaving Stamford Bridge he returned to League football with Leicester City after a spell in the Southern League, but never played in their senior side.

JOHNSON, Gary J. (1977–1980) Striker/Midfield

Born Peckham 14.9.59. Height 5ft 11in Weight 11st 7lb. Career Chelsea (September 1977), Brentford (December 1980, £15,000), P.G. Rangers, Aldershot.
Chelsea details Debut 15.1.79. 18(4) Appearances 9 Goals.

	Appearances			Goals		
	FL	FAC	LC	FL	FAC	LC
1978–79	1	1	–	1	–	–
1979–80	12(3)	0(1)	–	7	–	–
1980–81	3	–	1	1	–	–
Total	16(3)	1(1)	1	9	–	–

Joined Chelsea as a South London schools player, signing apprentice forms in May 1976. Primarily a striker, he promised more than he achieved and at one time he seemed on the verge of establishing a permanent place for himself in the first-team. He had a loan period with Crystal Palace during the 1978–79 season.

THOMAS FREDERICK JENKINS

GARY JOHNSON

| GEOFFREY H. JOHNSON | DEREK J. JOHNSTONE |

JOHNSON, Geoffrey H. (1911–1913) Full-back

Born London. Career Chelsea (March 1911), Portsmouth (1913).
Chelsea details Debut 16.3.12. 5 Appearances

	Appearances		Goals	
	FL	FAC	FL	FAC
1911–12	2	–	–	–
1912–13	2	1	–	–
Total	4	1	–	–

A full-back signed as cover for Walter Bettridge and Jock Cameron, he was unable to displace either of the reigning incumbents, and the signing of Jimmy Sharp further restricted his opportunities in the senior side.

JOHNSTONE, Derek J. (1983–1985) Striker

Born Dundee 4.11.53 Height 6ft, Weight 13st 2lb. Career St Columba's (Dundee), Glasgow Rangers, Chelsea (September 1983), Glasgow Rangers (January 1985).
Honours Scotland (14 caps), Scotland Schoolboy, Youth & Amateur International, Scotland under-23 International (6 caps), **Scottish League** (1 appearance), **Scottish League Championship** medals 1975, 1976, 1978, Scottish Cup winners' medals 1973, 1976, 1978, 1979, 1981, losers' medal 1971, Scottish League Cup winners' medals 1971, 1978, 1979, 1982, losers' medal 1983. European Cup Winners' Cup winners' medal 1972.
Chelsea details Debut 24.2.84. 1(3) Appearances

	Appearances		Goals	
	FL	FAC	FL	FAC
1983–84	0(2)	–	–	–
1984–85	1(1)	–	–	–
Total	1(3)	–	–	–

Famous Scottish international striker who was signed, at the age of 29, to provide cover for Kerry Dixon and David Speedie. In fact he had little opportunity to make his mark felt at Chelsea during his stay of 17 months in London.

JONES, Evan (1909–1911)

Born Aberdare. Height 5ft 8 in, Weight 11st 10lb. Career Aberdare, Chelsea (September 1909), Oldham Athletic (February 1911), Bolton Wanderers.
Chelsea details Debut 11.9.09. 21 Appearances 4 Goals

	Appearances		Goals	
	FL	FAC	FL	FAC
1909–10	18	–	3	–
1910–11	3	–	1	–
Total	21	–	4	–

An ebullient character, noted for his singing as well as his footballing ability who, after an extended run in the first-team during an injury to George Hilsdon, was unable to stake a regular claim for a slot in the League side. He continued to score goals regularly in the reserve team before moving to Oldham Athletic.

JONES, Joseph J. (1982–1985) Defender

Born Llandudno 4.3.55. Height 5ft 10in Weight 11st 7lb. Career Wrexham, Liverpool, Wrexham, Chelsea (October 1982, £34,500), Huddersfield Town (August 1985, £35,000).
Honours Wales (70 caps), Wales Under-23 (4 caps), Football League Championship medals 1976, 1977, Second Division Championship medal 1984, European Champions' Cup medal 1977, F.A. Cup losers' medal 1977.
Chelsea details Debut 26.3.83. 89(2) Appearances 2 Goals.

	Appearances			Goals		
	FL	FAC	LC	FL	FAC	LC
1982–83	28	3	–	1	–	–
1983–84	34	1	4	1	–	–
1984–85	14(2)	1	4	–	–	–
Total	76(2)	5	8	2	–	–

He had already had an eventful career with both his previous clubs before joining a Chelsea team where morale was low and success elusive. He at once helped to restore both these ingredients by his attitude in the dressing-room and his positive approach on the field. If lacking in the finer skills, his determination not to accept defeat lightly turned many a game, and few players established such an immediate and obvious rapport with the supporters. A resourceful defender whether at full-back or in the centre of the defence.

EVAN JONES

JOSEPH J. JONES

KEITH JONES	T. BENNY JONES

JONES, Keith (1983–   ) Midfield

Born Dulwich 14.10.65. Height 5ft 9in, Weight 10st 11lb. Career Chelsea (August 1983). Honours England Youth International, England Schoolboy International.
Chelsea details Debut 26.3.83. 57(12) Appearances 10 Goals

	Appearances				Goals			
	FL	FAC	FLC	FMC	FL	FAC	FLC	FMC
1982–83	0(2)	–	–	–	–	–	–	–
1984–85	17(2)	–	4(1)	–	2	–	2	–
1985–86	10(4)	1	3	3(1)	2	–	–	–
1986–87	16(1)	–	2(1)	1	3	–	1	–
Total	43(9)	1	9(2)	4(1)	7	–	3	–

A gifted and creative performer in midfield with a flair for scoring spectacular goals. Progressed through the junior and reserve ranks to have several spells of first-team experience. Won a "Robinson's Barley Water" regional award for Young Player of the Month in December 1984.

JONES, T. Benny (1947–1953) Outside-left

Born Frodsham 23.3.20, Died December 1972. Height 5ft 8½ins, Weight 12st 3lb. Career Tranmere Rovers, Chelsea (October 1947), Accrington Stanley (July 1953).
Chelsea details Debut 29.11.47. 62 Appearances 13 Goals

	Appearances		Goals	
	FL	FAC	FL	FAC
1947–48	11	2	–	–
1948–49	28	3	6	1
1949–50	6	–	2	–
1950–51	7	–	1	–
1951–52	3	2	2	1
Total	55	7	11	2

For most of his time at Chelsea he was on the fringe of the first-team. A most popular player with the fans, he was noted for his whole-hearted, bulldozing attacking play down the left-wing. Heavily-built, he possessed a strong shot, especially from his left foot, which made him a regular scorer of goals.

KELL, Leonard W. (1952–1954) Inside-forward

Born Billingham, Co. Durham 27.5.32. Height 5ft 8ins, Weight 10st 10lb. Career Chelsea (March 1952), Norwich City (June 1954).
Chelsea details Debut 8.9.53. 3 Appearances

	Appearances		Goals	
	FL	FAC	FL	FAC
1953–54	3	–	–	–
Total	3	–	–	–

Graduated to the ranks of full professional after four years as an apprentice on the Stamford Bridge staff. His time at Chelsea was spent almost entirely in the junior and reserve teams with Johnny McNichol and Les Stubbs the established first-team inside-forwards.

KEMBER, Steve D. (1971–1975) Midfield

Born Croydon 8.12.48. Height 5ft 8in Weight 11st. Career Crystal Palace, Chelsea (September 1971, £170,000), Leicester City (July 1975, £80,000), Crystal Palace, Vancouver Whitecaps, Whyteleafe.
Honours England Under-23 (3 caps), Second Division Championship medal 1979.
Chelsea details Debut 25.9.71. 144(6) Appearances 15 Goals.

	Appearances			Goals		
	FL	FAC	LC	FL	FAC	LC
1971–72	24(3)	2(1)	–	3	–	–
1972–73	35	5	6	–	–	2
1973–74	37	2	1	7	–	–
1974–75	29(2)	1	2	3	–	–
Total	125(5)	10(1)	9	13	–	2

A tireless runner in midfield and a strong tackler, his time at Chelsea coincided with the fragmentation of the 1970 and 1971 cup-winning squads and with a difficult financial period in the club. As a result, he was rarely able to do justice to his considerable ability. After retiring from the game he was Manager of Crystal Palace for a spell.

LEONARD W. KELL

STEVE D. KEMBER

GEORGE KENNEDY

DEREK T. KEVAN

KENNEDY, George (1908–1909) Half-back

Career Chelsea (May 1908), Brentford (1909).
Chelsea details Debut 10.10.08. 12 Appearances

	Appearances		Goals	
	FL	FAC	FL	FAC
1908–09	10	2	–	–
Total	10	2	–	–

Spending only one season at Stamford Bridge, he deputised for Bob McRoberts at centre-half in several matches and also appeared in both wing-half positions.

KEVAN, Derek T. (1963) Centre or inside-forward

Born Ripon 6.3.35. Height 6ft 1in, Weight 13st 8lb. Career Ripon YMCA, Bradford Park Avenue, West Bromwich Albion, Chelsea (March 1963, £45,000), Manchester City (August 1963, £40,000), Crystal Palace, Peterborough United, Luton Town, Stockport County. Honours England (14 caps), England Under-23 (4 caps), Football League XI.
Chelsea details Debut 23.3.63. 7 Appearances 1 Goal

	Appearances		Goals	
	FL	FAC	FL	FAC
1962–63	7	–	1	–
Total	7	–	1	–

His five-month sojourn at Chelsea was punctuated by the winning of promotion from Division II, as well as by differences of opinion with manager Tommy Docherty. A superbly built player, he scored nearly 250 goals in his League career, well over half of them for West Bromwich Albion, the only club he served for more than two seasons.

KEY, George (1905–1909) Wing-half

Born Dennistoun. Career Heart of Midlothian, Chelsea (August 1905).
Chelsea details Debut 2.9.05. 56 Appearances 2 Goals

	Appearances		Goals	
	FL	FAC	FL	FAC
1905–06	33	2	1	–
1906–07	4	–	1	–
1907–08	13	–	–	–
1908–09	4	–	–	–
Total	54	2	2	–

Chelsea's first right-half. "Geordie" had the reputation of possessing an inexhaustible supply of energy. No cause was ever lost for him and he only vacated his first-team spot through injury early in the 1905–06 season. However, he was then unable to displace George Henderson and was never an automatic choice afterwards.

KIRKUP, Joe (1966–1968) Full-back

Born Sunderland 17.12.39. Height 5ft 11in, Weight 12st 4lb. Career West Ham United, Chelsea (March 1966, £35,000), Southampton (February 1968, part-exchange David Webb). Honours England Under-23 (3 caps), Youth International, European Cup Winners' Cup winners' medal 1965.
Chelsea details Debut 12.3.66. 62(7) Appearances 2 Goals

	Appearances				Goals			
	FL	FAC	LC	FC	FL	FAC	LC	FC
1965–66	14	3	–	5	1	–	–	–
1966–67	24(2)	2(1)	3	–	1	–	–	–
1967–68	10(3)	1(1)	–	–	–	–	–	–
Total	48(5)	6(2)	3	5	2	–	–	–

A tall, stylish full-back, he became an important member of Chelsea's first-team squad during his two years with the club before manager Dave Sexton's exchange deal which brought the more aggressive Dave Webb to Stamford Bridge.

GEORGE KEY

JOE KIRKUP

JOHN KIRWAN | RAY A. KITCHENER

KIRWAN, John (1905–1908) Outside-left
Born Wicklow. Career Tottenham Hotspur, Chelsea (August 1905), Clyde (1908). Honours Ireland (17 caps).
Chelsea details Debut 2.9.05. 76 Appearances 18 Goals

	Appearances		Goals	
	FL	FAC	FL	FAC
1905–06	36	1	9	–
1906–07	35	2	8	1
1907–08	2	–	–	–
Total	73	3	17	1

Chelsea's outside-left for the club's first two seasons. Very fast and an accurate crosser of the ball, he was also a regular goalscorer. A great character and favourite with the crowd, he won four of his 17 international caps whilst at Stamford Bridge.

KITCHENER, Ray A. (1954–1956) Outside-left
Born Letchworth 31.10.30. Height 5ft 9in, Weight 11st. Career Hitchin Town, Chelsea (July 1954), Norwich City (September 1956).
Chelsea details Debut 11.2.56. 1 Appearance

	Appearances		Goals	
	FL	FAC	FL	FAC
1955–56	1	–	–	–
Total	1	–	–	–

A regular reserve player for his two seasons at Chelsea, his first professional club, he understudied Frank Blunstone and the further presence of amateur Jim Lewis meant that he had little prospect of ever gaining a regular first-team place.

KNOX, Thomas (1962–1965) Outside-left

Born Glasgow 5.4.39. Height 5ft 7½in, Weight 10st 4lb. Career East Stirling, Chelsea (June 1962, £5,000), Newcastle United (February 1965, £10,000), Mansfield Town, Northampton Town.
Chelsea details Debut 22.9.62. 21 Appearances

	Appearances			Goals		
	FL	FAC	LC	FL	FAC	LC
1962–63	6	–	–	–	–	–
1963–64	1	–	–	–	–	–
1964–65	13	–	1	–	–	–
Total	20	–	1	–	–	–

Joined Chelsea from East Stirling two months after Eddie McCreadie had arrived from the same club. Having remained on the fringe of the first-team for three years, he sought his fortune with Newcastle United, but again failed to establish himself as a regular and soon moved on into Third Division football two years later.

LAKE, George (1913–1918) Wing-half

Career Manchester City, Chelsea (1913).
Chelsea details Debut 14.4.14. 1 Appearance. Killed in action October 1918.

	Appearances		Goals	
	FL	FAC	FL	FAC
1913–14	1	–	–	–
Total	1	–	–	–

Signed professional early in the 1913–14 season after a period on trial. Any chance of establishing himself in the first-team was ended by the outbreak of World War I and he was one of the last men to be killed in action before the signing of the Armistice.

THOMAS KNOX

WANTED

If anyone has a photograph of **GEORGE**
It would be appreciated if you would allow us to copy it. Please forward it to Ron at 36 Lockier Walk, Wembley, Middx. It will be returned safely

GEORGE LAKE

TOM W. LANGLEY

JOSEPH LANGTON

LANGLEY, Tom W. (1975–1980) Striker

Born Lambeth 8.2.58. Height 5ft 11in, Weight 11st 7lb. Career Chelsea (March 1975), Queens Park Rangers (August 1980, £425,000), Crystal Palace, A.E.K. Athens, Coventry City, Wolverhampton Wanderers, Aldershot.
Honours England Under-21 (1 cap), England Schoolboy & Youth International.
Chelsea details Debut 9.11.74. 139(13) Appearances 43 Goals

	Appearances			Goals		
	FL	FAC	LC	FL	FAC	LC
1974–75	5(3)	–	–	1	–	–
1975–76	4(6)	–	–	1	–	–
1976–77	6	–	–	2	–	–
1977–78	39(2)	4	1	11	2	–
1978–79	40(1)	1	1	15	–	1
1979–80	35(1)	1	2	10	–	–
Total	129(13)	6	4	40	2	1

Made his Football League debut (v Leicester City) aged 16 years 9 months and signed professional forms four months later. An enthusiastic, fast and totally committed player, for three difficult seasons he bore the brunt of leading the Chelsea attack, often in discouraging circumstances and in the light of much unfair criticism.

LANGTON, Joseph (1919–1922) Wing-half

Career: Chelsea (October 1919) Free transfer 1922).
Chelsea details Debut: 2.5.21. 3 Appearances

	Appearances		Goals	
	FL	FAC	FL	FAC
1920–21	1	–	–	–
1921–22	2	–	–	–
Total	3	–	–	–

During his three years on the staff he was a regular member of the reserve team but could not displace such as Tommy Meehan, Tom Wilding and David Cameron from the senior side.

LAVERICK, Robert (1955–1959) Outside-left

Born: Trimdon, Co. Durham 11.6.38. Height 5ft 11in, Weight 12st 6lb.
Career: Chelsea (June 1955), Everton (February 1959), Brighton & Hove Albion, Coventry City
Honours: England Youth International
Chelsea details Debut: 2.2.57. 7 Appearances

	Appearances		Goals	
	FL	FAC	FL	FAC
1956–57	6	–	–	–
1957–58	1	–	–	–
Total	7	–	–	–

Joined Chelsea as a 15-year old groundstaff boy before signing professional. A powerful, sturdily-built winger of direct approach, he was contemporary with Frank Blunstone, Jim Lewis, and Mike Block on the staff and therefore found that few first-team opportunities came his way.

LAW, Thomas (1925–1939) Left-back

Born: Glasgow 1.4.08 Died February 17.2.76. Height 5ft 10in, Weight 12st.
Career: Waverley (Glasgow), Chelsea (June 1925, £10), Free-transfer (May 1939)
Honours: Scotland (2 caps)
Chelsea details Debut: 18.9.26. 319 Appearances, 19 Goals

	Appearances		Goals	
	FL	FAC	FL	FAC
1926–27	36	5	–	–
1927–28	38	1	1	–
1928–29	39	4	1	1
1929–30	41	1	–	–
1930–31	27	5	6	1
1931–32	27	7	1	2
1932–33	33	–	2	–
1933–34	25	2	4	–
1935–36	23	1	–	–
1937–38	4	–	–	–
Total	293	26	15	4

ROBERT LAVERICK

THOMAS LAW

THOMAS LAWTON

One of the most distinguished players in Chelsea's history whose entire professional career was spent at Stamford Bridge. Stockily built, he concealed his lack of pace with shrewd positional play. He was a fine passer of the ball and his constructive ideas launched many attacks from deep in his own half of the field. Strangely he was selected only twice by the Scottish selectors, on each occasion to play against England at Wembley, one of these being in 1928 for the team which won 5–1 and were dubbed the "Wembley Wizards". For most of his time in the Chelsea side he was also the recognised taker of penalty-kicks, seldom failing from the spot. He continued to live in London until the time of his death and remained a regular and familiar figure at The Bridge.

LAWTON, Thomas (1945–1947) Centre-forward

Born: Bolton 6.10.19. Height 6ft, Weight 12st 8lb
Career: Burnley, Everton, Chelsea (November 1945, £11,500), Notts County (November 1947, £20,000), Brentford, Arsenal
Honours: England (23 caps), Football League XI, Football League Championship medal 1939. Third Division (South) Championship medal 1950.
Chelsea details Debut: 5.1.46. 53 Appearances. 35 Goals

	Appearances		Goals	
	FL	FAC	FL	FAC
1945–46	–	6	–	1
1946–47	34	5	26	4
1947–48	8	–	4	–
Total	42	11	30	5

One of football's most famous centre-forwards. Magnificently built, he was a brilliant header of the ball as well as being an extremely skilful ball player with most delicate footwork for such a big man. One of those whose career was mutilated by World War II, he was one of Chelsea's big money signings designed to bring the game's top honours to Stamford Bridge. Unhappily, he fell into dispute with the management after only one "normal" season and then became Britain's first £20,000 transfer moving, perhaps unwisely, into Third Division football with Notts County. At his peak, both before and after the war, he was recognised as the finest centre-forward in the game. He managed both Brentford and Notts County for short periods.

LEADBETTER, James H. (1949–1952) Inside-forward

Born: Edinburgh 15.7.28. Height 5ft 8½, Weight 9st 10lb.
Career: Edinburgh Thistle, Chelsea (July 1949), Brighton & Hove Albion (August 1952), Ipswich Town
Honours: First Division Championship medal 1962, Second Division Championship medal 1961, Third Division Championship medal 1957
Chelsea details Debut: 12.4.52. 3 Appearances

	Appearances		Goals	
	FL	FAC	FL	FAC
1951–52	3	–	–	–
Total	3	–	–	–

Pencil-slim Scottish ball-playing inside-forward. Spent three seasons at Chelsea without his true potential being unearthed. After more than 100 games with Brighton he went on to win fame with Ipswich Town's team which won three Championship titles in six years, playing as a "withdrawn" left winger, a tactical role created for him by his manager Alf Ramsey.

LEE, Colin (1980–   ) Centre-forward/Full-back

Born: Plymouth 12.6.56 Height 6ft 1in, Weight 11st 9lb.
Career: Bristol City, Hereford United, Torquay United, Tottenham Hotspur, Chelsea (January 1980, £200,000)
Honours: Second Division Championship medal 1984, Full Members' Cup winners' medal 1986
Chelsea details Debut: 1.3.80. 200 (23) Appearances 41 Goals

	Appearances				Goals			
	FL	FAC	LC	FMC	FL	FAC	LC	FMC
1979–80	4(1)	–	–	–	1	–	–	–
1980–81	34(1)	1	1(1)	–	15	1	–	–
1981–82	40	6	3	–	11	1	–	–
1982–83	31(4)	3	2	–	5	–	–	–
1983–84	25(8)	–	4(1)	–	3	–	–	–
1984–85	20(2)	1	9	–	1	–	1	–
1985–86	12(1)	1	1	1(1)	–	–	–	2
1986–87	1(1)	–	0(2)	–	–	–	–	–
Total	167(18)	12	20(4)	1(1)	36	2	1	2

JAMES H. LEADBETTER

COLIN LEE

JOHN LEE

For the first part of his career he was recognised as a striker (32 goals from 99 League games before his arrival at Stamford Bridge), but the advent of David Speedie and Kerry Dixon limited his chances in the forward line and he developed into a sound, solid full-back, occupying that place during the latter part of the 1983-84 Second Division Championship season with distinction. However, in the Full Members' Cup final he was again pressed into service as a forward – and responded by scoring two goals!

LEE, John (1920–1924) Outside-left

Born: Sheffield 1890, Died 10.8.55. Height 5ft 10¼, Weight 11st 2lb.
Career: Bird in Hand (Sheffield), Hull City, Chelsea (February 1920, £1,500), Watford, Rotherham United
Chelsea details Debut: 13.3.20. 7 Appearances, 1 Goal

	Appearances		Goals	
	FL	FAC	FL	FAC
1919–20	4	–	1	–
1920–21	2	–	–	–
1922–23	1	–	–	–
Total	7	–	1	–

Signed for a relatively large fee, for those days, he won an immediate first-team place but failed to adjust to First Division football, playing mostly in the reserve team during his Stamford Bridge career.

LEWINGTON, Ray (1974–1979) Midfield

Born: Lambeth 7.9.56. Height 5ft 7in, Weight 10st 13lb.
Career: Chelsea (February 1974), Vancouver Whitecaps (February 1979, £40,000), Wimbledon (Loan), Fulham, Sheffield United, Fulham (Player-Manager)
Chelsea details Debut: 21.2.76. 87(5) Appearances, 4 Goals.

	Appearances			Goals		
	FL	FAC	LC	FL	FAC	LC
1975–76	8(1)	–	–	2	–	–
1976–77	42	2	3	–	–	–
1977–78	20(4)	2	–	2	–	–
1978–79	10	–	–	–	–	–
Total	80(5)	4	3	4	–	–

Ball-winning midfield player who first joined Chelsea as a schoolboy. He was an ever-present in the 1976–77 Second Division promotion winning team, but lacked the necessary pace to establish himself in the top class, and was not part of manager Danny Blanchflower's plans for Chelsea's future. Spent a brief period in North American football before returning to this country to resume his Football League career. Appointed Player-Manager of Fulham in the summer of 1986.

LEWIS, Frederick A. (1946–1953) Left-back

Born: Broughton Gifford (Wilts.) 27.7.23. Height 5ft 8in, Weight 10st 12lb.
Career: Aylesbury, Chelsea (March 1946), Colchester United (June 1953)
Chelsea details Debut: 31.8.46. 26 Appearances

	Appearances		Goals	
	FL	FAC	FL	FAC
1946–47	7	–	–	–
1947–48	12	–	–	–
1948–49	3	3	–	–
1952–53	1	–	–	–
Total	23	3	–	–

Compact full-back, with constructive ideas, who came to Chelsea following demobilisation from the Royal Navy. After a promising start he was unable to command a regular first-team place and spent most of his seven seasons on the staff in the reserve team.

RAY LEWINGTON

FREDERICK A. LEWIS

JAMES L. LEWIS FREDERICK LINFOOT

LEWIS, James L. (1952–1958) Winger/Centre-forward

Born: Hackney 26.6.27. Height 5ft 11in, Weight 12st.
Career: Walthamstow Avenue, Leyton Orient (amateur), Walthamstow Avenue, Chelsea (amateur, September 1952)
Honours: England Amateur International, Football League Championship medal 1955
Chelsea details Debut: 4.10.52. 95 Appearances, 40 Goals

| | Appearances || Goals ||
	FL	FAC	FL	FAC
1952–53	9	–	4	–
1953–54	20	–	9	–
1954–55	17	–	6	–
1955–56	9	2	2	1
1956–57	18	–	9	–
1957–58	17	3	8	1
Total	90	5	38	2

One of the famous amateur players who have assisted Chelsea down the years, he was also one of the most prolific scorers of goals from the wing. In the 1954–55 Championship season he shared the outside-left berth with Frank Blunstone. Of direct method he possessed both speed and clever footwork. The son of J.W. Lewis, also an England amateur international player, he was presented with an illuminated address in November 1959 to commemorate his distinguished career at Stamford Bridge over six seasons.

LINFOOT, Frederick (1920–1924) Outside-right

Born: Whitley Bay. Height 5ft 11in, Weight 11st 1lb
Career: Leeds City, Chelsea (July 1920), Fulham (March 1924), Lincoln City
Chelsea details Debut: 4.9.20. 41 Appearances, 1 Goal

| | Appearances || Goals ||
	FL	FAC	FL	FAC
1920–21	13	4	–	–
1921–22	2	–	–	–
1922–23	14	2	–	–
1923–24	5	1	1	–
Total	34	7	1	–

Remained on the fringe of the first-team during his four seasons on the Chelsea staff at a time when a series of different players were competing for the right-wing spot.

LIVESEY, Charles (1959–1961) Centre-forward

Born: West Ham 8.3.24. Height 5ft 11½in, Weight 12st 8lb
Career: Wolverhampton Wanderers (Amateur), Southampton, Chelsea (May 1959, part-exchange for Cliff Huxford), Gillingham (August 1961, £5,500), Watford, Northampton Town, Brighton & Hove Albion
Chelsea details Debut: 22.8.59. 42 Appearances, 18 Goals

	Appearances			Goals		
	FL	FAC	LC	FL	FAC	LC
1959–60	25	2	–	9	1	–
1960–61	14	–	1	8	–	–
Total	39	2	1	17	–	–

Robust centre-forward who was noted for his brisk and enthusiastic approach. Despite a most respectable scoring ratio, he never fully acclimatised to First Division football and moved on when losing his place in the first-team to Ron Tindall. He scored over 100 goals in his Football League career from some 360 games.

LIVINGSTONE, William (1955–1959) Centre-half

Born: Greenock 8.2.29. Height 6ft 1½in, Weight 12st 8lb
Career: Ardeer Recreation, Reading, Chelsea (June 1955), Brentford (August 1959)
Chelsea details Debut: 15.2.56. 22 Appearances

	Appearances		Goals	
	FL	FAC	FL	FAC
1955–56	1	–	–	–
1956–57	12	1	–	–
1957–58	8	–	–	–
Total	21	1	–	–

Powerfully built "stopper" centre-half who proved a reliable deputy following the retirement, through injury, of Stan Wicks and before the signing of John Mortimore. Most of his time at Chelsea, however, was spent in the reserve team.

CHARLES LIVESEY

WILLIAM LIVINGSTONE

BARRY D. LLOYD	TOM LOGAN

LLOYD, Barry D. (1966–1969) Inside-forward

Born: Hillingdon 19.2.49. Height 5ft 7½, Weight 10st 5lb
Career: Hillingdon, Chelsea (February 1966), Fulham (January 1969, £30,000), Hereford United, Brentford
Chelsea details Debut: 10.4.67. 8(2) Appearances

	Appearances		Goals	
	FL	FAC	FL	FAC
1966–67	4	–	–	–
1967–68	1	–	–	–
1968–69	3(2)	–	–	–
Total	8(2)	–	–	–

Joined Chelsea as an apprentice from his local club. Unable to win a first-team place at a time when Chelsea had a surfeit of talent on the books, he moved on to Fulham when John Dempsey made the reverse move and went on to play over 250 games for the "Cottagers". Appointed Manager of Brighton & Hove Albion in January 1987.

LOGAN, Tom (1913–1920) Centre-half

Born: Falkirk. Height 5ft 11in, Weight 13st 4lb.
Honours: Scotland (1 cap) F.A. Cup final losers' medal 1915
Career: Falkirk, Chelsea (May 1913)
Chelsea details Debut: 6.9.13. 117 Appearances, 8 Goals

	Appearances		Goals	
	FL	FAC	FL	FAC
1913–14	35	1	2	–
1914–15	35	6	4	–
1919–20	22	3	1	1
1920–21	15	–	–	–
Total	107	10	7	1

A fine resourceful centre-half whose career was bisected by World War I at a time when he was at his peak and well capable of adding to his undeserved tally of only one international cap. A powerful defender, he was never averse to moving forward to lend weight to attack, this in the days before the alteration on the off-side law.

LOCKE, Gary R. (1972–1982) Full-back

Born: Kingsbury 12.7.54. Height 5ft 11in, Weight 11st 5lb.
Career: Chelsea, Crystal Palace (January 1983)
Honours: England Youth International
Chelsea details Debut: 30.9.72. 315(2) Appearances, 4 Goals

	Appearances			Goals		
	FL	FAC	FC	FL	FAC	FC
1972–73	17(1)	3	6	–	–	–
1973–74	31	2	1	–	–	–
1974–75	41	2	4	1	–	–
1975–76	23	4	–	1	–	–
1976–77	42	2	3	–	1	–
1977–78	18	3	1	–	–	–
1978–79	8	–	1	–	–	–
1979–80	32	1	1	–	–	–
1980–81	21(1)	1	–	–	–	–
1981–82	31	6	2	1	–	–
1982–83	6	–	2	–	–	–
Total	270(2)	24	21	3	1	–

A product of the Chelsea Youth Scheme, he was a pillar of the defence for 11 seasons at a time when the club was in severe financial difficulty, which was reflected by a marked lack of success on the field. As a result, he often failed to win the credit he deserved. Further, his career was disrupted by injuries. At his best he was a sound defensive player with an attacking flair – his speedy "overlapping" runs leading to goals on many occasions.

LUKE, George (1967–68) Wing-half

Born: Hetton-le-Hole (Co. Durham) 9.11.48
Career: Newcastle United, Chelsea (March 1967), Durban City (August 1968)
Honours: England Schoolboy International
Chelsea details Debut: 9.5.67. 1 Appearance

	Appearances		Goals	
	FL	FAC	FL	FAC
1966–67	1	–	–	–
Total	1	–	–	–

Contemporary with such as John Hollins, Ron Harris and John Boyle, he was unable to win a first-team place despite his undoubted ability and sought his fortune in South African football after little more than a year at Stamford Bridge.

GARY R. LOCKE

GEORGE LUKE

FRANK LYON	JAMES A.R. MACAULAY

LYON, Frank (1907–1908) Full-back

Career: Queens Park Rangers, Chelsea (March 1907), Retired through injury May 1908.
Chelsea details Debut: 14.9.07. 6 Appearances

	Appearances		Goals	
	FL	FAC	FL	FAC
1907–08	6	–	–	–
Total	6	–	–	–

Started the 1907–08 season as first choice at right-back but the arrival of Jock Cameron limited his chances to become established and then injury forced his early retirement from the game. He subsequently opened a business in Crewe.

MACAULAY, James A.R. (1946–1951) Wing-half

Born: Edinburgh 19.10.22. Height 5ft 9in, Weight 11st 6lb
Career: Edinburgh Thistle, Chelsea (November 1946), Aldershot (August 1951)
Chelsea details Debut: 19.10.46. 94 Appearances, 5 Goals

	Appearances		Goals	
	FL	FAC	FL	FAC
1946–47	30	5	1	–
1947–48	15	–	–	–
1948–49	36	3	4	–
1949–50	5	–	–	–
Total	86	8	5	–

First came to Chelsea as a junior in 1940–41 and then signed professional forms on demobilisation from the R.A.F. in November 1946. A civil servant and part-time player, he was a strong, attacking wing-half in the immediate post-war period but lost his place to Frank Mitchell.

MACAULAY, Robert (1932–1936) Full-back

Born: Wishaw 28.8.04. Height 5ft 8in, Weight 12st
Career: Glasgow Rangers, Fall River (U.S.A.), Glasgow Rangers, Chelsea (May 1939), Cardiff City (December 1936), Workington, Raith Rovers
Honours: Scotland (2 caps) Scottish F.A. Cup winners' medal 1932, Scottish League (1 appearance)
Chelsea details Debut: 3.9.32. 74 Appearances, 1 Goal

	Appearances		Goals	
	FL	FAC	FL	FAC
1932–33	10	–	–	–
1933–34	13	3	–	–
1934–35	38	2	1	–
1935–36	5	3	–	–
Total	66	8	1	–

Scottish international full-back who arrived in London with a big reputation that he was never to fully justify. Stockily built, he lacked a little pace but was a good tackler and distributor of the ball. Was unable to hold a first-team place in competition with such as Tommy Law and George Barber.

MacFARLANE, Ian (1956–1958) Full-back

Born: Lanark 26.1.33. Height 6ft 1in, Weight 12st 7lb
Career: Aberdeen, Chelsea (August 1956), Leicester City (May 1958)
Chelsea details Debut: 22.8.56. 43 Appearances

	Appearances		Goals	
	FL	FAC	FL	FAC
1956–57	30	–	–	–
1957–58	10	3	–	–
Total	40	3	–	–

Powerfully built full-back, he was the regular first-choice during his first season on the Chelsea staff, but loss of form led to his transfer to Leicester City after two seasons. Later became Manager of Carlisle United for a spell and then Coach at Leicester City.

ROBERT MACAULAY

IAN MacFARLANE

ALEX H. MACHIN

STANLEY W. MACINTOSH

MACHIN, Alex H. (1944–1948) Inside-forward/Wing-half
Born: Shepherds Bush 6.7.20
Career: Chelsea (1944), Plymouth Argyle (June 1948)
Chelsea details Debut: 5.1.46. 61 Appearances, 9 Goals

	Appearances		Goals	
	FL	FAC	FL	FAC
1945–46	–	3	–	1
1946–47	37	5	7	–
1947–48	16	–	1	–
Total	53	8	8	1

He was first spotted by Chelsea while serving with the Royal Hampshire Regiment during World War II and became a full-time professional on demobilisation. Then 25, he had already lost too much vital training and experience during his formative years and, doubtless as a result, never quite fulfilled his potential. A strong, forceful player, he lost his place to Ken Armstrong after one season in the first-team and then moved to Plymouth Argyle where he played a handful of games in their League side.

MACINTOSH, Stanley W. (1930–1936) Goalkeeper
Born: Brighton. Height 6ft, Weight 10st 13lb
Career: London Caledonians, Chelsea (May 1930)
Chelsea details Debut: 6.12.30. 1 Appearance

	Appearances		Goals	
	FL	FAC	FL	FAC
1930–31	1	–	–	–
Total	1	–	–	–

A capable 'keeper who was content to remain at Stamford Bridge for six seasons without any real chance of displacing either Vic Woodley or Johnny Jackson, internationals both, and possibly the two best in their position in Britain.

MACKIE, Robert (1905–1908) Full-back

Born: Bannockburn
Career: Heart of Midlothian, Chelsea (August 1905), Leicester City (1908), Airdrieonians
Chelsea details Debut: 2.9.05 48 Appearances, 1 Goal

	Appearances		Goals	
	FL	FAC	FL	FAC
1905–06	35	2	1	–
1906–07	3	2	–	–
1907–08	6	–	–	–
1930–31	1	–	–	–
Total	44	4	1	–

Chelsea's first right-back. Extremely quick and a great-hearted player who was popular with the club's supporters, he lost his place through injury and the signing of Joe Walton prevented him from regaining it again on a regular basis.

MAIR, Tommy (1909–1910) Outside-left

Career: Leyton, Chelsea (January 1909)
Chelsea details Debut: 25.12.08. 9 Appearances, 1 Goal

	Appearances		Goals	
	FL	FAC	FL	FAC
1908–09	4	–	–	–
1909–10	5	–	1	–
Total	9	–	1	–

He was at Chelsea for just over a year and was one of a number of players who occupied the outside-left position at a time when Chelsea, unsuccessfully as it turned out, were struggling to maintain their First Division status.

ROBERT MACKIE

TOMMY MAIR

ANDREW MALCOLM | WILSON MARSH

MALCOLM, Andrew (1961–1962) Wing-half
Born: East Ham 4.5.33. Height 5ft 8in. Weight 11st 10lb
Career: West Ham United, Chelsea (November 1961, £12,000) Queens Park Rangers (October 1962, £12,000)
Honours: England Schoolboy & Youth International, Football League
Chelsea details Debut: 4.11.61. 28 Appearances, 1 Goal

	Appearances		Goals	
	FL	FAC	FL	FAC
1961–62	27	1	1	–
Total	27	1	1	–

He was signed after a long and distinguished career with West Ham (over 300 games) to add stability and experience to a young Chelsea team, in a move which also took Ron Tindall to Upton Park. Perhaps he was already past his peak, but, after one unhappy season during which Chelsea were relegated, manager Tommy Docherty placed his faith in 19-year old Terry Venables and he moved to Queens Park Rangers shortly afterwards.

MARSH, Wilson (1921–1924) Goalkeeper
Born: Woodhouse. Height 6ft 1½in, Weight 13st
Career: Eckington Works (Sheffield), Chelsea (December 1921), Dundee (Summer 1924)
Chelsea details Debut: 27.12.21

	Appearances		Goals	
	FL	FAC	FL	FAC
1921–22	1	–	–	–
1023–24	9	2	–	–
Total	27	1	1	–

For nearly three seasons he stood in the wings as deputy goalkeeper to Jim Molyneux, Colin Hampton and the great Corinthian, Howard Baker. Not surprisingly, his opportunities were limited and he was not retained at the end of the 1923–24 season, and he moved to Dundee. He was also a notable golfer.

MARSHALL, Owen Thomas (1913–1920) Full-back

Born: Nottingham
Career: Ilkeston United, Chelsea (March 1913), Gillingham (November 1920)
Chelsea details Debut: 8.9.13. 36 Appearances

	Appearances		Goals	
	FL	FAC	FL	FAC
1913–14	18	2	–	–
1913–15	11	–	–	–
1919–20	5	–	–	–
Total	34	2	–	–

Proved a reliable deputy for either Walter Bettridge or Jack Harrow whenever required and might have gone further in the game but for the interruption of his career by World War I.

MATTHEWS, Reginald D. (1956–1961) Goalkeeper

Born: Coventry 20.12.33. Height 6ft, Weight 11st 7lb
Career: Coventry City, Chelsea (December 1956, £20,000) Derby County (October 1961, £10,000)
Honours: England (5 caps), England Under-23 (4 caps), England "B" (3 caps) Football League
Chelsea details Debut 17.11.56. 148 Appearances

	Appearances				Goals			
	FL	FAC	LC	FC	FL	FAC	LC	FC
1956–57	22	2	–	–	–	–	–	–
1957–58	42	3	–	–	–	–	–	–
1958–59	32	2	–	3	–	–	–	–
1959–60	33	2	–	–	–	–	–	–
1960–61	6	–	1	–	–	–	–	–
Total	135	9	1	3	–	–	–	–

Was signed for a, then, record fee for a goalkeeper. He possessed lightning reflexes and was absolutely fearless, having already won his 5 England full international caps. At Chelsea he was not always seen at his best, being forced to play behind an unreliable and often square-lying defence. Ultimately he lost his place to Peter Bonetti and moved on to Derby County where he played more than 250 games, giving the midland club years of outstanding service.

OWEN THOMAS MARSHALL

REGINALD D. MATTHEWS

| EDWARD MAYBANK | ALAN K. MAYES |

MAYBANK, Edward (1974–1976) Striker

Born Lambeth 11.10.56. Height 5ft 10ins, Weight 10st 12lb. Career Chelsea (February 1974), Fulham (November 1976, £65,000), Brighton & Hove Albion, Fulham.
Chelsea details Debut 19.4.75. 32 Appearances 6 Goals

	Appearances		Goals	
	FL	FAC	FL	FAC
1974–75	3	–	1	–
1975–76	22	4	5	–
1976–77	3	–	–	–
Total	28	4	6	–

Signed professional after two years as an apprentice at Stamford Bridge. A talented, if at times unpredictable, striker who lost his place to Steve Finnieston and, with young Tommy Langley also in the wings, he was allowed to move on.

MAYES, Alan K. (1980–1983) Striker

Born London 11.12.53. Height 5ft 7in, Weight 10st 7lb. Career Queens Park Rangers, Watford, Northampton Town, Swindon Town, Chelsea (December 1980, £200,000), Swindon Town (Summer 1983, free transfer), Carlisle United, Blackpool.
Chelsea details Debut 26.12.80. 71(5) Appearances 24 Goals.

	Appearances			Goals		
	FL	FAC	LC	FL	FAC	LC
1980–81	13	–	–	4	–	–
1981–82	35(4)	6	1	12	4	–
1982–83	13(1)	3	–	3	1	–
Total	61(5)	9	1	19	5	–

A free scorer throughout his career spent, for the most part, in the lower divisions of the League. A neat ball-player with an accurate shot, he was especially adept at turning in a confined space to lose his marker. However, he became a victim of manager John Neal's "sell-and-buy" policy in the close-season of 1983, when the team was rebuilt.

MAYES, Arnold John (1933–1942) Wing-half

Born London. Career Barking, Chelsea (March 1933), Retired 1942.
Chelsea details Debut 28.12.35. 13 Appearances

	Appearances		Goals	
	FL	FAC	FL	FAC
1935–36	2	1	–	–
1937–38	4	–	–	–
1938–39	6	–	–	–
Total	12	1	–	–

A strong tackling wing-half who was understudy to Irish international Billy Mitchell in the four seasons leading up to the outbreak of World War II. He became a corporal in the Army during the hostilities and did not resume his football career afterwards.

McALLISTER, Kevin (1985–   ) Winger

Born Falkirk 8.11.62. Height 5ft 5in, Weight 11st. Career Falkirk, Chelsea (May 1985, £35,000).
Honours Full Members' Cup winners' medal 1986.
Chelsea details Debut 14.9.85. 28 (11) Appearances 2 Goals.

	Appearances			Goals		
	FL	FLC	FMC	FL	FLC	FMC
1985–86	13(7)	3(1)	3(2)	–	–	1
1986–87	7(1)	2	–	–	1	–
Total	20(8)	5(1)	3(2)	–	1	1

Lightweight winger with good ball control and a wide range of skills. Possessing a fine turn of speed, his chances at Stamford Bridge have been limited by the consistent form of Pat Nevin with his greater scoring ability.

ARNOLD JOHN MAYES

KEVIN McALLISTER

ANTHONY McANDREW | JAMES McCALLIOG

McANDREW, Anthony (1982–1984) Defender/Midfield

Born Glasgow 11.4.56. Height 5ft 11½in, Weight 13st 2lb. Career Middlesborough, Chelsea (August 1982), Middlesborough (October 1984).
Chelsea details Debut 4.9.82. 23 Appearances 4 Goals.

	Appearances			Goals		
	FL	FAC	LC	FL	FAC	LC
1982–83	7	–	2	–	–	–
1983–84	13	1	–	4	–	–
Total	20	1	2	4	–	–

A solid defender, or midfield player, whose Chelsea career was dogged by a series of injuries. Designed to add experience to the squad, he captained the side for a period during the 1983–84 Championship season. After recovering full fitness he was uable to win back his place in the first-team and soon returned to Middlesborough where he played nearly 300 senior games for the Teesside club.

McCALLIOG, James (1963–1965) Inside-forward

Born Clydebank 23.9.46. Height 5ft 9in, Weight 10st 5lb. Career Leeds United (amateur), Chelsea (September 1963), Sheffield Wednesday (October 1965, £37,500), Wolverhampton Wanderers, Manchester United, Southampton, Lincoln City, Runcorn.
Honours Scotland (5 caps), Scotland Under-23 (2 caps), Scottish Schoolboy International, F.A. Cup winners' medal 1976, losers' medal 1966, Second Division Championship medal 1975, Fairs' Cup losers' medal 1972.
Chelsea details Debut 23.9.64. 12 Appearances 3 Goals.

	Appearances			Goals		
	FL	FAC	LC	FL	FAC	LC
1964–65	3	–	5	2	–	1
1965–66	4	–	–	–	–	–
Total	7	–	5	2	–	1

Slim Scottish Schoolboy International who was unable to establish himself at a time when there was stiff competition for first-team places and, unwisely many thought, was allowed to move on. Ultimately played nearly 500 League games without, perhaps, ever quite fulfilling his very great potential.

McCARTNEY, David (1906–1907) Centre-half

Born Ayrshire. Career Dalbeattie, Glossop North End, Watford, Chelsea (August 1906), Northampton Town (Summer 1907).
Chelsea details Debut 12.1.07. 3 Appearances

	Appearances		Goals	
	FL	FAC	FL	FAC
1906–07	1	2	–	–
Total	1	2	–	–

Strong commanding centre-half whose first-team opportunities were limited by the consistent form of Bob McRoberts and he moved on after 12 months to seek a permanent spot in a senior team.

McCONNELL, English (1910–1911) Centre-half

Career Cliftonville, Glentoran, Sunderland, Sheffield Wednesday, Chelsea (April 1910, £1,000).
Honours Ireland (12 caps).
Chelsea details Debut 16.4.10. 21 Appearances

	Appearances		Goals	
	FL	FAC	FL	FAC
1909–10	3	–	–	–
1910–11	18	–	–	–
Total	21	–	–	–

He was signed, along with several other players, in an unavailing bid to avoid relegation in the closing weeks of the 1909–10 season after a long and distinguished career both in his native Ireland and in the north of England. A polished and stylish centre-half, very much in the "attacking" mould of those days, his football days came to an unfortunate end at Stamford Bridge due to a cartilage operation 12 months after his arrival on the Chelsea scene.

DAVID McCARTNEY

ENGLISH McCONNELL

EDWARD G. McCREADIE

McCREADIE, EDWARD G. (1962–1974) Full-back

Born Glasgow 15.4.40. Height 5ft 8½in, Weight 10st 8lb. Career Drumchapel Amateurs, Clydebank Juniors, East Stirlingshire, Chelsea (April 1962, £5,000), Retired November 1974. Honours Scotland (23 caps), F.A. Cup winners' medal 1970, losers' medal 1967, Football League Cup winners' medal 1965.

Chelsea details Debut 18.8.62. 405(5) Appearances 5 Goals.

	Appearances					Goals				
	FL	FAC	LC	FC	ECWC	FL	FAC	LC	FC	ECWC
1962–63	32	2	–	–	–	–	–	–	–	–
1963–64	35	3	1	–	–	1	–	–	–	–
1964–65	34	2	5	–	–	1	–	1	–	–
1965–66	30	5	–	9	–	–	–	–	–	–
1966–67	38	7	2	–	–	1	–	–	–	–
1967–68	36	5	1	–	–	–	–	–	–	–
1968–69	38	5	3	4	–	–	–	–	–	–
1969–70	29(1)	8	2	–	–	–	–	–	–	–
1970–71	13(1)	–	–	–	2	–	–	–	–	–
1971–72	7	1	1(1)	–	1	–	–	–	–	–
1972–73	31	3	6	–	–	1	–	–	–	–
1973–74	4(2)	–	–	–	–	–	–	–	–	–
Total	327(4)	41	21(1)	13	3	4	–	1	–	–

One of Chelsea's best-ever bargain buys at £5,000, was an "unknown" from the Scottish Second Division. At once he struck up a formidable full-back duo with Ken Shellito which was an important part of the 1962–63 Second Division promotion winning team. Aggressive and flamboyant in style, he went on to establish a, then, record number of international appearances for a Chelsea player. Latterly his career was plagued by injury and he was appointed Coach in November 1974 before taking over as Manager, from Ron Suart, 12 months later. In management, too, his forceful style was much in evidence and he guided the team back to the First Division in May 1976. Then, with his future apparently assured, a dispute over contract ended his always eventful 14-year stay at Stamford Bridge and he continued his career in North American football, with Memphis Rogues.

McDERMOTT, Thomas (1905–1907) Inside-forward

Born Glasgow. Career Everton, Chelsea (October 1905), Dundee (1906), Bradford City.
Chelsea details Debut 21.10.05. 32 Appearances 11 Goals

	Appearances		Goals	
	FL	FAC	FL	FAC
1905–06	22	1	7	1
1906–07	9	–	3	–
Total	31	1	10	–

A scheming inside-forward who contested the inside-left position with Jimmy Windridge during Chelsea's first two seasons. Despite undoubted ability and an impressive "scoring ratio" his play suffered from inconsistency and he moved on after two seasons to seek a permanent first-team spot elsewhere.

McEWAN, Marshall (1909–1911) Winger

Career Blackpool, Bolton Wanderers, Chelsea (March 1909, £1,000), Linfield (1911).
Chelsea details Debut 2.4.10. 35 Appearances 3 Goals

	Appearances		Goals	
	FL	FAC	FL	FAC
1909–10	5	–	1	–
1910–11	28	2	2	–
Total	33	2	3	–

A Scotsman and a ball-playing winger who was one of a group of players signed towards the end of the 1909–10 season in a bid to stave off relegation. "Slippery as an eel" was one description of this player who probably lacked the necessary physique to make a real impression in English football in those days.

WANTED
If anyone has a photograph of **THOMAS**
It would be appreciated if you would allow us to copy it.
Please forward it to Ron at 36 Lockier Walk, Wembley, Middx.
It will be returned safely
THOMAS McDERMOTT

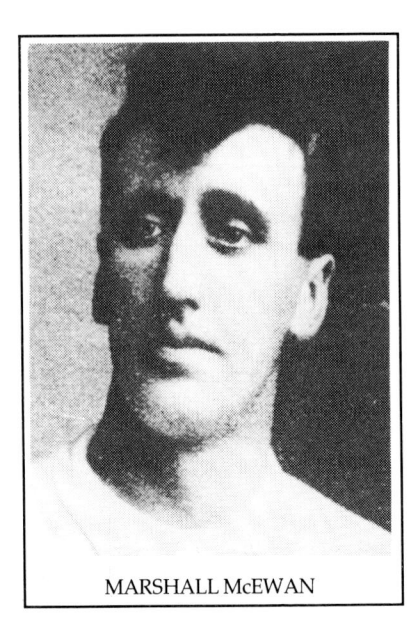

MARSHALL McEWAN

ROBERT McEWAN

ALEX McFARLAINE

McEWAN, Robert (1905–1906) Full-back
Career Glasgow Rangers, Heart of Midlothian, Chelsea (August 1905), Glossop (August 1906).
Chelsea details Debut 2.9.05. 20 Appearances

	Appearances		Goals	
	FL	FAC	FL	FAC
1905–06	19	1	–	–
Total	19	1	–	–

Scottish full-back who was an "ever-present" in Chelsea's first three months, but then lost his place to Tommy Miller through injury and was unable to displace him when he was fit again.

McFARLANE, Alex (1913–1915) Inside-forward
Career Dundee, Chelsea (April 1913).
Chelsea details Debut 13.9.13. 4 Appearances

	Appearances		Goals	
	FL	FAC	FL	FAC
1913–14	3	–	–	–
1914–15	1	–	–	–
Total	4	–	–	–

Any chance of "Sandy" establishing himself in English football was ruined by the outbreak of World War I and, apart from one isolated game in 1915–16, he never again played for Chelsea. He later managed both Dundee and Charlton Athletic.

McINNES, John S. (1947–1951) Outside-left

Born Glasgow 11.8.27, Died October 1973. Height 5ft 8in, Weight 10st. Career Morton, Chelsea (May 1947), Bedford Town (Summer 1951).
Chelsea details Debut 3.5.47. 37 Appearances 7 Goals

	Appearances		Goals	
	FL	FAC	FL	FAC
1946–47	3	–	1	–
1947–48	15	–	–	–
1948–49	18	–	6	–
1949–50	1	–	–	–
Total	37	–	7	–

This willowy outside-left spent five years at Stamford Bridge, fighting injury and ill-health for much of this time. Speedy, with clever ball control, it was sad that such talent never had the chance to blossom. He died, prematurely, in Bedford where his abbreviated playing career ended.

McKENNA, Peter J. (1924–1931) Goalkeeper

Born Liverpool. Height 5ft 10in, Weight 12st. Career Bangor, Chelsea (May 1924).
Chelsea details Debut 8.11.24. 66 Appearances

	Appearances		Goals	
	FL	FAC	FL	FAC
1924–25	14	1	–	–
1925–26	29	2	–	–
1926–27	10	–	–	–
1927–28	2	–	–	–
1928–29	4	1	–	–
1929–30	2	–	–	–
1930–31	1	–	–	–
Total	62	4	–	–

His seven years of loyal service to Chelsea was spent understudying, first the legendary Howard Baker and then Sam Millington. Reliable, he was just a little lacking in height to make him a dominant 'keeper. Nevertheless, he was consistently sound whenever called upon, which in his early seasons was frequently, as Baker was often away on duty with either the England Amateur side or with the Corinthians.

JOHN S. McINNES

PETER J. McKENNA

DUNCAN McKENZIE | KENNETH McKENZIE

McKENZIE, Duncan (1978–1979) Striker/Midfield

Born Grimsby 10.6.50. Height 5ft 9in, Weight 11st. Career Nottingham Forest, Mansfield Town, Leeds United, Everton, Chelsea (September 1978, £165,000), Blackburn Rovers (March 1979, £80,000).
Chelsea details Debut 9.9.78. 16 Appearances 4 Goals

	Appearances		Goals	
	FL	FAC	FL	FAC
1978–79	15	1	4	–
Total	15	1	4	–

A highly talented performer who, in a brief seven-month stay, never acclimatised himself to a side of limited ability, often doubtful commitment, and struggling to avoid, inevitable, relegation. He scored some spectacular goals but too often failed to produce his best form.

McKENZIE, Kenneth (1910–1911) Winger

Career Inverness Thistle, Chelsea (March 1910, £25).
Chelsea details Debut 26.4.11. 1 Appearance

	Appearances		Goals	
	FL	FAC	FL	FAC
1910–11	1	–	–	–
Total	1	–	–	–

Most of his brief career at Chelsea, lasting just over a year, was spent in the reserve team at a time when the staff was well-stocked with wingers.

McKENZIE, Kenneth W. (1920–1923) Centre-half

Born Montrose. Height 6ft, Weight 12st. 2lb. Career Queens Park, Chelsea (November 1920), Cardiff City (May 1923).
Chelsea details Debut 18.9.20. 22 Appearances

	Appearances		Goals	
	FL	FAC	FL	FAC
1920–21	3	–	–	–
1921–22	18	1	–	–
Total	21	1	–	–

Ideally built for a centre-half, he had an extended run in the autumn of 1921, deputising for the injured Harold Wilding, yet was not able to displace him on a permanent basis.

McKNIGHT, Philip (1947–1954) Wing-half

Born Camlachie 15.6.24. Height 5ft 8in, Weight 10st 7lb. Career Alloa Athletic, Chelsea (January 1947), Leyton Orient (July 1954).
Chelsea details Debut 1.5.48. 33 Appearances 1 Goal

	Appearances		Goals	
	FL	FAC	FL	FAC
1947–48	1	–	–	–
1948–49	2	–	–	–
1949–50	1	–	–	–
1950–51	5	–	–	–
1951–52	12	–	–	–
1952–53	4	–	1	–
1953–54	8	–	–	–
Total	33	–	1	–

Loyal reserve wing-half who deputised capably whenever required. A hard-working player with a long throw he went on to play almost 200 first-team games with Leyton Orient before retiring in 1959.

KENNETH W. McKENZIE

PHILIP McKNIGHT

JOSEPH McLAUGHLIN   ERIC McMILLAN

McLAUGHLIN, Joseph (1983–   ) Centre-half

Born Greenock 2.6.60. Height 6ft 1in, Weight 12st. Career Morton, Chelsea (May 1983, £95,000).
Honours Second Division Championship medal 1984, Full Members' Cup Winners' medal 1986.
Chelsea details Debut 27.8.83. 187 Appearances 5 Goals.

	Appearances				Goals			
	FL	FAC	FLC	FMC	FL	FAC	FLC	FMC
1983–84	41	1	5	–	–	–	–	–
1984–85	36	3	9	–	1	–	–	–
1985–86	40	1	5	5	1	–	1	–
1986–87	36	1	2	2	2	–	–	–
Total	153	6	21	7	4	–	1	–

Tall, commanding centre-half who had already played 200 or so games for Morton in the Scottish League before his arrival at Stamford Bridge. Immediately establishing himself in the first-team, he was the lynch-pin of the defence in the 1983–84 Second Division Championship side, and he continued his impressive form in First Division football, coming under the close scrutiny of the Scottish International selectors.

McMILLAN, Eric (1958–1960) Wing-half

Born Beverley 2.11.36. Height 5ft 10½ins, Weight 11st 10lb. Career Chelsea (April 1958), Hull City :June 1960, £2,000), Halifax Town, Scarborough, Port Elizabeth (South Africa).
Chelsea details Debut 5.9.59. 5 Appearances

	Appearances		Goals	
	FL	FAC	FL	FAC
1959–60	5	–	–	–
Total	5	–	–	–

Signed, first on amateur forms, after service with the R.A.F. Unable to break through into the first-team at Chelsea he returned to his native Humberside to play 150 League games for Hull City.

McMILLAN, Paul A. (1967–1968) Wing-half

Born Lennox Castle 13.7.50. Height 5ft 10½ins, Weight 11st 9lb. Career Chelsea (July 1967), Retired on medical advice February 1968.
Chelsea details Debut 2.9.67. 1 Appearance

	Appearances		Goals	
	FL	FAC	FL	FAC
1967–68	1	–	–	–
Total	1	–	–	–

Former Chelsea Junior whose career came to a most unfortunate end after eight months as a professional for medical reasons, although he did later play again, briefly, for Clydebank.

McNALLY, Errol (1961–1963) Goalkeeper

Born Lurgan 27.8.43. Height 5ft 10½ins, Weight 11st. Career Portadown, Chelsea (December 1967, £5,000), Glenavon (1963).
Chelsea details Debut 17.3.62. 9 Appearances

	Appearances		Goals	
	FL	FAC	FL	FAC
1961–62	8	–	–	–
1962–63	1	–	–	–
Total	9	–	–	–

One of several 'keepers saddled with the thankless task of playing second fiddle to Peter Bonetti, his one extended run taking place when a dispirited side were already doomed to relegation to Division II.

WANTED
If anyone has a photograph of **PAUL**
It would be appreciated if you would allow us to copy it. Please forward it to Ron at 36 Lockier Walk, Wembley, Middx.
It will be returned safely

PAUL A. McMILLAN

ERROL McNALLY

| | JOHN McNAUGHT | | | ROBERT McNEIL |

McNAUGHT, John (1986–   ) Midfield

Born Glasgow 19.6.64. Height 5ft 11in, Weight 11st 12lb. Career Auchengill Boys' Club, Hamilton Academical, Chelsea (May 1986, £70,000).
Chelsea details Debut 5.5.86. 11(1) Appearances 2 Goals.

	Appearances			Goals		
	FL	FAC	LC	FL	FAC	LC
1985–86	0(1)	–	–	–	–	–
1986–87	8	–	3	2	–	–
Total	8(1)	–	3	2	–	–

Rugged midfield player, strong in the tackle and with a liking for moving on to the attack at every opportunity. Had played three seasons with Hamilton Academical in the Scottish League before his arrival at Stamford Bridge, scoring 19 goals in 109 outings.

McNEIL, Robert (1914–1929) Winger

Born Springburn (Glasgow). Height 5ft 7ins, Weight 10st 10lb. Career Hamilton Academicals, Chelsea (Summer 1914), Retired May 1929.
Honours F.A. Cup final losers' medal 1915.
Chelsea details Debut 5.9.14. 307 Appearances 32 Goals

	Appearances		Goals	
	FL	FAC	FL	FAC
1914–15	37	8	3	1
1919–20	26	3	3	2
1920–21	39	8	6	1
1921–22	42	1	2	–
1922–23	41	3	4	–
1923–24	29	2	–	–
1924–25	35	1	3	–
1925–26	24	2	5	1
1926–27	6	–	1	–
Total	279	28	27	5

One of Chelsea's best-loved players over his 14 seasons with the club, interrupted, of course, by the First World War. But for this his total number of games would have exceeded 400. Signed, along with Jimmy Croal from Falkirk, he made up a left-wing partnership which took Chelsea to their first F.A. Cup final at the end of his first season at Stamford Bridge. Extremely fast, he possessed a clever football brain. Also a fine dribbler with the ball, although not a prolific scorer of goals, he could at times surprise friend and foe alike with the power and accuracy of his long-range shooting. After retiring, he returned to become Trainer to his first love, Hamilton Academicals.

McNICHOL, John (1952–1958) Inside-forward

Born Kilmarnock 20.8.25. Height 5ft 9in, Weight 11st. Career Hurlford Juniors, Newcastle United, Brighton & Hove Albion, Chelsea (August 1952, £12,000), Crystal Palace (March 1958).
Honours Football League Championship medal 1955.
Chelsea details Debut 23.8.52. 202 Appearances 66 Goals

	Appearances		Goals	
	FL	FAC	FL	FAC
1952–53	39	7	11	1
1953–54	41	1	18	–
1954–55	40	2	14	1
1955–56	24	6	2	–
1956–57	24	2	10	1
1957–58	13	3	4	4
Total	181	21	59	7

Manager Ted Drake's first signing for Chelsea. Then aged 27, he had played all his League football in the Third Division but immediately made an impact in the higher sphere. A clever ball-playing and forceful inside-forward, he was a regular scorer of goals as well as a creator of chances, especially for Roy Bentley. An integral part of the 1954–55 Championship winning side, he stayed in the game after retiring as a player, being employed at Crystal Palace in their commercial department.

JOHN McNICHOL

ROBERT McROBERTS

THOMAS MEEHAN

McROBERTS, Robert (1905–1909) Centre-half/Centre-forward

Born Coatbridge. Career Small Heath, Chelsea (August 1905, £100).
Chelsea details Debut 2.9.05. 106 Appearances 10 Goals

	Appearances		Goals	
	FL	FAC	FL	FAC
1905–06	34	1	9	–
1906–07	35	–	1	–
1907–08	20	1	–	–
1908–09	15	–	–	–
Total	104	2	10	–

Equally at home in either the centre-half or centre-forward position, Bob ws in the team for Chelsea's inaugural game at Stockport. Noted for his sound positional play as a defender, particularly, he was a fine header of the ball and was appointed club captain at the start of the 1907–08 season. He subsequently became Manager of Birmingham.

MEEHAN, Thomas (1920–1924) Wing-half

Born Manchester, Died 18.8.24. Height 5ft 5in, Weight 10st 7lb. Career Newtown, Walkden Central, Rochdale Town, Manchester United, Chelsea (December 1920).
Honours England (1 cap), Football League XI (1 appearance).
Chelsea details Debut 27.12.20. 133 Appearances 4 Goals

	Appearances		Goals	
	FL	FAC	FL	FAC
1920–21	19	4	–	–
1921–22	37	–	–	–
1922–23	42	3	3	–
1923–24	26	2	1	–
Total	124	9	4	–

One of the most stylish and outstanding wing-halves of his time. Both a soung defensive player and a constructive user of the ball, he was also extremely popular. A non-smoker and teetotaller, his career was ended by his tragic death while still at the height of his powers. Some 2,000 attended his funeral at Wandsworth and a match between Chelsea and a Football League XI at Stamford Bridge in October 1924 raised £1,500 for his dependants. His one international appearance for England was made only months before he died.

MEDHURST, Harry E. (1946–1952) Goalkeeper

Born Byfleet 5.2.16, Died April 1984. Height 5ft 9in, Weight 10st 10lb. Career Woking, West Ham United, Chelsea (December 1946, exchange Joe Payne), Brighton & Hove Albion (November 1952).
Chelsea details Debut 25.12.46. 157 Appearances

	Appearances		Goals	
	FL	FAC	FL	FAC
1946–47	20	5	–	–
1947–48	27	2	–	–
1948–49	26	–	–	–
1949–50	41	7	–	–
1950–51	28	–	–	–
1951–52	1	–	–	–
Total	143	14	–	–

Already past his 30th birthday when he arrived at Chelsea to play in the First Division for the first time in his career, he immediately established himself in the senior side and gave sterling service as a player for five seasons. On the small side for a goalkeeper, he compensated for this by his wonderful agility and his reliability. Originally an outside-left he was pressed into service in goal in an emergency and remained there afterwards. After leaving Stamford Bridge he had six months at Brighton before returning as Assistant-Trainer in the summer of 1953. He then became Head Trainer in 1960 and Physiotherapist in 1973, a post he held until his retirement in April 1984.

MEREDITH, John (1928–1930) Outside-right

Born Grimsby. Height 5ft 6½in, Weight 10st. Career Scunthorpe, Blackpool, Chelsea (May 1928), Reading (October 1930).
Chelsea details Debut 27.10.28. 23 Appearances 6 Goals

	Appearances		Goals	
	FL	FAC	FL	FAC
1928–29	16	–	5	–
1929–30	7	–	1	–
Total	23	–	6	–

A lightweight right-winger who was on the staff for two seasons as deputy for Jackie Crawford. Most of his football was played in the reserve team where was a regular scorer of goals.

HARRY E. MEDHURST

JOHN MEREDITH

NILS MIDDELBOE   JOHN MILLAR

MIDDELBOE, Nils (1913–1921) Half-back

Born Denmark, Died in Copenhagen September 1976. Career Chelsea (1913–21).
Honours Denmark (13 caps).
Chelsea details **Debut** 15.11.13. 46 Appearances

	Appearances		Goals	
	FL	FAC	FL	FAC
1913–14	6	–	–	–
1914–15	7	–	–	–
1919–20	9	2	–	–
1920–21	14	3	–	–
1921–22	5	–	–	–
Total	41	5	–	–

Famous Danish amateur half-back who appeared, all too irregularly, for Chelsea over a period of ten years, interrupted by the First World War. With his long raking stride and great skill he was a most popular personality at Stamford Bridge. Amateur in every sense of the word, he never claimed even his expenses. His team colleagues presented him with a silver cigarette box inscribes to "our captain and comrade – one of the best" at the end of his playing career.

MILLAR, John (1984–1987) Full-back

Born Coatbridge 8.12.66. Height 5ft 7in, Weight 12st. Career Clyde Amateurs, Chelsea (August 1984), Blackburn Rovers (July 1987).
Honours Scotland Youth International.
Chelsea details **Debut** 8.2.86. 11 Appearances

	Appearances		Goals	
	FL	FAC	FL	FAC
1985–86	7	–	–	–
1986–87	4	–	–	–
Total	11	–	–	–

Scottish full-back who graduated to the first-team via the Juniors (whom he captained) and reserves. A sound left-back who made his debut as a 19-year-old, he has also played cricket for Scotland and was a student at London University. He had periods on loan to both Hamilton Academical and Northampton Town in the 1986–87 season.

MILLER, Harold S. (1923–1939) Inside-forward/Wing-half

Born St Albans. Height 5ft 8in, Weight 9st 4lb. Career St Albans City, Charlton Athletic, Chelsea (June 1923), Free-transfer (May 1939).
Honours England (1 cap).
Chelsea details Debut 25.8.23. 363 Appearances 44 Goals

	Appearances		Goals	
	FL	FAC	FL	FAC
1923–24	32	2	3	–
1924–25	30	1	6	–
1925–26	20	–	2	–
1926–27	20	–	3	–
1927–28	11	–	1	–
1928–29	22	4	4	2
1929–30	40	1	13	–
1930–31	10	–	1	–
1931–32	22	4	3	1
1932–33	17	1	3	–
1933–34	23	5	1	–
1934–35	34	2	–	–
1935–36	34	4	1	–
1936–37	16	2	–	–
1937–38	6	–	–	–
Total	337	26	41	3

One of the longest-serving players in the history of Chelsea F.C. Having won amateur honours, "Dusty" turned professional with Charlton Athletic and came to Chelsea as an inside-forward with a reputation for scoring goals. Indeed, his ability had already been rewarded with an England international cap. In the First Division he found life harder and was not always assured of his place in the team, especially when the big-money names began to arrive after the 1929–30 promotion season. Then, however, he converted to wing-half and his "second" career began. Lightly built, he was, surprisingly, a hard tackler, but his forté was his constructive use of the ball. A good dribbler, he possessed dainty footwork and was also noted for his wonderful consistency.

HAROLD S. MILLER

THOMAS MILLER | SIMEON MILLINGTON

MILLER, Thomas (1905–1909) Full-back

Born Falkirk. Career: Chelsea (August 1905), Not retained (May 1909)
Chelsea details Debut 2.9.05. 120 Appearances

	Appearances		Goals	
	FL	FAC	FL	FAC
1905–06	24	2	–	–
1906–07	38	2	–	–
1907–08	30	1	–	–
1908–09	20	3	–	–
Total	112	8	–	–

Small and very fast, he was anything but the popular image of a full-back of those days in the early part of the century. Winning his first-team place as a result of an injury to Bob McEwan, he then remained first choice for the next three seasons. A constructive user of the ball, if a little over-elaborate at times, after a couple of pints of beer he once claimed to be the "best back in England"!

MILLINGTON, Simeon (1926–1932) Goalkeeper

Born Walsall. Height 5ft 10in, Weight 11st 4lb. Career Wellington, Chelsea (January 1926), Retired through illness 1932.
Chelsea details Debut 2.10.26. 245 Appearances

	Appearances		Goals	
	FL	FAC	FL	FAC
1926–27	32	5	–	–
1927–28	40	1	–	–
1928–29	38	3	–	–
1929–30	38	1	–	–
1930–31	40	5	–	–
1931–32	35	7	–	–
Total	223	22	–	–

A most reliable goalkeeper who spanned the period between Howard Baker, who retired at the end of the 1925–26 season, and Vic Woodley. A familiar figure in his cloth cap, he was never absent, other than through a rare injury, from his debut until illness forced his retirement from the game six seasons later. After missing out on promotion in the first four of these years, "Sam" was very much an integral part of the side which eventually regained its First Division place in the spring of 1930.

MILLS, George R. (1929–1943) Centre-forward

Born Deptford 29.12.08, Died July 1978. Height 6ft, Weight 11st 12lb. Career Bromley, Chelsea (December 1929), Retired 1943.
Honours England (3 caps), Football League XI (1 appearance).
Chelsea details Debut 21.12.29. 239 Appearances 123 Goals

	Appearances		Goals	
	FL	FAC	FL	FAC
1929–30	20	1	14	–
1930–31	7	4	1	2
1931–32	14	7	8	4
1932–33	31	1	13	–
1933–34	24	–	14	–
1934–35	20	–	8	–
1935–36	19	–	11	–
1936–37	32	2	22	1
1937–38	27	1	13	–
1938–39	26	3	12	–
Total	220	19	116	7

Plucked out of amateur football to be pitchforked into the Chelsea first-team at Christmas 1929, the side winning 5–0, he was one of the corner-stones of the team in the ten seasons leading up to World War II. Tall, well-built and with an infectious enthusiasm for the game, he went on to become Chelsea's first "centurion". Strangely, he spent most of his Stamford Bridge career contesting his place with a series of internationals, all of whom had been signed at great expense – in contrast to George's £10 signing-on fee. Hughie Gallacher, Joe Bambrick and "ten goal" Joe Payne all at times ousted him from the side. Yet he ended the 1938–39 season as first choice for the centre-forward position. But for such rivalry his figures would have been still more impressive than they are. Scored a hat-trick on his debut for England against Northern Ireland and was Coach of the "A" Team for a period after the war.

GEORGE R. MILLS

| FRANK R. MITCHELL | WILLIAM MITCHELL |

MITCHELL, Frank R. (1949–1952) Wing-half

Born Goulburn (Australia) 3.6.22, Died 4.4.84. Height 5ft 11in, Weight 12st 12lb. Career Coventry City (amateur), Birmingham City, Chelsea (January 1949), Watford (August 1952).
Chelsea details Debut 5.2.49. 85 Appearances 1 Goal

	Appearances		Goals	
	FL	FAC	FL	FAC
1948–49	11	–	1	–
1949–50	33	7	–	–
1950–51	27	1	–	–
1951–52	4	2	–	–
Total	75	10	1	–

A stylish, constructive wing-half back whose career was delayed by the Second World War. He was particularly adept in his use of the long pass crossfield which he directed with pin-point accuracy. His all-too-brief Chelsea career ended when he lost his place to Bill Dickson, but he went on to play some 200 games for Watford. He was also a useful cricketer who played 17 games for Warwickshire between 1946 and 1948.

MITCHELL, William (1933–1945) Wing-half

Born Co. Lurgan 1911, Died 1978. Height 5ft 7in, Weight 11st 4lb. Career Distillery, Chelsea (June 1933), Bath City (1945).
Honours Northern Ireland (15 caps).
Chelsea details Debut 24.2.34. 117 Appearances 3 Goals

	Appearances		Goals	
	FL	FAC	FL	FAC
1933–34	2	–	–	–
1934–35	4	–	–	–
1935–36	31	3	–	1
1936–37	27	–	–	–
1937–38	21	–	2	–
1938–39	23	6	–	–
Total	108	9	2	1

Already capped by Northern Ireland when he arrived at Stamford Bridge, Billy was a terrier-type wing-half – small of stature but immensely strong and especially so in the tackle. His somewhat fiery temperament sometimes got him into trouble with the authorities but he was a magnificent team man and it was sad that the outbreak of World War II prematurely ended his Chelsea career.

MOLYNEUX, James (1910–1922) Goalkeeper

Born Port Sunlight. Height 5ft 9in, Weight 11st 9lb. Career Stockport County, Chelsea (August 1910), Stockport County (January 1923).
Honours F.A. Cup final losers' medal 1915.
Chelsea details Debut 3.9.10. 239 Appearances

	Appearances		Goals	
	FL	FAC	FL	FAC
1910–11	37	4	–	–
1911–12	12	–	–	–
1912–13	18	2	–	–
1913–14	34	2	–	–
1914–15	37	8	–	–
1919–20	27	5	–	–
1920–21	36	8	–	–
1921–22	9	–	–	–
Total	210	29	–	–

Signed as understudy to Jack Whitley, in fact he won a first-team place immediately and was then almost an automatic choice for his 12 seasons (including the war years) on the staff. Despite his lack of inches, he was extremely agile with a good sense of anticipation and he became one of the most respected 'keepers in the game. "Moly" was also immensely popular with the Chelsea supporters and won an "unofficial" honour when he kept goal in the 1919 London Victory Cup final against Fulham at Highbury.

JAMES MOLYNEUX

| GRAHAM MOORE | MARTIN MORAN |

MOORE, Graham (1961–1963) Centre/Inside-forward

Born Hengoed 7.3.41. Height 5ft 11½in, Weight 13st 11lb. Career Cardiff City, Chelsea (December 1961, £35,000), Manchester United (November 1963, £35,000), Northampton Town, Charlton Athletic, Doncaster Rovers.
Honours Wales (21 caps), Wales Under-23 (9 caps), Football League XI.
Chelsea details Debut 23.12.61. 72 Appearances 14 Goals

	Appearances		Goals	
	FL	FAC	FL	FAC
1961–62	17	–	2	–
1962–63	36	4	8	1
1963–64	15	–	3	–
Total	68	4	13	1

Tommy Docherty paid a, then, record club fee to obtain the services of the established Welsh international forward. But he failed to make the expected impact in the First Division – especially in the all-important matter of scoring goals. Soon Barry Bridges had forced his way into the first-team and, with other young players of promise in the pipeline, he was allowed to move on.

MORAN, Martin (1905–1908) Outside-right

Born Glasgow. Career Heart of Midlothian, Chelsea (Summer 1905), Glasgow Celtic (1908).
Chelsea details Debut 2.9.05. 67 Appearances 8 Goals

	Appearances		Goals	
	FL	FAC	FL	FAC
1905–06	34	2	5	1
1906–07	19	2	2	–
1907–08	10	–	–	–
Total	63	4	7	1

"The muscular midget", as he was affectionately known, was Chelsea's first right-winger and became renowned for his speedy dashes down the right-wing. Already a mature and experienced player, he was also described as the type of player "to delight the heart of a manager".

MORRISON, William (1924–1927) Inside-forward

Born Bo'ness. Career Linlithgow Rovers, Chelsea (June 1924).
Chelsea details Debut 20.4.25. 1 Appearance

	Appearances		Goals	
	FL	FAC	FL	FAC
1924–25	1	–	–	–
Total	1	–	–	–

A regular reserve team player for his two seasons on the Stamford Bridge staff, he was unable to displace such as Andy Wilson, Albert Thain and Harold Miller from the inside-forward positions.

MULHOLLAND, James (1962–1964) Forward

Born Knightswood 10.4.38. Height 5ft 8in, Weight 10st 10lb. Career East Stirling, Chelsea (October 1962, £8,000), Morton (September 1964, part-exchange Billy Sinclair), Barrow, Stockport County, Crewe Alexandra.
Chelsea details Debut 3.11.62. 12 Appearances 3 Goals

	Appearances		Goals	
	FL	FAC	FL	FAC
1962–63	4	1	1	1
1963–64	7	–	1	–
Total	11	1	2	1

After a promising start he failed to win a permanent place in the first-team, either at centre-forward or on the wing, in the face of the stream of talent emerging from the Chelsea Juniors.

WILLIAM MORRISON

JAMES MULHOLLAND

JOHN A. MORTIMORE

MORTIMORE, John A. (1957–1965) Centre-half

Born Farnborough 23.9.34. Height 6ft, Weight 11st 9lb. Career Woking, Aldershot (amateur), Chelsea (August 1957), Queens Park Rangers (September 1965, £8,000), Sunderland.
Honours England amateur international, England Youth international, Football League Cup winners' medal 1965.
Chelsea details Debut 28.4.56. 279 Appearances 10 Goals

	Appearances				Goals			
	FL	FAC	LC	FC	FL	FAC	LC	FC
1955–56	1	–	–	–	–	–	–	–
1956–57	2	–	–	–	–	–	–	–
1957–58	39	3	–	–	1	–	–	–
1958–59	37	1	–	3	1	1	–	–
1959–60	33	–	–	–	–	–	–	–
1960–61	12	–	3	–	1	–	1	–
1961–62	14	–	–	–	–	–	–	–
1962–63	42	4	–	–	1	–	–	–
1963–64	41	3	–	–	2	–	–	–
1964–65	28	5	8	–	2	–	–	–
Total	249	16	11	3	8	1	1	–

A commanding centre-half, especially powerful in the air who was still an amateur with Woking when he made his Chelsea debut. Strangely, for two seasons he was displaced by, first, Bobby Evans (well past his best and not a centre-half in any event) and then by Mel Scott, both of whom were lesser performers in his position. But he was an "ever-present" in the Second Division promotion team of 1962–63 and lent invaluable experience to manager Tommy Docherty's youthful proteges. Later Assistant Manager of Southampton after gaining coaching and managerial experience abroad.

MULLIGAN, Pat (1969–1972) Full-back/Centre-half

Born Dublin 17.3.45. Height 5ft 7in, Weight 11st 9lb. Career Shamrock Rovers, Chelsea (October 1969, £17,500), Crystal Palace (September 1972, £75,000), West Bromwich Albion. Honours Eire (51 caps), Football League Cup losers' medal 1972.
Chelsea details Debut 20.12.69. 74(5) Appearances 2 Goals

	Appearances				Goals			
	FL	FAC	LC	ECWC	FL	FAC	LC	ECWC
1969–70	6(2)	–	–	–	–	–	–	–
1970–71	16(1)	–	3	5(1)	1	–	–	–
1971–72	27	3	5	1(1)	1	–	–	–
1972–73	6	–	1	–	–	–	–	–
Total	55(3)	3	9	6(2)	2	–	–	–

(also 1 F.A. Charity Shield appearance 1972–73)

His move to Chelsea set up a record fee for any Eire player up to that time. A rugged and powerful defender whose turn of speed made him a dangerous overlapping raider down the flanks. For a comparatively small man he was surprisingly good in the air and, although rarely certain of a permanent place in the team, it was a disappointment when he left the club.

MURPHY, Jerry M. (1985–   ) Midfield

Born Stepney 23.9.59. Height 5ft 9in, Weight 11st 10lb. Career Crystal Palace, Chelsea (August 1985, free-transfer).
Honours Republic of Ireland (3 caps), England Schoolboy International.
Chelsea details Debut 17.8.85. 37 Appearances 3 Goals

	Appearances				Goals			
	FL	FAC	FLC	FMC	FL	FAC	FLC	FMC
1985–86	21	1	3	1	3	–	–	–
1986–87	11	–	–	–	–	–	–	–
Total	32	1	3	1	3	–	–	–

After ten years as a professional with Crystal Palace (229 League games), he was snapped up by Chelsea and immediately made an impact in the first-team. A creative left-side midfield player, as well as a powerful tackler, his early Stamford Bridge days were punctuated by a series of injuries which hampered his progress in establishing himself as a regular member of the League side.

PAT MULLIGAN

JERRY M. MURPHY

ALBERT G. MURRAY | PATRICK K.F.M. NEVIN

MURRAY, Albert G. (1961–1966) Winger/Midfield

Born Shoreditch 22.9.42. Height 5ft 7½in, Weight 10st 8lb. Career Chelsea (May 1961), Birmingham City (August 1966, £25,000), Brighton & Hove Albion, Peterborough United. Honours England Under-23 (6 caps), England Schoolboy & Youth International, Football League Cup Final winners' medal 1965.
Chelsea details Debut 21.10.61. 179(4) Appearances 44 Goals

	Appearances				Goals			
	FL	FAC	LC	FC	FL	FAC	LC	FC
1961–62	18	1	–	–	4	–	–	–
1962–63	39	4	–	–	4	1	–	–
1963–64	37	3	–	–	12	2	–	–
1964–65	40	5	6	–	17	1	–	–
1965–66	22(4)	1	–	3	2	–	–	1
Total	156(4)	14	6	3	39	4	–	1

Signed professional forms after three years as a Chelsea junior. A most versatile player who began life as an orthodox right-winger, then converted into a midfield operator, before playing most of the latter part of his career at full-back. He was also a capable "emergency" goalkeeper. Lightly built, he possessed clever and intricate footwork and his total of 17 League goals in the 1964–65 season was the highest for a Chelsea winger since Dick Spence (19 in 1934–35).

NEVIN, Patrick K.F.M. (1983–   ) Winger

Born Glasgow 6.9.63. Height 5ft 6in, Weight 10st. Career Clyde, Chelsea (May 1983, £95,000).
Honours Scotland (4 caps), Scotland Under-21 International (5 caps), Scotland Youth International, Second Division Championship medal 1984, Full Members' Cup winners' medal 1986.
Chelsea details Debut 13.9.83. 193(3) Appearances 38 Goals

	Appearances				Goals			
	FL	FAC	FLC	FMC	FL	FAC	FLC	FMC
1983–84	38	1	3(1)	–	14	–	–	–
1984–85	41	3	9	–	4	1	2	–
1985–86	39(1)	2	8	6	7	–	3	2
1986–87	36(1)	2	3	2	5	–	–	–
Total	154(2)	8	23(1)	8	30	1	5	2

An artistic ball player in the true Scottish tradition. A prolific creator of goalscoring chances for colleagues, he is also a strong and accurate finisher himself. A thoughtful person and severe self-critic, he is one of the outstanding entertainers in modern football and has been a most important ingredient in Chelsea's rise from the basement of Second Division football to the top bracket of clubs in the First Division.

NICHOLAS, Anthony W.L. (1955–1960) Inside-forward

Born West Ham 16.4.38. Height 5ft 10in, Weight 12st 3lb. Career Chelsea (May 1955), Brighton & Hove Albion (November 1960), Leyton Orient.
Honours England Youth International.
Chelsea details Debut 22.8.65. 63 Appearances 21 Goals

	Appearances				Goals			
	FL	FAC	LC	FC	FL	FAC	LC	FC
1956–57	20	1	–	–	6	–	–	–
1957–58	11	–	–	–	6	–	–	–
1958–59	21	–	–	2	5	–	–	1
1959–60	7	–	–	–	1	–	–	–
1960–61	–	–	1	–	–	–	1	–
Total	59	1	1	2	18	–	1	1

Signing professional after service as a Chelsea Junior, this strongly-built player never wholly fulfilled his potential as a free-scoring inside-forward. With thrust, as well as clever ball skills, it was his misfortune to be a contemporary of Jimmy Greaves, who restricted his opportunities. Yet it was surprising that he failed to make much of an impact with either of his two subsequent clubs.

ANTHONY W.L. NICHOLAS

C. BRIAN NICHOLAS   EDDIE A. NIEDZWIECKI

NICHOLAS, C. Brian (1955–1958) Wing-half
Born Aberdare 20.4.33. Height 5ft 9½ins, Weight 11st 7lb. Career Queens Park Rangers, Chelsea (July 1955), Coventry City (February 1958).
Honours England Schoolboy International.
Chelsea details Debut 5.9.55. 29 Appearances 1 Goal

	Appearances		Goals	
	FL	FAC	FL	FAC
1955–56	10	3	–	–
1956–57	7	–	1	–
1957–58	9	–	–	–
Total	26	3	1	–

Signed after five years at Queens Park Rangers, mostly as a first-team player, he understudied Ken Armstrong for two seasons and then, after the latter retired, was overlooked in favour of John Mortimore. As a result he moved on and played several seasons in Coventry City's League side. A tough tackler and sound defensive player.

NIEDZWIECKI, Eddie A. (1983–   ) Goalkeeper
Born Bangor 3.5.59. Height 6ft, Weight 11st. Career Wrexham, Chelsea (May 1983, £45,000).
Honours Wales (1 cap), Wales Schoolboy International, Second Division Championship medal 1984.
Chelsea details Debut 27.8.83. 159 Appearances

	Appearances				Goals			
	FL	FAC	FLC	FMC	FL	FAC	FLC	FMC
1983–84	42	1	5	–	–	–	–	–
1984–85	40	3	9	–	–	–	–	–
1985–86	30	2	8	5	–	–	–	–
1986–87	10	2	1	1	–	–	–	–
Total	122	8	23	6	–	–	–	–

After seven months with Wrexham he came to Stamford Bridge, immediately won his place in the first-team, and became a vital member of the Second Division Championship team of 1983–84. An outstanding goalkeeper, respected and liked throughout the game, he is an excellent handler of the ball, with fine anticipation as well as being agile and courageous. The recognised deputy to Neville Southall in the Welsh goal, his career suffered a major setback in March 1986 when he severely injured a knee and was incapacitated for six months, before resuming still some way short of full fitness.

NUTTON, Michael W. (1977–1983) Central defender

Born St John's Wood 3.10.59. Height 5ft 11in, Weight 10st 12lb. Career Chelsea (October 1977), Millwall (March 1983).
Chelsea details Debut 23.12.78. 81(2) Appearances

	Appearances			Goals		
	FL	FAC	LC	FL	FAC	LC
1978–79	15	–	–	–	–	–
1979–80	19	–	–	–	–	–
1980–81	18	–	1	–	–	–
1981–82	17(2)	3	–	–	–	–
1982–83	8	–	–	–	–	–
Total	77(2)	3	1	–	–	–

Joined Chelsea as a schoolboy, graduating to professional after 18 months as an apprentice. A competent defender in the middle of the back-four, he had several spells in the first-team without ever establishing himself as an automatic choice. His misfortune was to come into a struggling team virtually doomed to relegation and in an era of many comings and goings. Lacked the height to dominate in defence but was a useful foil in partnership with Micky Droy.

OAKTON, A. Eric (1932–1937) Winger

Born Kiveton Park (Yorkshire). Height 5ft 9in, Weight 11st. Career Grimsby Town (amateur), Rotherham United, Worksop Town, Sheffield United, Scunthorpe United, Bristol Rovers, Chelsea (May 1932), Nottingham Forest (Summer 1937).
Chelsea details Debut 27.8.32. 112 Appearances 28 Goals

	Appearances		Goals	
	FL	FAC	FL	FAC
1932–33	34	–	8	–
1933–34	41	5	12	1
1934–35	8	–	1	–
1935–36	8	–	3	–
1936–37	16	–	3	–
Total	107	5	27	1

At home on either flank, he was a fast, direct wingman with a flair for scoring goals. For two seasons he was a regular choice in the first-team but the arrival of Dick Spence and Willie Barraclough restricted his opportunities after that.

MICHAEL W. NUTTON

A. ERIC OAKTON

SEAMUS D. O'CONNELL | LESLIE F. ODELL

ODELL, Leslie F. (1924–1936) Full-back

Born Sandy (Bedfordshire). Height 6ft, Weight 13st 4lb. Career Sandy, Biggleswade Town, Luton Town (amateur), Chelsea (amateur, August 1924; professional, September 1924), Retired May 1936.
Chelsea details Debut 20.12.24. 103 Appearances 7 Goals

	Appearances		Goals	
	FL	FAC	FL	FAC
1924–25	2	–	–	–
1925–26	1	–	–	–
1927–28	6	–	–	–
1928–29	7	–	2	–
1929–30	13	–	–	–
1930–31	23	–	5	–
1931–32	11	1	–	–
1932–33	17	1	–	–
1933–34	14	–	–	–
1934–35	5	–	–	–
1935–36	2	–	–	–
Total	101	2	7	–

Curiously, this tall, commanding full-back could never claim a regular place throughout his 12 seasons at Stamford Bridge – and this despite chalking up a century of appearances. He began in the Smith-Harrow era, partnered Scottish internationals Law and Macaulay, and finished as Barber and O'Hare were becoming established. A loyal servant whose strength was, not least, the length and power of his kicking, which was also put to good use from the penalty spot.

O'CONNELL, Seamus D. (1954–1956) Inside-forward

Born Carlisle. Career Queens Park, Middlesborough (amateur), Bishop Auckland, Chelsea (amateur, August 1954), Crook Town, Carlisle (amateur).
Honours England Amateur International, Football League Championship medal 1955, F.A. Amateur Cup winners' medals 1955, 1956, losers' 1954.
Chelsea details Debut 16.10.54. 17 Appearances 12 Goals

	Appearances		Goals	
	FL	FAC	FL	FAC
1954–55	10	1	7	1
1955–56	6	–	4	–
Total	16	1	11	1

Marked his debut with a hat-trick in the 5–6 defeat at home to Manchester United and, when available, proved himself a prolific scorer of goals at this top level in the game. Well-built and a fine mover with the ball, his accurate shooting was his greatest asset. How much he might have achieved in the professional game will never be known, since he disappeared – to help his father in his cattle-dealing business – and made only spasmodic appearances thereafter for Crook Town and Carlisle United, and never relinquished his amateur status.

O'DOWD, Peter (1931–1934) Centre-half

Born Halifax. Height 5ft 11in, Weight 10st 5lb. Career Blackburn Rovers, Burnley, Chelsea (November 1931, £5,250), Valenciennes (1934, £3,000).
Honours England (3 caps).
Chelsea details Debut 14.11.31. 87 Appearances

	Appearances		Goals	
	FL	FAC	FL	FAC
1931–32	24	7	–	–
1932–33	36	–	–	–
1933–34	20	–	–	–
Total	80	7	–	–

Those who were fortunate enough to see his all-too-brief Chelsea career mostly agree that he was Chelsea's finest-ever centre-half. Quietly spoken, he was a stylist, an intelligent player with time in which to use the ball constructively, and always with an eye to move forward to lend weight to the attack. His performance for England against Scotland in 1932 was universally admired and applauded. Then, at the height of his powers, he fell out with the Stamford Bridge management, went off to play in France for much greater financial reward and was lost to English football for ever.

PETER O'DOWD

RALPH OELOFSE   FRANCIS O'HARA

OELOFSE, Ralph (1951–1953) Centre-half
Born Johannesburg 12.11.26. Height 5ft 11in, Weight 12st 4lb. Career Berea Park (South Africa), Chelsea (October 1951), Watford (July 1953).
Chelsea details Debut 1.3.52. 8 Appearances

	Appearances		Goals	
	FL	FAC	FL	FAC
1951–52	3	–	–	–
1952–53	5	–	–	–
Total	8	–	–	–

One of several South African players who tried their hand in English football after the Second World War. A dominating figure in defence, he played a few games as a deputy for John Harris before moving to Watford, then in the Third Division South.

O'HARA, Francis (1905–1906) Centre-forward
Career Chelsea (August 1905), Not retained (May 1906).
Chelsea details Debut 7.10.05. 3 Appearances 3 Goals

	Appearances		Goals	
	FL	FAC	FL	FAC
1905–06	1	2	–	3
Total	1	2	–	3

One of the large squad assembled to launch Chelsea into the Football League. "Pat" was unable to force his way into the first-team and was at Stamford Bridge for only one season.

O'HARE, John (1932–1941) Full-back

Born Armadale. Height 5ft 8in, Weight 11st 4lb. Career Shawfield Juniors, Chelsea (June 1932), Retired 1941.
Chelsea details Debut 27.4.35. 108 Appearances

	Appearances		Goals	
	FL	FAC	FL	FAC
1933–34	1	–	–	–
1934–35	2	–	–	–
1935–36	27	1	–	–
1936–37	36	2	–	–
1937–38	22	–	–	–
1938–39	14	3	–	–
Total	102	6	–	–

Fearless tackler who lacked the pace to become a top-class full-back. Nevertheless, he was a dependable player who was in, or around, the first-team in the four seasons leading up to World War II, despite competing for his place with the likes of George Barber, Ned Barkas, Tommy Law and Jack Smith.

ORMISTON, Andrew (1909–1915) Centre-half

Born Peebles. Height 5ft 11½in, Weight 12st 6lb. Career Hebburn Argyle, Lincoln City, Chelsea (Summer 1909), Lincoln City (1918).
Chelsea details Debut 4.9.09. 102 Appearances 1 Goal

	Appearances		Goals	
	FL	FAC	FL	FAC
1909–10	24	2	–	–
1910–11	6	–	–	–
1911–12	37	1	1	–
1912–13	20	3	–	–
1913–14	8	1	–	–
Total	95	7	–	–

"Alec" was a commanding centre-half and a particularly fine header of the ball. One of several players who followed manager David Calderhead from Lincoln City to Chelsea at that time, he never quite succeeded in coming to terms with the demands of a higher class of football, but played in the majority of the games in the promotion season of 1912–13.

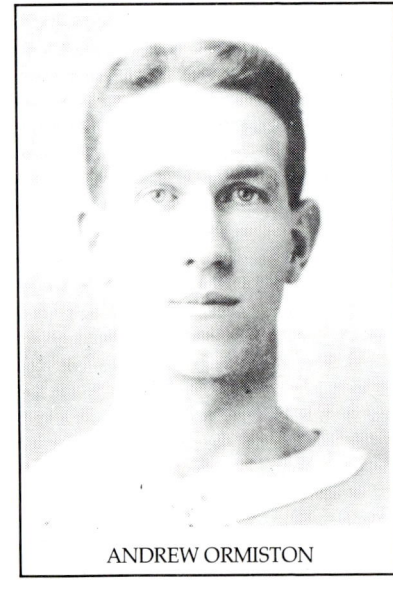

JOHN O'HARE

ANDREW ORMISTON

| JOHN O'ROURKE | THOMAS ORD |

O'ROURKE, John (1962–1963) Centre-forward

Born Northampton 11.12.45. Height 5ft 8½in, Weight 10st 10lb. Career Arsenal (amateur), Chelsea (April 1962), Luton Town (December 1963), Middlesborough, Ipswich Town, Coventry City, Queens Park Rangers, Bournemouth & Boscombe Athletic.
Chelsea details Debut 25.9.63. 1 Appearance

	Appearances			Goals		
	FL	FAC	LC	FL	FAC	LC
1963–64	–	–	1	–	–	–
Total			1			

One of soccer's nomads, he topped the Combination goalscorers list in 1962–63 but failed to win a first-team place at a time when Barry Bridges and Graham Moore were the recognised choices for the central spearhead positions in the attack. He went on to notch some 150 League goals with six different clubs.

ORD, Thomas (1972–1974) Midfield

Born London 15.10.52. Height 5ft 9in, Weight 11st 7lb. Career Erith & Belvedere, Chelsea (October 1972), Bristol City (loan), Rochester Lancers (U.S.A.) (Summer 1974), Bexley United.
Chelsea details Debut 7.4.73. 3 Appearances 1 Goal

	Appearances		Goals	
	FL	FAC	FL	FAC
1972–73	3	–	1	–
Total	3	–	1	–

Despite scoring on his debut he never succeeded in winning a first-team place at a time when the professional staff was being pruned for reasons of finance.

OSGOOD, Peter (1964–1974 & 1978–1979) Striker/Midfield

Born Windsor 20.2.47. Height 6ft 2in, Weight 12st 9lb. Career Chelsea (September 1964), Southampton (March 1974, £275,000), Norwich City (loan), Philadelphia Furies (U.S.A.), Chelsea (December 1978, £25,000), Retired September 1979.

Honours England (4 caps), England Under-23 (6 caps), England Youth International, Football League XI (3 appearances), F.A. Cup winners' medals 1970, 1976, European Cup Winners' Cup winners' medal 1971, Football League Cup losers' medal 1972.

Chelsea details Debut 16.12.64 376(4) Appearances 150 Goals

	Appearances					Goals				
	FL	FAC	LC	FC	ECWC	FL	FAC	LC	FC	ECWC
1964–65	–	–	1	–	–	–	–	2	–	–
1965–66	31(1)	5	–	11	–	7	1	–	3	–
1966–67	10	–	2	–	–	6	–	–	–	–
1967–68	42	5	1	–	–	16	1	–	–	–
1968–69	35	5	3	3(1)	–	9	3	–	1	–
1969–70	36(2)	7	3	–	–	23	8	–	–	–
1970–71	27	3	3	–	7	5	1	2	–	4
1971–72	36	3	9	–	4	18	1	4	–	8
1972–73	38	5	7	–	–	11	4	2	–	–
1973–74	21	–	1	–	–	8	–	–	–	–
1978–79	9	1	–	–	–	2	–	–	–	–
1979–80	1	–	–	–	–	–	–	–	–	–
Total	286(3)	34	30	14(1)	11	105	19	10	4	12

(also 1 F.A. Charity Shield appearance 1970–71)

An immensely talented player, whether as a striker or operating in midfield. He arrived on the Stamford Bridge scene as an "unknown" amateur in March 1964, scored two goals on his debut, nine months later, and then became an automatic choice in the first-team for nine seasons until differences of opinion with manager Dave Sexton led to his departure. His flair and opportunism made him one of the most exciting players of his generation. High-spirited, and often unpredictable, off the field he was not the easiest of players to handle and at time his irresponsible actions landed him in trouble with the authorities. But, equally, it must be said that he was not always sympathetically handled and it makes little sense that a player of such rare ability was recognised so infrequently at international level. In October 1966 he broke a leg and missed the rest of that season through injury. After an interval of more than four years he returned to Chelsea, at the age of 31, but some of the old magic, and pace, was missing and he was unable to retain a first-team place.

PETER OSGOOD

ERIC G. PARSONS

PARSONS, Eric G. (1950–1956) Outside-right

Born Worthing 9.11.23. Height 5ft 7in, Weight 10st 4lb. Career West Ham United, Chelsea (November 1950, £23,000), Brentford (November 1956).
Honours England "B" (2 caps), Football League Championship medal 1955.
Chelsea details Debut 2.12.50. 177 Appearances 42 Goals

	Appearances		Goals	
	FL	FAC	FL	FAC
1950–51	5	–	–	–
1951–52	11	2	1	–
1952–53	33	7	8	3
1953–54	29	1	9	–
1954–55	42	3	11	1
1955–56	33	5	7	1
1956–57	5	–	1	–
Total	158	18	37	5

(also 1 F.A. Charity Shield appearance 1955–56)

A fast and clever outside-right who, after a cartilage operation, developed into one of the outstanding players of the 1954–55 Championship team. An ever-present in this side he scored many vital goals, as well as laying on others – especially for Roy Bentley. A firm favourite with the Chelsea crowd, who affectionately nicknamed him the "rabbit", he played nearly 500 senior games despite losing several seasons through World War II at the start of his career.

PATES, Colin G. (1979–) Defender/Midfield

Born Mitcham 10.8.61. Height 5ft 11in, Weight 11st. Career Chelsea (July 1979). Honours England Youth International, Second Division Championship medal 1984, Full Members' Cup winners' medal 1986.
Chelsea details Debut 10.10.79. 309 Appearances 9 Goals

	Appearances				Goals			
	FL	FAC	FLC	FMC	FL	FAC	FLC	FMC
1979–80	16	1	–	–	–	–	–	–
1980–81	15	–	–	–	–	–	–	–
1981–82	42	7	3	–	1	–	–	–
1982–83	35	3	2	–	4	–	–	–
1983–84	42	1	5	–	–	–	–	–
1984–85	36	3	9	–	1	–	–	–
1985–86	35	2	8	5	1	–	–	–
1986–87	33	2	2	2	2	–	–	–
Total	254	19	29	7	9	–	–	–

First came to Stamford Bridge as a schoolboy apprentice in July 1977. A talented central defender who played in all 11 England Youth internationals in the "Little World Cup" tournament of 1980–81. He quickly established himself as a member of Chelsea's first-team squad and was appointed captain in April 1984, for the last few matches of the Second Division Championship season. He has also played in midfield on occasions but is happiest in his defensive role, operating on the left side.

PATON, John A. (1946–1949) Outside-left

Born Glasgow 2.4.23. Career St Mungo's Academy, Dennistoun Waverley, Glasgow Celtic, Chelsea (November 1946, £7,000), Glasgow Celtic (Summer 1947), Brentford, Watford.
Chelsea details Debut 7.12.46. 23 Appearances 3 Goals

	Appearances		Goals	
	FL	FAC	FL	FAC
1946–47	18	5	3	–
Total	18	5	3	–

A press photographer by profession, he was a Chelsea player for less than one season but was the recognised first choice for the outside-left berth during his short stay. With clever footwork and accurate crosses his play produced goals for others and, after returning north of the border, he again came south to play a further 200 games or so in English football.

COLIN G. PATES

JOHN A. PATON

| JOSEPH PAYNE | FRANK PEARSON |

PAYNE, Joseph (1938–1946) Centre-forward

Born Bolsover 17.1.14, Died April 1975. Height 6ft, Weight 12st. Career Bolsover Colliery, Biggleswade Town, Luton Town, Chelsea (March 1938, £5,000), West Ham United (December 1946, part-exchange Harry Medhurst), Millwall.
Honours England (1 cap).
Chelsea details Debut 12.3.38. 47 Appearances 23 Goals

	Appearances		Goals	
	FL	FAC	FL	FAC
1937–38	10	–	4	–
1938–39	26	6	17	2
1945–46	–	5	–	–
Total	36	11	21	2

The statistic that Joe Payne scored 110 goals in his 118 League games is an impressive one yet, even so, does not tell the full story of this remarkable player who scored ten goals on his first appearance at centre-forward for Luton Town against Bristol Rovers in April 1936. His Chelsea career was truncated by the outbreak of the Second World War and, later, by injury. A fine header of the ball and blessed with powerful and accurate shooting from either foot, he was a lethal finisher. As Sergeant Payne (R.A.F.) he scored 50 goals (39 games) in the "unofficial" season of 1943–44 and 40 (29 games) the following season. Sadly, he played little football after the ending of hostilities despite several brave attempts to overcome injury. He also played minor county cricket for Bedfordshire.

PEARSON, Frank (1905–1906) Centre-forward

Born Manchester 18.5.84. Height 5ft 9½in, Weight 12st 7lb. Career Preston North End, Manchester City, Chelsea (October 1905, £250), Hull City (October 1906), Luton Town, Rochdale, Eccles Borough.
Chelsea details Debut 14.10.05. 30 Appearances 18 Goals

	Appearances		Goals	
	FL	FAC	FL	FAC
1905–06	29	1	18	–
Total	29	1	18	–

After an outstandingly successful first season for Chelsea, when he frequently captained the side he, surprisingly, was allowed to move on and was never able to reproduce his best form subsequently.

PEARSON, George W.M. (1926–1933) Outside-left

Born West Stanley. Height 5ft 2in, Weight 10st 11lb. Career Chelsea (February 1926), Luton Town (Summer 1933).
Chelsea details Debut 3.4.26. 215 Appearances 35 Goals

	Appearances		Goals	
	FL	FAC	FL	FAC
1925–26	1	–	–	–
1926–27	35	5	3	–
1927–28	35	1	4	–
1928–29	32	4	6	–
1929–30	38	1	12	–
1930–31	26	–	4	–
1931–32	27	7	4	2
1932–33	3	–	–	–
Total	197	18	33	2

He came to Stamford Bridge from his native north-east via Bury, where he had been a trialist. Succeeding Bobby McNeil (the last survivor from the 1915 Cup Final team) he took over the left-wing position and became an automatic choice for the next six seasons. One of the smallest men ever to play for Chelsea, he was extremely fast and direct with a powerful shot and his most successful season with the club was that of 1929–30, when Chelsea returned to the First Division after an absence of six seasons.

PHILLIPS, John T.S. (1970–1980) Goalkeeper

Born Shrewsbury 7.7.51. Height 5ft 10½in, Weight 10st 10lb. Career Shrewsbury Town, Aston Villa, Chelsea (August 1970, £25,000), Crewe Alexandra (loan), Brighton & Hove Albion (March 1980, £15,000), Charlton Athletic, Crystal Palace.
Honours Wales (4 caps), Wales Under-23 (4 caps).
Chelsea details Debut 24.10.70. 149 Appearances

GEORGE W.M. PEARSON   JOHN T.S. PHILLIPS

PETER B. PICKERING

	Appearances				Goals			
	FL	FAC	LC	ECWC	FL	FAC	LC	ECWC
1970–71	14	–	–	4	–	–	–	–
1971–72	7	–	1	–	–	–	–	–
1972–73	16	5	2	–	–	–	–	–
1973–74	22	2	–	–	–	–	–	–
1974–75	34	2	4	–	–	–	–	–
1975–76	3	–	–	–	–	–	–	–
1976–77	11	2	1	–	–	–	–	–
1977–78	11	–	1	–	–	–	–	–
1978–79	7	–	–	–	–	–	–	–
Total	125	11	9	4	–	–	–	–

He spent the majority of his career at Chelsea understudying Peter Bonetti, although, as his total of first-team games suggests, he had several lengthy spells of duty in the senior side, notably when playing a crucial part in steering the club to the final of the European Cup Winners' Cup final in 1971. At his best a very fine 'keeper, his game did, however, suffer from inconsistency.

PICKERING, Peter B. (1948–1951) Goalkeeper

Born York 24.3.26. Height 5ft 11ins, Weight 12st 6lb. Career Earswick, York City, Chelsea (May 1948), Kettering Town (Summer 1951), Northampton Town.
Chelsea details Debut 9.10.48. 35 Appearances

	Appearances		Goals	
	FL	FAC	FL	FAC
1948–49	16	3	–	–
1949–50	1	–	–	–
1950–51	10	5	–	–
Total	27	8	–	–

A magnificently-built and spectacular goalkeeper who shared the goalkeeping duties with Harry Medhurst for some three seasons. A lack of consistency prevented him going further in the game but he totalled 160 League games in his career, delayed by World War II. A good cricketer, he played one match for Northamptonshire and later became a first-class umpire in South Africa.

PINNER, Michael J. (1961) Goalkeeper

Born Boston 16.2.34. Career Cambridge University, Pegasus, Aston Villa (amateur), Sheffield Wednesday (amateur), Queens Park Rangers (amateur), Manchester United (amateur), Chelsea (amateur, 1961), Swansea City (amateur), Leyton Orient.
Honours England Amateur International.
Chelsea details Debut 20.4.62. 1 Appearance

	Appearances		Goals	
	FL	FAC	FL	FAC
1961–62	1	–	–	–
Total	1	–	–	–

Famous amateur goalkeeper who made occasional appearances for six League clubs, Chelsea included, before signing professional forms for Leyton Orient.

PLUM, Seth L. (1924–1926) Wing-half

Born Tottenham. Height 5ft 7½in, Weight 10st 5lb. Career Charlton Athletic (amateur), Chelsea (May 1924), Southend United (Summer 1926).
Honours England Amateur International.
Chelsea details Debut 30.8.24. 27 Appearances 1 Goal

	Appearances		Goals	
	FL	FAC	FL	FAC
1924–25	17	1	1	–
1925–26	9	–	–	–
Total	26	1	1	–

A wing-half who arrived having won amateur international honours and began his Chelsea career in the first-team. However, he was unable to establish his place and played most of his football in the reserve-team thereafter.

MICHAEL J. PINNER

SETH L. PLUM

WANTED
If anyone has
a photograph
of
WILLIAM
It would be appreciated if you
would allow us to copy it.
Please forward it to Ron at
36 Lockier Walk,
Wembley, Middx.
It will be returned safely

WILLIAM PORTER

ANTHONY J. POTRAC

PORTER, William (1906–1907) Outside-left
Career London Caledonians, Chelsea (amateur, 1905–07), Luton Town.
Chelsea details Debut 14.4.06. 2 Appearances

	Appearances		Goals	
	FL	FAC	FL	FAC
1905–06	1	–	–	–
1906–07	1	–	–	–
Total	2	–	–	–

One of several amateurs linked with Chelsea in their early days. His two first team games, separated by 11 months, were both occasioned when he deputised for the injured Johnny Kirwan.

POTRAC, Anthony J. (1970–1973) Inside-forward
Born Victoria 21.1.53. Height 5ft 9½ins, Weight 11st. Career Chelsea (August 1970), Durban City (Summer 1973).
Chelsea details Debut 8.1.72. 1 Appearance

	Appearances		Goals	
	FL	FAC	FL	FAC
1971–72	1	–	–	–
Total	1	–	–	–

He was unable to break into the first-team at a time when financial cuts were being forced on the club, and a large number of other junior players were also pressing for places.

PRIESTLEY, John (1920–1928) Inside-forward

Born Glasgow. Height 5ft 8ins, Weight 10st 2lb. Career Johnstone, Chelsea (May 1920), Grimsby Town (May 1928).
Chelsea details Debut 2.5.21. 204 Appearances 19 Goals

	Appearances		Goals	
	FL	FAC	FL	FAC
1920–21	1	–	–	–
1922–23	20	3	1	–
1923–24	40	2	2	–
1924–25	35	–	1	–
1925–26	39	2	4	–
1926–27	39	5	6	1
1927–28	17	1	4	–
Total	191	13	18	1

Originally a wing-half, he turned out to be a wonderful investment for Chelsea, remaining a pillar of the first-team for six seasons. A strong tackler, he was an accurate passer of the ball and a consistent "provider" of goals for others. Well-liked and respected throughout the game.

PRIESTLEY, Thomas J.M. (1933–1934) Inside-forward

Born Belfast, Died 1986. Height 5ft 9ins, Weight 11st. Career Coleraine, Linfield, Chelsea (June 1933, £2,000).
Honours Northern Ireland (2 caps).
Chelsea details Debut 26.8.33. 27 Appearances 2 Goals

	Appearances		Goals	
	FL	FAC	FL	FAC
1933–34	23	4	1	1
Total	23	4	1	1

Chelsea secured his services in fierce competition with other English clubs. Easily identified by the fact that he wore a skull-cap to conceal his total baldness, he was a gifted player on the field and quiet and withdrawn off it. After one season he returned home, without being in dispute with the club, never returned and never played professional football again. He remained on Chelsea's list of retained players for many years.

JOHN PRIESTLEY

THOMAS J.M. PRIESTLEY

| PETER PROUDFOOT | STANLEY PROUT |

PROUDFOOT, Peter (1906–1907) Wing-half

Born Wishaw. Career Lincoln City, Millwall, Clapton Orient, Chelsea (April 1906), Manchester United.
Chelsea details Debut 13.4.06. 12 Appearances

	Appearances		Goals	
	FL	FAC	FL	FAC
1905–06	4	–	–	–
1906–07	7	–	–	–
1907–08	1	–	–	–
Total	12	–	–	–

A terrier-type defender whose energetic and constructive play were the features of his game. Unable to win a regular first-team place at Chelsea, he was appointed Manager of Clapton Orient in April 1922, after his playing career had ended and having held a commission in the Army during the First World War.

PROUT, Stanley (1932–1934) Outside-left

Born Fulham. Height 5ft 8in, Weight 10st 5lb. Career Park Royal, Chelsea (Summer 1932), Bristol Rovers (July 1934).
Chelsea details Debut 12.11.32. 17 Appearances 3 Goals

	Appearances		Goals	
	FL	FAC	FL	FAC
1932–33	16	1	3	–
Total	16	1	3	–

Having made the step-up from amateur to professional football with apparent ease, he lost his place to Jack Horton and, after a season in the reserves, moved into the Third Division.

RANDALL, Ernest A.W. (1950–1953) Centre-forward

Born Bognor 13.1.26. Height 6ft, Weight 12st 1lb. Career Bognor Town, Chelsea (December 1950), Crystal Palace (June 1953).
Chelsea details Debut 13.10.51. 3 Appearances 1 Goal

	Appearances		Goals	
	FL	FAC	FL	FAC
1951–52	3	–	1	–
Total	3	–	1	–

Powerfully-built centre-forward and former policeman, he was unable to displace Roy Bentley from the first-team, but was a regular goalscorer in the reserve and "A" teams.

RANKIN, John P. (1930–1934) Inside-forward

Born Coatbridge. Height 5ft 8½in, Weight 10st 2lb. Career Dundee, Charlton Athletic, Chelsea (May 1930), Notts County (Summer 1934).
Chelsea details Debut 25.3.31. 66 Appearances 9 Goals

	Appearances		Goals	
	FL	FAC	FL	FAC
1930–31	6	–	1	–
1931–32	24	3	4	–
1932–33	29	1	4	–
1933–34	3	–	–	–
Total	62	4	9	–

An engineer by profession, he was an artistic, ball-playing inside-forward who had played over 200 first-team games with Charlton. At a period when Chelsea were spilling out large sums of money on new "star" players, he never quite established himself as a regular first-teamer and the arrival of George Gibson virtually ended his opportunities in the senior side.

ERNEST A.W. RANDALL

JOHN P. RANKIN

WILLIAM READ

WANTED
If anyone has a photograph of **ERNEST**
It would be appreciated if you would allow us to copy it. Please forward it to Ron at 36 Lockier Walk, Wembley, Middx.
It will be returned safely

ERNEST J. REID

READ, William (1911–1912) Winger
Career Sunderland, Chelsea (May 1911), Dundee (March 1913).
Chelsea details Debut 20.1.12. 4 Appearances

	Appearances		Goals	
	FL	FAC	FL	FAC
1911–12	3	1	–	–
Total	3	1	–	–

Spent almost two seasons in the reserves as deputy to Billy Bridgeman on the left-wing.

REID, Ernest J. (1937–1939)
Born Pentrebach 25.3.14. Career Troedyrhiw, Chelsea (September 1937), Swansea Town (Summer 1939), Norwich City, Bedford Town.
Chelsea details Debut 5.11.38. 1 Appearance

	Appearances		Goals	
	FL	FAC	FL	FAC
1938–39	1	–	–	–
Total	1	–	–	–

Spotted in Welsh League football, he spent two seasons in the reserve-team, deputising on one occasion for Sammy Weaver, but never quite fulfilled his promise.

REILLY, Edward J. (1908–1909) Half-back/Inside-forward

Career Chelsea (amateur, 1908–09), Fulham (1909).
Chelsea details Debut 3.4.09. 1 Appearance

	Appearances		Goals	
	FL	FAC	FL	FAC
1908–09	1	–	–	–
Total	1	–	–	–

One of several amateurs associated with Chelsea in their early days, he was "on the books" for two seasons, but received only one opportunity in the first-team.

RHOADES-BROWN, Peter (1979–1984) Winger

Born Hampton 2.1.62. Height 5ft 11in, Weight 10st 12lb. Career Chelsea (July 1979), Oxford United (January 1984, £50,000).
Chelsea details Debut 29.12.79. 97(12) Appearances 5 Goals.

	Appearances			Goals		
	FL	FAC	LC	FL	FAC	LC
1979–80	1(3)	–	–	–	–	–
1980–81	30(4)	1	–	1	–	–
1981–82	24(3)	3(2)	3	1	1	–
1982–83	25	3	–	1	–	–
1983–84	6	–	1	1	–	–
Total	86(10)	7(2)	4	4	1	–

First came to Chelsea as a schoolboy, then becoming an apprentice before signing professional. A skilful and speedy left-side striker, his output of goals was disappointing and, partly as a result, the advent of Paul Canoville and Mickey Thomas rendered him superfluous to the needs of the first-team squad.

EDWARD J. REILLY

PETER RHOADES-BROWN

FREDERICK A. RICHARDSON	JAMES ROBERTSON

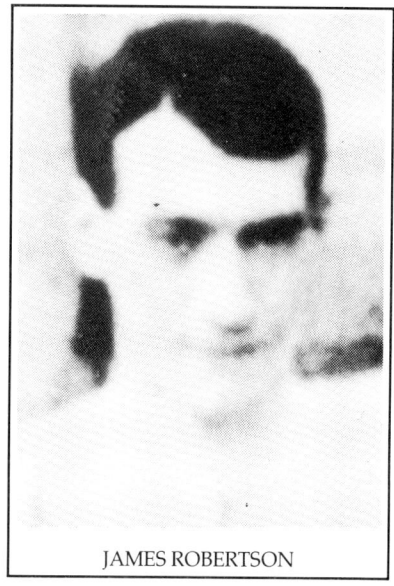

RICHARDSON, Frederick A. (1946–1947) Centre-forward

Born Middlestone 18.8.25. Height 5ft 9in, Weight 11st 7lb. Career Bishop Auckland, Chelsea (September 1946), Hartlepool United (October 1947), Barnsley, West Bromwich Albion, Chester, Hartlepool United.
Chelsea details Debut 12.4.47. 2 Appearances

	Appearances		Goals	
	FL	FAC	FL	FAC
1946–47	2	–	–	–
Total	2	–	–	–

Kept in the reserve-team by Tommy Lawton in the first season after World War II, he subsequently achieved success with his other clubs, chalking up nearly 250 League games (66 goals).

ROBERTSON, James (1905–1907) Inside-forward

Born Glasgow. Career Small Heath, Chelsea (August 1905, £50), Glossop (Summer 1907), Partick Thistle, Ayr United, Leeds City.
Chelsea details Debut 30.9.05. 31 Appearances 22 Goals

	Appearances		Goals	
	FL	FAC	FL	FAC
1905–06	16	2	13	1
1906–07	13	–	8	–
Total	29	2	21	1

A member of Chelsea's first-ever League side and a regular scorer of goals on his appearances during the first two seasons in the club's history. Strangely, in view of his impressive striking record, he was by no means assured of his first-team place – especially after the arrival of Billy Bridgeman in the autumn of 1906.

ROBERTSON, John Tait (1905–1906) Wing-half

Born Dumbarton 25.2.77, Died 24.1.35. Career Morton, Everton, Southampton, Glasgow Rangers, Chelsea (May 1905), Glossop (October 1906), Coventry City.
Honours Scotland (16 caps), Scottish League (6 appearances), Scottish League Championship medals 1900, 1901, 1902, Scottish F.A. Cup winners' medal 1903, losers' medal 1904, 1905.
Chelsea details Debut 2.9.05. 39 Appearances 4 Goals

	Appearances		Goals	
	FL	FAC	FL	FAC
1905–06	33	3	4	–
1906–07	3	–	–	–
Total	36	3	4	–

"Jackie" was appointed Chelsea's first, and only, Player-Manager in the spring of 1905 and his experience of both Scottish and English football was crucial in assembling a squad of players ready to do battle in the Football League at very short notice. For the princely salary of £4 a week, his shrewd judgement of talent enabled him to build a team with a nice blend of experience and youth which took the club to 3rd position in the Second Division at the very first attempt. He was also still a fine player and played regularly in the left-half position throughout that season.

JOHN TAIT ROBERTSON

WILLIAM GIBB ROBERTSON

ROBERTSON, William Gibb (1946–1960) Goalkeeper

Born Glasgow 13.11.28, Died June 1973. Height 6ft, Weight 13st. Career Arthurlie, Chelsea (July 1946), Leyton Orient (September 1960, £1,000).
Honours Football League Championship medal 1955.
Chelsea details Debut 21.4.51. 215 Appearances

	Appearances			Goals		
	FL	FAC	FC	FL	FAC	FC
1950–51	4	–	–	–	–	–
1951–52	41	9	–	–	–	–
1952–53	27	–	–	–	–	–
1953–54	34	–	–	–	–	–
1954–55	26	1	–	–	–	–
1955–56	34	4	–	–	–	–
1956–57	20	–	–	–	–	–
1958–59	10	–	1	–	–	–
1959–60	3	–	–	–	–	–
Total	199	14	1	–	–	–

(also 1 F.A. Cup Charity Shield appearance 1955–56)

Wonderfully solid and reliable goalkeeper who spent five years in the reserves understudying Harry Medhurst before making his debut against Liverpool on 21st April 1951 when, after 14 League games without a win Chelsea were four points adrift at the bottom of the First Division and "certainties" for relegation. Winning the last four games the drop was avoided on goal average, by 0.44 of a goal, and Bill's career as first-choice 'keeper was well and truly launched.

ROBERTSON, William Harold (1945–1948) Goalkeeper

Born Lossiemouth 25.3.23. Height 6ft 1½ins, Weight 12st 9lb. Career R.A.F. Lossiemouth, Chelsea (October 1945), Birmingham City (December 1948), Stoke City.
Chelsea details Debut 5.1.46. 43 Appearances

	Appearances		Goals	
	FL	FAC	FL	FAC
1945–46	–	6	–	–
1946–47	22	–	–	–
1947–48	15	–	–	–
Total	37	6	–	–

Had the unenviable task of succeeding Vic Woodley as Chelsea's first choice goalkeeper. Played regularly in the 1945–46 "transitional" season but lost his place with the arrival of Harry Medhurst. Later made over 200 first-team appearances for Stoke City.

ROBINSON, Arthur C. (1908–1910) Goalkeeper

Career Small Heath, Birmingham, Chelsea (Summer 1908), Not retained May 1910. Honours Irish League XI, Scottish League XI.
Chelsea details Debut 7.9.08. 3 Appearances

	Appearances		Goals	
	FL	FAC	FL	FAC
1908–09	2	–	–	–
1909–10	1	–	–	–
Total	3	–	–	–

Signed on in the 1908 close-season as deputy for Jack Whitley. An experienced 'keeper, he was given few opportunities to prove himself in his two seasons at Chelsea.

WILLIAM HAROLD ROBERTSON

ARTHUR C. ROBINSON

WANTED
If anyone has
a photograph
of
BRYAN
It would be appreciated if you
would allow us to copy it.
Please forward it to Ron at
36 Lockier Walk,
Wembley, Middx.
It will be returned safely

BRYAN S. ROBSON

TOM H. ROBSON

ROBSON, Bryan S. (1982–1983) Striker
Born Sunderland 11.11.45. Height 5ft 7in, Weight 11st 8lb. Career Newcastle United, West Ham United, Sunderland, West Ham United, Sunderland, Carlisle United, Chelsea (July 1982), Sunderland (Summer 1983), Carlisle United.
Honours England Under-23 (2 caps), Football League XI.
Chelsea details Debut 28.8.82. 12(5) Appearances 5 Goals.

	Appearances			Goals		
	FL	FAC	LC	FL	FAC	LC
1982–83	11(4)	–	1(1)	3	–	2
Total	11(4)	–	1(1)	3	–	2

After a long and distinguished career, "Pop" arrived at Stamford Bridge as senior professional just short of his 37th birthday. He was also involved in coaching duties with the juniors. But unable to hold a first-team place, he returned to Sunderland, for a third spell, after one season. At his prime he was a prolific goalscorer as his tally of some 250 League goals proves.

ROBSON, Tom H. (1965–1966) Outside-left
Born Gateshead 3.7.44. Height 5ft 7½in, Weight 10st 3lb. Career Northampton Town, Chelsea (November 1965, £30,000), Newcastle United (December 1966, £20,000), Peterborough United.
Honours England Youth International.
Chelsea details Debut 4.12.65. 6(1) Appearances

	Appearances		Goals	
	FL	FAC	FL	FAC
1965–66	6(1)	–	–	–
Total	6(1)	–	–	–

A speedy left-winger whose chances at Chelsea were stifled by the form and consistency of Bobby Tambling. On the staff for only 13 months, he later played some 500 first-team games for Peterborough United, scoring well over a century of goals.

RODGER, George B. (1924–1931) Centre-half

Born Cambusland. Height 5ft 10in, Weight 11st 2lb. Career Kilsyth Rangers, Chelsea (June 1924), Clachnacuddin (Coach/Manager, 1931).
Chelsea details Debut 17.1.25. 122 Appearances 2 Goals

	Appearances		Goals	
	FL	FAC	FL	FAC
1924–25	10	–	–	–
1925–26	32	2	–	–
1926–27	20	–	–	–
1927–28	13	–	1	–
1928–29	2	–	–	–
1929–30	28	1	1	–
1930–31	14	–	–	–
Total	119	3	2	–

Throughout his time at Stamford Bridge he faced keen competition for his place in the first-team, both from Harry Wilding and, later, Jack Townrow. However, he played a vital role in the 1929–30 promotion season and, before he had a real chance to establish himself in the First Division, a knee injury terminated his career.

ROFE, Dennis (1980–1982) Full-back

Born Fulham 1.6.50. Height 5ft 7½in, Weight 11st 7lb. Career Leyton Orient, Leicester City, Chelsea (February 1980, £80,000), Southampton (Summer 1982).
Honours England Under-23 (1 cap).
Chelsea details Debut 23.2.80. 61(2) Appearances

	Appearances			Goals		
	FL	FAC	LC	FL	FAC	LC
1979–80	14	–	–	–	–	–
1980–81	38	1	2	–	–	–
1981–82	6(1)	0(1)	–	–	–	–
Total	58(1)	1(1)	2	–	–	–

After a distinguished career with Orient and Leicester City, involving some 500 senior appearances, this hard-tackling, aggressive full-back was appointed captain in his first full season at Stamford Bridge and played 54 consecutive first-team games before, surprisingly, losing his place to Chris Hutchings. Soon he moved on to Southampton, where he subsequently became a member of the coaching staff.

GEORGE B. RODGER

DENNIS ROFE

DOUGLAS ROUGVIE   W. FRED ROUSE

ROUGVIE, Douglas (1984–1987) Defender

Born Ballingry (Fifeshire) 24.5.56. Height 6ft 1in, Weight 12st. Career Dunfermline United, Aberdeen, Chelsea (July 1984, £150,000), Brighton & Hove Albion (June 1987, £50,000). Honours Scotland (1 cap), Scottish League Championship medals 1980, 1984, Scottish F.A. Cup winners' medals 1982, 1983, 1984, Scottish League Cup losers' medals 1979, 1980, European Cup Winners' Cup winners' medal 1983, Full Members' Cup winners' medal 1986.
Chelsea details Debut 25.8.84 100 Appearances 3 Goals

	Appearances				Goals			
	FL	FAC	FLC	FMC	FL	FAC	FLC	FMC
1984–85	27	2	8	–	1	–	–	–
1985–86	35	2	5	4	2	–	–	–
1986–87	13	–	3	2	–	–	–	–
Total	74	4	16	6	3	–	–	–

Came to Chelsea at the age of 28 after 12 highly successful years with Aberdeen. A tall, strong defender, at home in any of the back-four positions, he is a hard tackler, good in the air, and quick coming forward. Popular with the crowd he has played mainly in the left-back position at Chelsea competing for the "number three" shirt with Keith Dublin.

ROUSE, W. Fred (1907–1909) Inside-forward

Born Cranford (Middlesex). Career Shepherd's Bush, Grimsby Town, Stoke City, Everton, Chelsea (October 1907, £1,000), Brentford (February 1909), West Bromwich Albion. Honours Football League XI.
Chelsea details Debut 19.10.07. 42 Appearances 11 Goals

	Appearances		Goals	
	FL	FAC	FL	FAC
1907–08	20	1	6	–
1908–09	18	3	5	–
Total	38	4	11	–

Chelsea's first-ever four-figure transfer signing. A vigorous, bustling inside-forward, he played in all three inside-forward positions for Chelsea and was a strong finisher.

RUSSELL, Robert I. (1944–1948) Wing-half

Born Aberdour 27.12.19. Height 5ft 7in, Weight 10st 10lb. Career Airdrieonians, Chelsea (December 1944), Notts County (August 1948), Leyton Orient.
Chelsea details Debut 5.1.46. 4 Appearances

	Appearances		Goals	
	FL	FAC	FL	FAC
1945–46	–	2	–	–
1946–47	2	–	–	–
Total	2	2	–	–

While the official record books show that Bobby played only four "official" first-team games for Chelsea, as a member of the renowned "Russell-Harris-Foss" half-back line which formed the backbone of so many war-time games from 1943–1945, his total number of such appearances was 85 and included the two Football League (South) Cup finals at Wembley in 1944 and 1945. Unfortunately, injury limited his football once the war ended.

RUSSELL, William (1927–1936) Wing-half

Born Hamilton. Height 5ft 7½in, Weight 10st. Career Blantyre Victoria, Chelsea (June 1927), Heart of Midlothian (January 1936), Rhyl (Player-Manager).
Chelsea details Debut 9.4.28. 160 Appearances 6 goals

	Appearances		Goals	
	FL	FAC	FL	FAC
1927–28	2	–	–	–
1928–29	13	1	–	–
1929–30	20	1	–	–
1930–31	17	–	1	–
1931–32	24	7	3	–
1932–33	31	–	1	–
1933–34	29	–	–	–
1934–35	14	1	1	–
Total	150	10	6	–

ROBERT I. RUSSELL

WILLIAM RUSSELL

| ARTHUR A. SALES | ROBERT SALMOND |

Like his namesake Bobby, he was a flame-haired wing-half. An intelligent player, renowned for his strength in the tackle he was primarily a defensive player, but his clever use of the ball initiated many an attack ("the man who gets into the open space makes things easy", he once said). A welcome guest at the 1967 F.A. Cup final banquet he was still following the fortunes of his old club – attending the Liverpool game on Merseyside in November 1986.

SALES, Arthur A. (1924–1928) Centre-half

Born Lewes 14.3.00, Died 1977. Career Redhill, Chelsea (September 1924), not retained May 1928.
Chelsea details Debut 30.8.24. 7 Appearances

	Appearances		Goals	
	FL	FAC	FL	FAC
1924–25	5	–	–	–
1925–26	1	–	–	–
1926–27	1	–	–	–
Total	7	–	–	–

Came to Stamford Bridge having established a high reputation for himself in amateur football. With George Rodger, Harry Wilding and Jack Townrow all on the books during his four seasons with the club, first-team opportunities were necessarily limited. He was also a fine athlete who had once run the 100 yards in 10.5 seconds.

SALMOND, Robert (1938–1945) Centre-half

Born Kilmarnock. Height 5ft 11½in, Weight 12st 7lb. Career Dundee North End, Portsmouth, Chelsea (November 1938), Banbury Spencer (1945).
Chelsea details Debut 12.11.38. 29 Appearances

	Appearances		Goals	
	FL	FAC	FL	FAC
1938–39	24	5	–	–
Total	24	5	–	–

This tall and dominating centre-half was signed after eight years' service with Portsmouth to take over from Allan Craig who was nearing the end of his long career. The outbreak of World War II, however, terminated his League career and at the end of hostilities he moved to Banbury Spencer as Player-Manager. It was a matter of surprise that he never received international recognition from the Scottish selectors.

SAUNDERS, Derek W. (1953–1959) Wing-half

Born Ware 6.1.28. Height 5ft 10in, Weight 11st 7lb. Career Walthamstow Avenue, Chelsea (June 1953), Retired May 1959.
Honours England Amateur International, Football League Championship medal 1955, F.A. Amateur Cup winners' medal 1952.
Chelsea details Debut 5.9.53. 223 Appearances 9 Goals.

	Appearances			Goals		
	FL	FAC	FC	FL	FAC	FC
1953–54	33	1	–	1	–	–
1954–55	42	3	–	1	–	–
1955–56	37	7	–	–	–	–
1956–57	41	2	–	6	–	–
1957–58	31	3	–	–	–	–
1958–59	19	1	2	1	–	–
Total	203	17	2	9	–	–

(Appearances also include 1 F.A. Charity Shield, 1955–56)

This red-haired and highly-skilled wing-half was an ever-present in the 1954–55 Championship team and his strong tackling and defensive play, as well as his constructive ideas, were crucial factors in that success. Appointed captain of Chelsea in August 1957, he joined the coaching staff on retirement as a player. Later, he was Groundsman and Chief Football Coach at Westminster School before joining Hampstead Cricket Club as Groundsman.

DEREK W. SAUNDERS

F. JOHN SAUNDERS

JAMES SAUNDERS

SAUNDERS, F. John (1948–1954) Centre-half

Born Middlesbrough 24.8.24. Height 6ft, Weight 12st. Career Darlington, Chelsea (May 1948), Crystal Palace (August 1954), Chester.
Chelsea details Debut 10.12.49. 60 Appearances

	Appearances		Goals	
	FL	FAC	FL	FAC
1949–50	3	1	–	–
1950–51	7	–	–	–
1951–52	13	–	–	–
1952–53	20	7	–	–
1953–54	9	–	–	–
Total	52	8	–	–

Understudied John Harris in the centre-half position for five seasons until the arrival of Ron Greenwood and Stan Wicks. A tall, craggy defender he made over 250 appearances in his League career, having first been spotted in Army football.

SAUNDERS, James (1909–1910) Goalkeeper

Born Birmingham. Height 5ft 9in, Weight 11st 7lb. Career Glossop, Manchester United, Lincoln City, Chelsea (May 1909), not retained (May 1910).
Chelsea details Debut 25.12.09. 2 Appearances

	Appearances		Goals	
	FL	FAC	FL	FAC
1909–10	2	–	–	–
Total	2	–	–	–

Deputised for Jack Whitley twice during his only season on the staff, one of the games being the home fixture against Newcastle United at Christmas, when over 70,000 spectators were present. He had previously been with manager Dave Calderhead at Lincoln City.

SCOTT, Mel (1956–1963) Centre-half

Born: Claygate. Height 6ft, Weight 11st 9lb.
Career: Chelsea (November 1956), Brentford (March 1963, £10,000)
Honours: England Under-23 (4 caps), England Youth International
Chelsea details Debut 11.3.58. 104 Appearances.

	Appearances			Goals		
	FL	FAC	FC	FL	FAC	FC
1957–58	9	–	–	–	–	–
1958–59	34	2	2	–	–	–
1959–60	9	2	–	–	–	–
1960–61	9	–	–	–	–	–
1961–62	36	1	–	–	–	–
Total	97	5	2	–	–	–

One of the many products of the Chelsea Youth Scheme in its most prolific and successful period, his early career as a professional was interrupted by National Service and he never quite, thereafter, fulfilled his true potential. Lack of domination in the air caused him to lose his place to John Mortimore, but he went on to become Brentford's regular pivot for five seasons.

SHARP, Buchanan (1919–1923) Inside-forward

Born: Dumbarton. Height 5ft 11in, Weight 12st 2lb.
Career: Vale of Leven, Chelsea (November 1919), Tottenham Hotspur (March 1923), Leicester City, Nelson, Southport
Chelsea details Debut: 28.2.20. 72 Appearances, 23 Goals

	Appearances		Goals	
	FL	FAC	FL	FAC
1919–20	11	2	3	2
1920–21	8	3	–	1
1921–22	21	–	7	–
1922–23	25	2	10	–
Total	65	7	20	3

Renowned for his close, Scottish-style, dribbling and ball control, as well as for his strong shooting powers. He played for Chelsea in the F.A. Cup semi-final against Aston Villa at

MEL SCOTT

BUCHANAN SHARP

JAMES SHARP	COLIN M. SHAW

Bramall Lane in March 1920, yet took some time to find his bearings in English League football. Even so, it was a surprise when he was allowed to move on towards the end of his most successful season at Stamford Bridge.

SHARP, James (1912–1915) Full-back

Born: Jordanstone 11.10.80 Died 18.11.49, Ayrshire. Height 5ft 9½in, Weight 13st 7lb.
Career: Dundee, Fulham, Woolwich, Arsenal, Fulham, Chelsea (November 1912, £1,750)
Honours: Scotland (5 caps)
Chelsea details Debut: 23.11.12. 64 Appearances

	Appearances		Goals	
	FL	FAC	FL	FAC
1912–13	23	2	–	–
1913–14	21	–	–	–
1914–15	17	1	–	–
Total	61	3	–	–

Was signed as an already experienced player to take over from Jock Cameron at full-back. A fine defender, with a good tactical sense, he was a little lacking in pace and the emergence of Jack Harrow limited his first-team opportunities, which were ended altogether by the outbreak of the First World War. Subsequently became trainer-coach with Fulham and was later associated both with Walsall and Cliftonville.

SHAW, Colin M. (1961–1963) Centre-forward

Born: St Albans 19.6.43. Height 5ft 6½in. Weight 10st 6lb.
Career: Chelsea (May 1961), Norwich City (August 1963, £5,000), Leyton Orient
Honours: England Youth International
Chelsea details Debut: 3.2.62. 1 Appearance

	Appearances		Goals	
	FL	FAC	FL	FAC
1961–62	1	–	–	–
Total	1	–	–	–

A prodigous scorer of goals in junior and reserve football (including 7 against Fulham in an F.A. Youth cup-tie on one occasion), he never established himself at senior level and with his three professional clubs (11 appearances in all) he failed to find the net in a League fixture.

SHELLITO, Kenneth (1957–1969) Full-back

Born: East Ham 18.4.40. Height 5ft 10in, Weight 12st 6lb
Career: Chelsea (April 1957), Retired January 1969
Honours: England (1 cap), England Under-23 (1 cap)
Chelsea details Debut: 15.4.59. 123 Appearances, 2 Goals

	Appearances				Goals			
	FL	FAC	LC	FC	FL	FAC	LC	FC
1958–59	2	–	–	–	–	–	–	–
1959–60	5	–	–	–	–	–	–	–
1961–62	26	1	–	–	–	–	–	–
1962–63	34	3	–	–	–	–	–	–
1963–64	18	–	–	–	1	–	–	–
1964–65	13	–	1	–	1	–	–	–
1965–66	16	–	–	4	–	–	–	–
Total	114	4	1	4	2	–	–	–

Joined Chelsea as a Junior in 1955. An outstanding and aggressive full-back whose career was dogged, and prematurely ended, by injury. Finally, after four operations on his left knee he was forced to retire, months before he might well have been part of England's triumphant 1966 World Cup campaign. As it was, he had only one full season in Chelsea's first-team, partnering Eddie McCreadie in one of the best young full-back duos in the League in the 1962–63 Second Division promotion season. After coaching the Juniors he succeeded Frank Blunstone as Manager of the Youth Section and was appointed Manager of Chelsea F.C. before the start of the 1977-78 season, resigning after 15 months. Later he was associated with both Queens Park Rangers and Crystal Palace and Cambridge United (as Manager).

SHEARER, Duncan (1983–1986) Striker

Born Fort William 28.9.66 Height 5ft 10in, Weight 10st 9lb.
Career Clachnacuddin, Chelsea (November 1983), Huddersfield Town (March 1986 £10,000).
Chelsea details Debut 1.2.86 2 Appearances 1 Goal.

	Appearances		Goals	
	FL	FAC	FL	FAC
1985-86	2	–	1	–
Total	2	–	1	–

KENNETH SHELLITO

DUNCAN SHEARER

JACK SHERBORNE	STEPHEN SHERWOOD

Tall centre-forward who scored goals regularly in the reserve team. With opportunities restricted by the consistent form of Kerry Dixon and David Speedie, he moved to Huddersfield Town where he was an instant success – scoring 5 goals in his first two full games.

SHERBORNE, Jack (1939–1945) Forward
Born: Bolton 1.5.16
Career: Chorley, Chelsea (February 1936), Retired 1945
Chelsea details Debut: 18.12.37. 5 Appearances

	Appearances		Goals	
	FL	FAC	FL	FAC
1937–38	5	–	–	–
Total	5	–	–	–

Apart from a brief spell in the League side in February and March 1937 he had to be content with reserve team football, although he played a handful of games in the first season of wartime "regional" football before joining the Army. After suffering wounds on his active service in France he never played again.

SHERWOOD, Stephen (1971–1976) Goalkeeper
Born: Selby 10.12.53. Height 6ft 3in, Weight 14st.
Career: Chelsea (July 1971), Millwall (loan), Brentford (loan), Watford (November 1976, £5,000)
Honours: F.A. Cup losers' medal 1984
Chelsea details Debut 1.1.72. 17 Appearances

	Appearances			Goals		
	FL	FAC	LC	FL	FAC	LC
1971–72	1	–	–	–	–	–
1972–73	3	–	–	–	–	–
1975–76	12	–	1	–	–	–
Total	16	–	1	–	–	–

Recommended to Chelsea whilst playing football in the West Riding, he was an Apprentice for a year before signing professional forms. The son of a former Huddersfield Town 'keeper and brother of Olympic hurdle, John, he began the 1975–76 season as first choice goalkeeper, before the re-signing of Peter Bonetti effectively ended his opportunities.

SILLETT, John C. (1954–1962)

Born: Southampton 20.7.36. Height 6ft, Weight 12st 12lb.
Career: Southampton (amateur), Chelsea (May 1954), Coventry City (April 1962, £3,000), Plymouth Argyle
Honours: Football League XI (1 appearance)
Chelsea details Debut: 1.1.57. 102 Appearances, 1 Goal

	Appearances				Goals			
	FL	FAC	LC	FC	FL	FAC	LC	FC
1956–57	2	1	–	–	–	–	–	–
1957–58	1	–	–	–	–	–	–	–
1958–59	27	2	–	2	–	–	–	–
1959–60	21	2	–	–	–	–	–	–
1960–61	30	–	2	–	–	–	1	–
1961–62	12	–	–	–	–	–	–	–
Total	93	5	2	2	–	–	1	–

Came to Stamford Bridge as an amateur with brother Peter in May 1953 and signed professional twelve months later. A strong, hard-tackling full-back he was in partnership with his brother on the flanks of the defence for some three seasons before losing his place to Ken Shellito. After retiring as a player, he was a Coach with Bristol City, managed Hereford United before being appointed Chief Coach with Coventry City.

SILLETT, R. Peter (1953–1962) Full-back

Born: Southampton 1.2.33. Height 6ft 1in, Weight 14st 9lb
Career: Southampton, Chelsea (May 1953 £12,000), Guildford City (June 1962, Free-transfer)
Honours: England (3 caps), England Under-23 (3 caps), England "B" (1 cap), England Youth International, Football League XI (1 appearance), Football League Championship medal 1955.
Chelsea details Debut: 19.8.53. 288 Appearances, 34 Goals

JOHN C. SILLETT    PETER R. SILLETT

JOSEPH SIMNER

	Appearances				Goals			
	FL	FAC	LC	FC	FL	FAC	LC	FC
1953–54	12	–	–	–	–	–	–	–
1954–55	21	3	–	–	6	–	–	–
1955–56	41	7	–	–	2	1	–	–
1956–57	30	2	–	–	2	–	–	–
1957–58	40	3	–	–	4	–	–	–
1958–59	35	2	–	4	7	–	–	1
1959–60	41	2	–	–	6	1	–	–
1960–61	37	1	3	–	2	–	2	–
1961–62	3	–	–	–	–	–	–	–
Total	260	20	3	4	29	2	2	1

(Appearances also include 1 F.A. Charity Shield, 1955–56)

A sound and respected full-back who was a particularly fine kicker of the ball. He obtained most of his goals either from the penalty spot or from free-kicks. A member of the 1954–55 Football League Championship side, he shared the right-back position with John Harris, and is well remembered for his goal against Wolverhampton Wanderers in front of 75,000 spectators, which virtually clinched the title, hitting a penalty-kick with stunning power past international 'keeper Bert Williams. Lacking the pace to make a permanent impact on the international scene, he was Manager of both Ashford Town, Folkestone and Poole Town for spells, after retiring as a player.

SIMNER, Joseph (1947–1949) Centre-forward

Born: Sedgley 13.3.23
Career: Folkestone Town, Chelsea (October 1947), Swindon Town (July 1949)
Chelsea details Debut: 6.3.48. 1 Appearance

	Appearances		Goals	
	FL	FAC	FL	FAC
1947–48	1	–	–	–
Total	1	–	–	–

Spent two years in the reserve team at a time when Roy Bentley and Hugh Billington were vying for the centre-forward berth before moving to Swindon Town, where he remained for three years.

SINCLAIR, William I. (1964–1966) Midfield

Born: Glasgow 21.3.47. Height 5ft 6in, Weight 11st 2lb.
Career: Greenock Morton, Chelsea (September 1964, part-exchange Jim Mulholland), Released, (March 1966), Glentoran
Chelsea details Debut: 24.4.65. 1 Appearance

	Appearances		Goals	
	FL	FAC	FL	FAC
1964–65	1	–	–	–
Total	1	–	–	–

After playing in the junior and reserve sides he made one League appearance, then went on the club tour of Australia the following summer but did not receive any futher first-team opportunities.

SISSONS, John L. (1974–1975) Outside-left

Born: Hayes 30.9.45. Height 5ft 7in, Weight 10st 12lb.
Career: West Ham United, Sheffield Wednesday, Norwich City, Chelsea (August 1974, £70,000), Contract cancelled (May 1975), Cape Town City
Honours: England Under-23 (10 caps), England Youth International, England Schoolboy International, F.A. Cup winners' medal 1964, European Cup Winners' Cup winners' medal 1965, Football League Cup losers' medal 1966
Chelsea details Debut: 17.8.74. 12(1) Appearances

	Appearances			Goals		
	FL	FAC	LC	FL	FAC	LC
1974–75	10(1)	1	1	–	–	–
Total	10(1)	1	1	–	–	–

A left-winger who had already played over 400 senior games, most of them for West Ham United, when he arrived at Stamford Bridge. Already past his best, he failed to establish himself in a team struggling to maintain its First Division status.

WILLIAM I. SINCLAIR

JOHN L. SISSONS

JOHN E. SITTON

WANTED
If anyone has
a photograph
of
DOUGLAS
It would be appreciated if you
would allow us to copy it.
Please forward it to Ron at
36 Lockier Walk,
Wembley, Middx.
It will be returned safely

DOUGLAS M. SMALE

SITTON, John E. (1977–1980) Central-defender
Born: Hackney 21.10.59. Height 6ft, Weight 12st 2lb
Career: Chelsea (October 1977), Millwall (February 1980, "nominal"), Gillingham, Orient
Chelsea details Debut: 21.2.79. 12(2) Appearances

	Appearances			Goals		
	FL	FAC	LC	FL	FAC	LC
1978–79	11(1)	–	–	–	–	–
1979–80	0(1)	–	1	–	–	–
Total	11(2)	–	1	–	–	–

A strongly-built centre-half who first came to Chelsea as an Apprentice in May 1976. He had a run of games in the first-team towards the end of the 1978–79 season, in a side already doomed to relegation from the First Division, but did not figure in manager Geoff Hurst's plans and played mostly reserve team football thereafter.

SMALE, Douglas M. (1937–1945) Outside-left
Born: Victoria (London) 27.3.16. Height 5ft 7in, Weight 11st.
Career: Kingstonian, Chelsea (March 1937), Retired 1945.
Chelsea details Debut: 29.3.37. 9 Appearances

	Appearances		Goals	
	FL	FAC	FL	FAC
1936–37	6	–	–	–
1937–38	2	–	–	–
1938–39	1	–	–	–
Total	9	–	–	–

One of many players whose career was terminated by the Second World War. He was on the fringe of the first-team at the outbreak of hostilities, as deputy for regular left-winger Alf Hanson, but had retired by the time normal football resumed in 1946. During the war he served with the R.A.F. in India.

SMART, James (1965–1966) Inside-forward

Born: Dundee 9.1.47. Height 5ft 7½in, Weight 10st 8lb.
Career: Greenock Morton, Chelsea (January 1965) Contract cancelled (March 1966), Highlands Park (South Africa)
Chelsea details Debut: 24.4.65. 1 Appearance

	Appearances		Goals	
	FL	FAC	FL	FAC
1964–65	1	–	–	–
Total	1	–	–	–

Spending only just over twelve months at Stamford Bridge in the reserves, he was unable to make an impact in English football and, with a stream of young talent emerging from the Juniors at that time was allowed to move on.

SMETHURST, Derek (1968–1971) Striker

Born: Durban 24.10.47. Height 6ft 1in, Weight 11st 7lb.
Career: Durban University, Chelsea ("permit-player" December 1968, professional January 1971), Millwall, (September 1971, £35,000)
Honours: European Cup Winners' Cup winners' medal 1971
Chelsea details Debut: 1.9.70, 18(1) Appearances, 5 Goals

	Appearances				Goals			
	FL	FAC	LC	ECWC	FL	FAC	LC	ECWC
1970–71	12	–	1	3(1)	4	–	–	1
1971–72	2	–	–	–	–	–	–	–
Total	14	–	1	3(1)	4	–	–	1

He proved himself an extremely able deputy for such as Peter Osgood and Ian Hutchinson during his time at The Bridge and he played an important role in semi-final and final stages of the successful European Cup Winners' Cup campaign in 1970–71. Surprisingly, he was allowed to move on but made little impact with his only other English club, Millwall.

JAMES SMART

DEREK SMETHURST

ARTHUR J. SMITH	GEORGE W. SMITH

SMITH, Arthur J. (1938–1945) Full-back
Born: Merthyr. Height 5ft 10in, Weight 11st 7lb
Career: Swindon Town, Chelsea (March 1938), Retired 1945.
Chelsea details Debut: 12.3.38. 49 Appearances

	Appearances		Goals	
	FL	FAC	FL	FAC
1937–38	11	–	–	–
1938–39	34	4	–	–
Total	45	4	–	–

An excellent acquisition from Third Division football, Jack went straight into the first-team at left-back and a very promising career was then truncated by the outbreak of World War II, during which he served as a Flight/Sgt in the R.A.F. Unfortunately, any chance of resuming his career afterwards was ruined by injuries received in a road accident. Won an "unofficial" war-time cap for Wales and was later Trainer to Wolverhampton Wanderers and Manager of West Bromwich Albion, guiding them back to the First Division during his first season at the helm.

SMITH, George W. (1921–1932) Full-back
Born: Parkhead. Height 5ft 9½in, Weight 11st 12lb
Career: Parkhead, Chelsea (Summer 1921), East Fife (1932).
Chelsea details Debut: 27.8.21. 370 Appearances

	Appearances		Goals	
	FL	FAC	FL	FAC
1921–22	35	–	–	–
1922–23	42	3	–	–
1923–24	39	2	–	–
1924–25	40	1	–	–
1925–26	34	2	–	–
1926–27	42	5	–	–
1927–28	40	1	–	–
1928–29	37	4	–	–
1929–30	30	1	–	–
1930–31	11	–	–	–
1931–32	1	–	–	–
Total	351	19	–	–

One of the best bargains for a £10 signing-on fee Chelsea have ever made. For almost ten full seasons this dependable and resourceful full-back was a permanent fixture in the first-team, having made his debut within weeks of his arrival from Scottish junior football. During the 1920s few English club teams were better served at full-back than Chelsea were by Smith and his two distinguished partners, Jack Harrow and, later, Tommy Law. Further, few men were more noted for their sportsmanship and fair play – and few were more respected and liked by supporters. George's final full season saw Chelsea return to the First Division after a six-year interval and soon afterwards a serious injury effectively ended his career.

SMITH, James H. (1951–1955) Winger

Born: Sheffield 6.12.30
Career: Shildon, Chelsea (April 1951), Leyton Orient (May 1955)
Chelsea details Debut: 8.9.51. 23 Appearances, 3 Goals

	Appearances		Goals	
	FL	FAC	FL	FAC
1951–52	16	4	3	–
1952–53	1	–	–	–
1953–54	2	–	–	–
Total	19	4	3	–

This nippy, clever winger never quite fulfilled his early promise and the consistency of Eric Parsons and Frank Blunstone condemned him to reserve football for his last three years on the staff. Surprisingly, he never made a big impact during his three seasons with Leyton Orient and he played no further League football afterwards.

JAMES H. SMITH

PHILIP SMITH | ROBERT A. SMITH

SMITH, Philip (1910) Centre-forward
Career: Crewe Alexandra, Chelsea (April 1910, £250)
Chelsea details Debut: 16.4.10. 1 Appearance

	Appearances		Goals	
	FL	FAC	FL	FAC
1909–10	1	–	–	–
Total	1	–	–	–

One of several players who were signed in the final weeks of the 1909–10 season in an unavailing bid to stave off relegation. After one game he never received a further opportunity and played only a handful of reserve games at the start of the following season.

SMITH, Robert A. (1950–1955) Centre-forward
Born: Langdale (Yorkshire) 22.2.23. Height 5ft 9in, Weight 12st
Career: Chelsea (May 1950), Tottenham Hotspur (December 1955, £16,000), Brighton & Hove Albion
Honours: England (15 caps), Football League Championship medal 1961, F.A. Cup winners' medals 1961, 1962
Chelsea details Debut: 4.9.50. 86 Appearances, 30 Goals

	Appearances		Goals	
	FL	FAC	FL	FAC
1950–51	16	5	7	2
1951–52	32	7	11	5
1952–53	7	–	1	–
1953–54	8	–	–	–
1954–55	4	–	–	–
1955–56	7	–	4	–
Total	74	12	23	7

One of the outstanding products of the Chelsea Youth Scheme, he came to Stamford Bridge as a schoolboy from Redcar in 1948. Making his debut as a 17-year old, this strongly-built and aggressive centre-forward made an immediate impact with his enthusiasm and bustling methods. Yet, he lost his place to Roy Bentley and never quite fitted into the scheme of things, but it was a matter of regret when he moved to Tottenham just at a time when further chances were coming his way. Once at White Hart Lane, he proved the folly of his release from Stamford Bridge, by winning a string of international caps and being a member of the famous Spurs "double" side.

SMITH, Stephen (1920–1923) Wing-half

Born: Byker. Height 5ft 7in, Weight 10st 1lb
Career: Chelsea (1920–22), Merthyr Tydfil.
Chelsea details Debut: 29.8.21. 23 Appearances, 1 Goal

	Appearances		Goals	
	FL	FAC	FL	FAC
1921–22	20	1	1	–
1922–23	2	–	–	–
Total	22	1	1	–

Although he had an extended run in the first-team in 1921–22 he never succeeded in establishing a permanent place in the League team, and the switching of Harry Wilding from centre to wing-half in September 1922 effectively ended his Chelsea career.

SORRELL, Dennis (1962–1964) Wing-half

Born: Lambeth 7.10.40. Height 5ft 5½in, Weight 10st 10lb
Career: Leyton Orient, Chelsea (March 1962, £10,000), Leyton Orient (September 1964, £3,000), Romford
Chelsea details Debut: 9.3.62. 4 Appearances, 1 Goal

	Appearances		Goals	
	FL	FAC	FL	FAC
1961–62	1	–	–	–
1962–63	–	1	–	1
1963–64	2	–	–	–
Total	3	1	–	1

Strong-tackling wing-half who was on the staff at a time when Terry Venables and Ron Harris were establishing themselves in his position. He played over 100 games for Leyton Orient in his two spells with that club.

STEPHEN SMITH

DENNIS SORRELL

NIGEL J. SPACKMAN

JOHN P. SPARROW

SPACKMAN, Nigel J. (1983–1987) Midfield
Born: Romsey 2.12.60. Height 6ft 1in, Weight 12st 4lb
Career: Andover, A.F.C. Bournemouth, Chelsea (June 1983 £40,000), Liverpool (February 1987, £400,000)
Honours: Second Division Championship medal 1984, Full Members' Cup winners' medal 1986.
Chelsea details Debut 27.8.83. 176(3) Appearances, 14 Goals

	Appearances				Goals			
	FL	FAC	LC	FC	FL	FAC	LC	FC
1983–84	40	1	5	–	3	–	–	–
1984–85	42	3	10	–	1	1	–	–
1985–86	37(2)	2	7(1)	6	7	–	–	–
1986–87	20	2	–	1	1	–	–	1
Total	139(2)	8	22(1)	7	12	1	–	1

Powerful midfield player, strong in the tackle with boundless energy. Ever ready to move up in support of, and in front of, his forward men, he had a good shot especially from long range. The practical joker of the side, he was a highly popular player with colleagues and fans alike and was an integral, and ever-present, member of the 1984 Second Division Championship team.

SPARROW, John P. (1974–1981) Full-back
Born: Bethnal Green 3.6.57. Height 5ft 10in, Weight 12st
Career: Chelsea (June 1974), Millwall (loan), Exeter City (January 1981, £10,000)
Honours: England Youth International, England Schoolboy International
Chelsea details Debut: 13.3.74. 68(6) Appearances, 2 Goals

	Appearances			Goals		
	FL	FAC	FC	FL	FAC	FC
1973–74	8	–	–	–	–	–
1974–75	12	–	–	1	–	–
1975–76	8(1)	–	1	–	–	–
1976–77	12(2)	–	–	1	–	–
1977–78	12(3)	1	1	–	–	–
1979–80	11	1	1	–	–	–
Total	63(6)	2	3	2	–	–

Made his debut as a 16-year old in March 1974, three months before signing professional forms and after two years as an apprentice. Promised rather more than he achieved and was never able to hold down a regular place at a time of instability within the club.

SPECTOR, Miles D. (1952–1953) Outside-left

Born: Hendon 4.8.34
Career: Hendon, Chelsea (1952–53, amateur), Hendon.
Honours: England Youth International, England Amateur International
Chelsea details Debut: 7.2.53. 6 Appearances

	Appearances		Goals	
	FL	FAC	FL	FAC
1952–53	2	3	–	–
1953–54	1	–	–	–
Total	3	3	–	–

As an 18-year Hendon Grammar Schoolboy he made an immediate impact in both the League and F.A. Cup competitions, with his speedy, direct raids down the left flank. Unable to be assured of a regular place, with Frank Blunstone and Jim Lewis (another amateur player) available, little more was seen of him and he remained in amateur football throughout his career thereafter.

SPEEDIE, David R. (1982–   ) Striker

Born: Glenrothes 20.2.60. Height 5ft 7in, Weight 11st Career: Barnsley, Darlington, Chelsea (May 1982, £80,000) Coventry City (July 1987, £750,000).
Honours: Scotland (5 caps), Scotland Under 21 international (1 cap), Second Division Championship medal 1984, Full Members' Cup winners' medal 1986
Chelsea details Debut: 18.9.82 197(8) Appearances 64 Goals.

	Appearances				Goals			
	FL	FAC	LC	FC	FL	FAC	LC	FC
1982–83	34	3	3	–	7	–	2	–
1983–84	32(5)	1	2(1)	–	13	–	–	–
1984–85	33(2)	3	9	–	10	2	4	–
1985–86	34	2	8	5	14	2	1	5
1986–87	22	3	1	2	3	1	–	–
Total	155(7)	12	23(1)	7	47	5	7	5

Highly talented striker, or occasional midfield player. His lightning quick reactions and skill on the ball are a menace to opponents as, on occasions is his excitable temperament. For a comparatively small man he is a powerful header with the ability to outjump taller opponents. His relentless determination and aggression were vital components of Chelsea's surge from the Second Division to the upper reaches of the First.

MILES D. SPECTOR

DAVID R. SPEEDIE

RICHARD SPENCE

SPENCE, Richard (1934–1950) Outside-right

Born: Barnsley 18.7.08. Died: March 1983, Height 5ft 7in, Weight 9st
Career: Thorpe Colliery, Barnsley, Chelsea (October 1934, £5,000), Retired 1950
Honours: England (2 caps)
Chelsea details Debut: 6.10.34, 246 Appearances, 65 Goals.

	Appearances		Goals	
	FL	FAC	FL	FAC
1934–35	34	2	19	–
1935–36	40	5	13	–
1936–37	39	2	8	2
1937–38	28	–	4	–
1938–39	41	6	11	–
1945–46	–	6	–	1
1946–47	33	4	7	–
1947–48	6	–	–	–
Total	221	25	62	3

A loyal and well-loved servant of Chelsea F.C. for more than 40 years. A bargain signing from his home town team of Barnsley, he was an automatic choice for the right-wing position in the five seasons leading to the outbreak of the Second World War, during which he served in the Police Force and, later, in the Army. A wiry light-weight man to whom fitness came easily, he resumed his career again in 1945 and when he made his final first-team appearance on September 13th 1947, at 40 years and 57 days, he was the oldest player to appear for Chelsea in a League fixture. Before the war he was unfortunate enough to have been a contemporary of international wingers Sammy Crooks and Stanley Matthews, but still played twice for England. Extremely fast, he was very much a winger of the old school and loved to make direct tracks on goal. He possessed a surprisingly powerful shot for such a small man and his tally of 19 goals in his first season on the staff remains a record for any Chelsea wingman – this after arriving with eight games of that season already played. During the war he made 170 "unofficial" appearances (50 goals) to show what further records could have come his way but for the hostilities. He joined the training staff on his retirement as a player and continued to be a frequent visitor to Stamford Bridge almost to the time of his death.

SPOTTISWOOD, Joseph (1919–1920) Outside-left
Born: Carlisle. Height 5ft 9in, Weight 12st
Career: Chelsea (1919), Swansea Town (January 1920), Queens Park Rangers
Chelsea details Debut: 3.1.20, 1 Appearance

	Appearances		Goals	
	FL	FAC	FL	FAC
1919–1	–	–	–	–
Total	1	–	–	–

Signed for Chelsea soon after the resumption of normal football in August 1919, but was unable to make an impression with Chelsea, although subsequently enjoying considerably more success with his other clubs.

STANLEY, Garry E. (1971–1979) Midfield
Born: Burton-on-Trent 4.3.54. Height 5ft 9½in, Weight 11st 7lb
Career: Chelsea (March 1971), Fort Lauderdale Strikers (1979), Everton (August 1979, £300,000), Swansea City, Portsmouth
Chelsea details Debut: 16.8.75. 115(5) Appearanes, 15 Goals

	Appearances			Goals		
	FL	FAC	LC	FL	FAC	LC
1975–76	29	2	1	3	–	–
1976–77	33	2	3	6	–	–
1977–78	11	–	1	1	–	–
1978–79	32(4)	0(1)	1	5	–	–
Total	105(4)	4(1)	6	15	–	–

An attacking midfield player recommended to Chelsea by former player, Frank Upton, who had spotted him in Derbyshire Schools football. His forceful play was an important ingredient in the 1976–77 promotion team and, in many ways, he reflected his manager, Eddie McCreadie's, attitude towards the game. Was allowed to move on in order to ease the financial situation at Stamford Bridge but never quite fulfilled his true potential.

| JOSEPH SPOTTISWOOD | GARRY E. STANLEY |

JAMES STARK | WILLIAM H.O. STEER

STARK, James (1907–1908) Centre-half
Born: Ruchzie (Glasgow) 1880.
Career: Mansewood, Pollokshaws Eastwood, Glasgow Perthshire, Glasgow Rangers, Chelsea (May 1907), Glasgow Rangers (October 1908), Greenock Morton
Honours: Scotland (2 caps), Scottish League (2 appearances). Scottish League Championship medal 1901, Scottish Cup winners' medal 1903, losers' medals 1904, 1905, 1909.
Chelsea details Debut: 5.10.07. 32 Appearances, 2 Goals

	Appearances		Goals	
	FL	FAC	FL	FAC
1907–08	30	2	2	–
Total	30	2	2	–

Scottish international centre-half who was signed early in the 1907–08 season in order to establish Chelsea in their first experience of First Division football. However, and disappointingly from the club's point of view, he decided to return to his native land after one season in London. He was a dominating defender, but one who enjoyed moving upfield to lend weight to his attackers.

STEER, William H. O. (1912–1918) Centre-forward
Born Kingston-upon-Thames. Career, Queens Park Rangers, Chelsea (July 1912), Retired 1918.
Honours England Amateur International (4 caps)
Chelsea details Debut 21.12.12. 4 Appearances 1 Goal

	Appearances		Goals	
	FL	FAC	FL	FAC
1912–13	4	–	1	–
Total	4	–	1	–

Former amateur international who signed professional forms for Chelsea but never succeeded in winning a regular first-team place. Played irregularly in 'regional' football during the First World War, after which he retired.

STEFFEN, Willi (1946–1947) Full-back

Career Swiss football, Chelsea (1946–47), amateur
Honours Switzerland (7 caps)
Chelsea details Debut 30.11.46. 20 Appearances

	Appearances		Goals	
	FL	FAC	FL	FAC
1946–47	15	5	–	–
Total	15	5	–	–

A former pilot in the Swiss Air Force, this outstanding defender played for Chelsea, as an amateur, while in London in the first season after World War II. Superbly built and standing over 6ft tall, he made an immediate impression. A strong tackler and dominating in the air he was universally popular with his fellow players and with supporters, and it was a matter of great regret when he returned home after his 5-month stay in England.

STEPNEY, Alex C. (1966) Goalkeeper

Born Mitcham 18.9.44. Height 6ft, Weight 12st 8lb.
Career Tooting & Mitcham, Millwall, Chelsea (May 1966, £50,000), Manchester United (September 1966, £50,000), Altrincham
Honours England (1 cap), England Under-23 (3 caps), Football League XI, Football League Championship medal 1968, FA Cup winners' medal 1977, losers' medal 1976
Chelsea details Debut 3.9.66. 1 Appearance

	Appearances		Goals	
	FL	FAC	FL	FAC
1966–67	1	–	–	–
Total	1	–	–	–

Signed at a time when Peter Bonetti's future with Chelsea was uncertain, he remained at Stamford Bridge for four months only before moving on to Manchester United where he played some 500 first-team games.

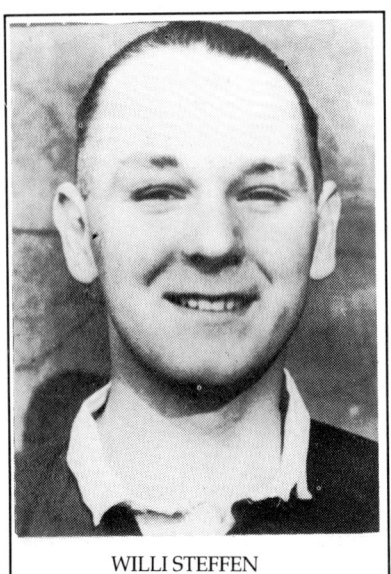

WILLI STEFFEN   ALEX C. STEPNEY

| GEORGE STONE | LESLIE STUBBS |

STONE, George (1924–1928) Outside-left

Born: 27.7.1894 Died February 1940. Career Hemel Hempstead, Chelsea (September 1924). Not retained May 1928.
Chelsea details Debut 29.8.25. 25 Appearances 2 Goals

	Appearances		Goals	
	FL	FAC	FL	FAC
1925–26	22	–	2	–
1926–27	3	–	–	–
Total	25	–	2	–

After playing regularly in the first-team during the first half of the 1925–26 season he lost his place to the veteran Bobby McNeil and was never again recognised as a first choice for the left-wing position.

STUBBS, Leslie (1952–1958) Inside-forward

Born Great Wakering 18.2.29 Height 5ft 10ins, Weight 12st. Career Great Wakering, Southend United, Chelsea (November 1952, £10,000), Southend United (November 1958, £12,000 combined fee with Alan Dicks)
Honours Football League Championship medal 1956
Chelsea details Debut 15.11.52 123 Appearances 35 Goals

	Appearances		Goals	
	FL	FAC	FL	FAC
1952–53	5	–	–	–
1953–54	30	1	9	–
1954–55	27	3	5	1
1955–56	17	4	10	–
1956–57	18	1	7	–
1957–58	13	1	3	–
1958–59	2	–	–	–
Total	112	10	34	1

(Appearances also include 1 FA Charity Shield, 1955–56)

Forceful inside-forward who was a regular goalscorer and who played an important role in the 1954–55 Championship team. Strongly-built, he possessed a powerful shot, if somewhat lacking pace and mobility.

STRIDE, David R. (1976–1979) Full-back

Born Lymington 14.3.58 Height 5ft 9in Weight 11st 5lb. Career Chelsea (January 1976), Memphis Rogues (USA, £90,000), Millwall
Chelsea details Debut 23.9.78. 37 Appearances

	Appearances			Goals		
	FL	FAC	FC	FL	FAC	FC
1978–79	32	1	–	–	–	–
1979–80	3	–	1	–	–	–
Total	35	1	1	–	–	–

Joined Chelsea as an apprentice and was converted to full-back from his previous position as a left-winger. He developed into a speedy, overlapping defender before his career was interrupted by a hairline fracture of the skull, after having apparently established himself in the first-team.

SWAIN, Kenneth J. (1973–1978) Striker/Full-back

Born Birkenhead 28.1.52 Height 5ft 9in Weight 11st 7lb. Career Wycombe Wanderers, Chelsea (August 1973), Aston Villa (December 1978, £100,000), Nottingham Forest, Portsmouth
Chelsea details Debut 16.3.74. 127(5) Appearances 29 Goals.

	Appearances			Goals		
	FL	FAC	LC	FL	FAC	LC
1973–74	4(3)	–	–	1	–	–
1975–76	24(1)	3	1	4	1	–
1976–77	36	2	3	13	–	1
1977–78	35(1)	2	1	4	1	–
1978–79	15	–	1	4	–	–
Total	114(5)	7	6	26	2	1

Although after leaving Chelsea he played almost exclusively as a full-back, at Stamford Bridge he was primarily a left-winger. With clever footwork and the ability to cross the ball accurately he was an effective attacker, if lacking a little pace. It was a matter of regret when financial economies, as much as anything else, dictated his move to Aston Villa.

DAVID R. STRIDE

KENNETH J. SWAIN

ROBERT TAMBLING

TAMBLING, Robert (1958–1970) Forward

Born Storrington 18.9.41 Height 5ft 8½in Weight 12st 6lb. Career Chelsea (September 1958), Crystal Palace (January 1970, £40,000)
Honours England (3 caps), England Under-23 (13 caps), England Schoolboy International, Football League XI (1 appearance), FA Cup losers' medal 1966, Football League Cup winners' medal 1965.
Chelsea details Debut 7.2.59 366(4) Appearances 202 Goals

	Appearances				Goals			
	FL	FAC	LC	FC	FL	FAC	LC	FC
1958–59	1	–	–	–	1	–	–	–
1959–60	4	–	–	–	1	–	–	–
1960–61	24	1	3	–	9	–	3	–
1961–62	34	1	–	–	20	2	–	–
1962–63	40	4	–	–	35	2	–	–
1963–64	35	2	1	–	17	2	–	–
1964–65	33	5	7	–	15	4	6	–
1965–66	26	6	–	10	16	5	–	2
1966–67	36	7	3	–	21	6	1	–
1967–68	24	5	1	–	12	3	–	–
1968–69	36(2)	5	3	4	17	1	–	1
1969–70	5(2)	–	–	–	–	–	–	–
Total	298(4)	36	18	14	164	25	10	3

The most prolific goalscorer in Chelsea's history, his total of 202 being more than fifty ahead of his nearest rivals, Roy Bentley and Peter Osgood. Also, only Jimmy Greaves (41) has ever bettered his 35 League goals in the Second Division promotion season of 1962–63. First came to Chelsea as a 15-year-old junior in July 1957 and made his senior debut, aged 17, scoring a goal against West Ham United in front of a crowd of over 52,000. Bobby possessed great speed and acceleration, qualities which, allied to his accurate shooting – especially with his left foot – brought him a regular harvest of goals. He scored 5 times in the away fixture against Aston Villa in September 1966 and 4 times on four separate occasions. After his move to Crystal Palace he returned to Chelsea to be presented with an illuminated address to commemorate his outstanding feats of scoring goals throughout his remarkable Chelsea career.

TAYLOR, Frederick (1909–1920) Wing-half

Born Rotherham Height 5ft 8½ins, Weight 12st 5lb. Career Gainsborough Trinity, Chelsea (1909), Brentford (July 1919)
Honours Football League XI (1 appearance), FA Cup losers' medal 1915
Chelsea details Debut 25.12.09. 171 Appearances 4 Goals

	Appearances		Goals	
	FL	FAC	FL	FAC
1909–10	20	2	1	–
1910–11	14	–	–	–
1911–12	27	2	2	–
1912–13	32	3	–	–
1913–14	31	1	1	–
1914–15	31	8	–	–
Total	155	16	4	–

A strong wing-half who was especially noted for his speed. He became a cornerstone of the Chelsea defence in the seasons leading up to World War I, which ended his first-team career – apart from isolated games made in the 'regional' football played during the hostilities. In recognition of his loyal service to the club he was granted a benefit in 1920 which realised £120.

TENNANT, Albert E. (1934–1953) Inside-forward/Wing-half/Full-back

Born: Ilkeston 29.10.17 Died: 1986. Height 5ft 9in, Weight 12st.
Career: Stanton Iron Works, Chelsea (November 1934), Retired May 1953
Chelsea details Debut 5.1.46. 8 Appearances

	Appearances		Goals	
	FL	FAC	FL	FAC
1945–46	–	6	–	–
1946–47	1	–	–	–
1948–49	1	–	–	–
Total	2	6	–	–

FREDERICK TAYLOR

ALBERT E. TENNANT

ALBERT E. THAIN

It was only during World War II that he blossomed into a valuable first-team player, albeit in the less demanding climate of "regional football". He had been unable to break through previously appearing in the reserve and "A" teams, as an inside-forward, in the five seasons leading up to the war. Then, he played no fewer than 148 "unofficial" games, first at wing-half and latterly as a most dependable full-back. Injury struck him down early in the 1946–47 season and he played little football thereafter, becoming Coach in 1953 before, finally leaving Stamford Bridge to take over as Manager of Guildford City in the summer of 1959.

THAIN, Albert E. (1922–1931) Inside-forward

Born: Southall. Height 5ft 9in, Weight 10st 3lb.
Career: Metropolitan Railway, Southall, Chelsea (April 1922), Bornemouth & Boscombe Athletic (Summer 1931).
Chelsea details Debut 30.9.33. 153 Appearances, 50 Goals

	Appearances		Goals	
	FL	FAC	FL	FAC
1922–23	9	–	–	–
1923–24	6	–	1	–
1924–25	2	–	–	–
1925–26	32	1	15	1
1926–27	39	5	14	5
1927–28	31	–	10	–
1928–29	23	3	4	–
1929–30	2	–	–	–
Total	144	9	44	6

A clever ball player with a long-striding run which frequently took him clear of all opposition to score a regular supply of goals. Having learnt his football with a local railway works team, he jokingly said he chose Chelsea as his professional club because he could listen to the underground trains passing during games at Stamford Bridge which made him feel at home. Injury abbreviated a fine career, after which this loyal clubman would often pay his fare to support his team at away matches.

THOMAS, Michael R. (1984–85) Midfield

Born: Mochdre 7.7.54. Height 5ft 6in, Weight 10st 7lb
Career: Wrexham, Manchester United, Everton, Brighton & Hove Albion, Stoke City, Chelsea (January 1984, £75,000), West Bromwich Albion (September 1985, £100,000), Derby County (loan)
Honours: Wales (51 caps), Wales Under-23 (2 caps), F.A. Cup losers's medal 1979, Third Division Championship medal 1978, Second Division Championship medal 1984
Chelsea details Debut 14.1.84. 53(1) Appearances, 11 Goals

	Appearances			Goals		
	FL	FAC	LC	FL	FAC	LC
1983–84	17	–	–	4	–	–
1984–85	26(1)	3	7	5	–	2
Total	43(1)	3	7	9	–	2

A vital signing midway through the 1983–84 Second Division Championship season. An ebbulient left-sided midfield player, or winger, he was very fast, extremely tenacious and determined both as defender and attacker. After a somewhat chequered career he quickly settled at Stamford Bridge, became one of the most popular players the club has had, and it was a matter of some concern amongst supporters when he was allowed to leave.

THOMPSON, James W. (1927–1929) Forward

Born: West Ham. Height 5ft 11in, Weight 12st 1lb
Career: Millwall, Coventry City, Luton Town, Chelsea (May 1927), Norwich City (Summer 1929)
Chelsea details Debut 27.8.27. 42 Appearances, 34 Goals

MICHAEL R. THOMAS	JAMES W. THOMPSON

CHARLES R. THOMSON

	Appearances		Goals	
	FL	FAC	FL	FAC
1927–28	29	1	25	–
1928–29	8	4	8	1
Total	37	5	33	1

Came to Chelsea having played mainly as a left-winger, but, once at Stamford Bridge, he was converted into a highly successful centre-forward. Indeed no other player in the club's history can match his goal "average" over a comparable number of games. Most surprisingly, he was dropped at the start of his second season, returned briefly to score a few more goals, and was then allowed to leave the following summer. Despite such outstanding feats of goalscoring he is perhaps even better remembered as the scout who unearthed so much youthful talent for Chelsea, particularly from the East End of London, during the years after World War II.

THOMSON, Charles R. (1952–1957) Goalkeeper

Born: Perth 2.3.30. Height 5ft 11in, Weight 12st
Career: Clyde, Chelsea (October 1952), Nottingham Forest (August 1957)
Honours: F.A. Cup winners' medal 1959, Football League Championship medal 1955
Chelsea details Debut 26.12.52. 59 Appearances

	Appearances		Goals	
	FL	FAC	FL	FAC
1952–53	15	7	–	–
1953–54	7	1	–	–
1954–55	16	2	–	–
1955–56	8	3	–	–
Total	46	13	–	–

"Chick" was a sound and reliable 'keeper who shared the duties of guarding Chelsea's net with Bill Robertson for four seasons, playing an especially valuable role in the 1954–55 Championship season. His father had also been a professional goalkeeper in the Scottish League.

THOMSON, James (1965–1968) Defender

Born: Provenside, Glasgow 1.10.46. Height 5ft 10½in, Weight 11st 3lb
Career: Provenside Hibernian, Chelsea (January 1965), Burnley (September 1968, £40,000)
Chelsea details Debut: 4.5.66. 40(7) Appearances, 1 Goal

	Appearances			Goals		
	FL	FAC	FC	FL	FAC	FC
1965–66	2	–	–	–	–	–
1966–67	21(4)	3	1	1	–	–
1967–68	10(2)	2(1)	1	–	–	–
Total	33(6)	5(1)	2	1	–	–

A reliable defender who was in, or on the verge of, the first-team during his three and a half years on the staff, playing in any of the defensive positions. Unable to claim a regular spot, he moved on to Burnley where he went on to play over 300 senior games.

THOMSON, Robert J. (1911–1922) Centre-forward

Born: Croydon. Height 5ft 6in, Weight 11st
Career: Croydon Common, Chelsea (September 1911), Charlton Athletic (March 1922)
Honours: F.A. Cup losers' medal 1915
Chelsea details Debut: 21.10.11. 95 Appearances, 29 Goals

	Appearances		Goals	
	FL	FAC	FL	FAC
1911–12	21	2	7	–
1912–13	10	–	1	–
1913–14	9	–	1	–
1914–15	30	8	12	6
1920–21	13	2	2	–
Total	83	12	23	6

ROBERT J. THOMSON

JAMES THOMSON

SIDNEY TICKRIDGE

He succeeded George Hilsdon as first-team centre-forward yet was rarely assured of a permanent place during more than seven "normal" seasons with the club, interrupted by World War I. He is, perhaps, remembered for two reasons not directly connected with his performances on the field. First, he was renowned for having only one eye ("I just shut the other one and play from memory", he once said), and, secondly he played in the F.A. Cup final even though the famous amateur, Vivian Woodward (normally first-choice) was unexpectedly available, having been given leave from his duties in the Army. Having played in every cup-tie up to the final, Woodward, sportingly, insisted that Bob should play.

TICKRIDGE, Sidney (1951–1955) Full-back

Born: Stepney 10,4.23. Height 5ft 10in, Weight 11st 11lb
Career: Tottenham Hotspur, Chelsea (March 1951), Brentford (July 1955)
Honours: England Schoolboy International
Chelsea details Debut: 23.3.51, 73 Appearances

	Appearances		Goals	
	FL	FAC	FL	FAC
1950–51	8	–	–	–
1951–52	41	8	–	–
1952–53	12	4	–	–
Total	61	12	–	–

Came to Chelsea after fifteen years on the Tottenham staff which he had joined, as an amateur, in 1936. Although he played only one full season in the first-team, he proved an excellent signing, first in lending stability to a suspect defence and, secondly, in doing the same job in the reserve team where his experience helped the younger players.

TINDALL, Ronald A.E. (1953–1961) Centre-forward/Full-back

Born: Streatham 23.9.35. Height 5ft 10in, Weight 10st 9lb
Career: Camberley Wanderers, Chelsea (April 1953), West Ham United (November 1961, part-exchange Andy Malcolm), Reading, Portsmouth
Honours: Football League XI (1 appearance)
Chelsea details Debut 12.11.55. 174 Appearances, 70 Goals

	Appearances				Goals			
	FL	FAC	LC	FC	FL	FAC	LC	FC
1955–56	15	3	–	–	7	1	–	–
1956–57	26	1	–	–	10	–	–	–
1957–58	36	2	–	–	16	1	–	–
1958–59	29	2	–	2	13	–	–	–
1959–60	24	–	–	–	6	–	–	–
1960–61	25	1	3	–	16	–	–	–
1961–62	5	–	–	–	–	–	–	–
Total	160	9	3	2	68	2	–	–

Tall, speedy centre-forward who turned professional after working in the Chelsea F.C. offices. Spotted by Ted Drake, he was an industrious player, strong in the air, who in the latter part of his time played almost exclusively at full-back. In emergency he could also perform creditably in goal. Played over 400 senior games in his career, scoring almost a century of goals. From 1956 to 1966 he played 172 games for Surrey C.C.C. and was a most useful all-rounder.

TOOMER, James (1905–1906) Forward

Career: Chelsea (Amateur, Summer 1905), Southampton (Amateur, Summer 1906)
Chelsea details Debut: 18.11.05. 1 Appearance

	Appearances		Goals	
	FL	FAC	FL	FAC
1906–06	–	1	–	–
Total	1	–	–	–

One of the large squad of players signed for Chelsea inaugural season of 1905–06, he played regularly in the reserve team but made only one first-team appearance, in an F.A. Cup tie when the recognised first choice players were fulfilling a League fixture.

RONALD A.E. TINDALL

WANTED
If anyone has
a photograph
of
JAMES
It would be appreciated if you
would allow us to copy it.
Please forward it to Ron at
36 Lockier Walk,
Wembley, Middx.
It will be returned safely

JAMES TOOMER

JOHN E. TOWNROW

PETER G. TUCK

TOWNROW, John E. (1927–1932) Centre-half

Born: London. Height 5ft 11½in, Weight 13st 7lb
Career: Clapton Orient, Chelsea (February 1927), Bristol Rovers (Summer 1932)
Honours: England (2 caps), England Schoolboy International
Chelsea details Debut: 26.2.27. 140 Appearances, 3 Goals

	Appearances		Goals	
	FL	FAC	FL	FAC
1926–27	9	–	–	–
1927–28	25	1	–	–
1928–29	41	4	2	–
1929–30	14	–	–	–
1930–31	27	5	1	–
1931–32	14	–	–	–
Total	130	10	3	–

Already an international player when he signed for Chelsea, Jack was one of the most capable and respected centre-halves of his time. Very much an "attacking" pivot by nature, he was forced to change his game once the new offside law was introduced, although he always enjoyed moving upfield when given the opportunity. He was a fine tackler, very strong in the air and with the ability to use the ball constructively. His Chelsea career was hampered by injuries but he was an important member of the 1929–30 promotion team and he also helped to establish the side in the First Division the following season.

TUCK, Peter G. (1951–1954) Inside-forward

Born: Plaistow 14.5.32. Height 5ft 8in, Weight 10st 6lb
Career: Chelsea (May 1951), Retired 1954.
Chelsea details Debut: 20.10.51. 3 Appearances, 1 Goal

	Appearances		Goals	
	FL	FAC	FL	FAC
1951–52	3	–	1	–
Total	3	–	1	–

Signing professional after graduating from the Chelsea Juniors, any hopes of a successful career were dashed when he broke his leg and never played serious football again.

TURNBULL, James (1912–1913) Inside/Centre-forward

Born: Bannockburn. Height 5ft 10in, Weight 12st 11lb
Career: Falkirk, East Stirlingshire, Falkirk, Dundee, Glasgow Rangers, Preston North End, Leyton, Manchester United, Bradford, Chelsea (Summer 1912)
Honours: Football League championship medal 1908
Chelsea details Debut: 2.9.12. 22 Appearances, 8 Goals

	Appearances		Goals	
	FL	FAC	FL	FAC
1912–13	19	2	8	–
1913–14	1	–	–	–
Total	20	2	8	–

One of the best-known centre forwards of his day, he was considered most unlucky never to have won international honours. A contemporary writing of him said that in 1907–08 when he led Manchester United's championship winning forward line he gave "one of the finest expositions of centre-forward play we have seen in the present decade". His season at Chelsea came at the end of his long career, but was instrumental in helping the club to avoid relegation.

TURNBULL, Robert (1925–1928) Centre-forward

Born: Dumbarton. Height 5ft 8in, Weight 11st 7lb
Career: Arsenal, Charlton Athletic, Chelsea (February 1925), Clapton Orient (March 1928)
Chelsea details Debut: 7.2.25. 87 Appearances, 58 Goals

	Appearances		Goals	
	FL	FAC	FL	FAC
1924–25	9	–	3	–
1925–26	36	2	29	1
1926–27	32	5	17	6
1927–28	3	–	2	–
Total	80	7	51	7

Was signed in order to solve Chelsea's scoring "famine" during their first season after relegation from Division I and this he did with great success, achieving one of the best scoring "ratios" of any player in the club's history. Lost his place to Jimmy Thompson early in the 1927–28 season. A whole-hearted and enthusiastic player he was skilful with a strong shot from either foot.

JAMES TURNBULL

ROBERT TURNBULL

WANTED
If anyone has
a photograph
of
EDWARD
It would be appreciated if you
would allow us to copy it.
Please forward it to Ron at
36 Lockier Walk,
Wembley, Middx.
It will be returned safely

EDWARD TYE

FRANK UPTON

TYE, Edward (1914–1915) Full-back
Career: Chelsea 1914–15
Chelsea details Debut: 28.12.14. 1 Appearance

	Appearances		Goals	
	FL	FAC	FL	FAC
1914–15	1	–	–	–
Total	1	–	–	–

A diminutive full-back whose speed unfortunately did not compensate for his slight physique. Played consistently well for the reserves in the last season before the outbreak of World War I but was never able to displace either Bettridge or Harrow.

UPTON, Frank (1961–1965) Wing-half
Born: Ainsley Hill 18.10.34. Height 6ft, Weight 13st 4lb
Career: Nuneaton, Northampton Town, Derby County, Chelsea (August 1961, £15,000 – contract cancelled, September 1965), Derby County, Notts County, Worcester City, Workington
Chelsea details Debut: 19.8.61. 86 Appearances, 3 Goals

	Appearances			Goals		
	FL	FAC	LC	FL	FAC	LC
1961–62	10	–	–	–	–	–
1962–63	37	4	–	3	–	–
1963–64	24	3	–	–	–	–
1964–65	3	1	4	–	–	–
Total	74	8	4	3	–	–

A strongly-built, hard-tackling wing-half who played a crucial part in the 1962-63 promotion team. In his long career he played nearly 400 League games and was Player-Manager of Workington for a brief period. Later he returned to the Stamford Bridge coaching staff and was also associated in a similar capacity at Aston Villa, Wolverhampton Wanderers and Coventry City.

VENABLES, Terry (1960–1966) Midfield

Born: Bethnal Green 6.1.43. Height 5ft 8½in, Weight 11st 6lb
Career: Chelsea (August 1960), Tottenham Hotspur (May 1966, £80,000), Queens Park Rangers, Crystal Palace
Honours: England (2 caps), England Under-23 (4 caps), England Schoolboy, Youth & Amateur International, Football League XI (1 Appearance), Football League Cup winners' medal 1966, F.A. Cup winners' medal 1967
Chelsea details Debut: 6.2.60. 237 Appearances, 31 Goals

	Appearances				Goals			
	FL	FAC	LC	FC	FL	FAC	LC	FC
1959–60	1	–	–	–	–	–	–	–
1960–61	36	1	3	–	–	–	–	–
1961–62	12	–	–	–	1	–	–	–
1962–63	42	4	–	–	2	1	–	–
1963–64	38	3	–	–	8	–	–	–
1964–65	39	5	5	–	7	–	1	–
1965–66	34	6	–	8	8	–	–	3
Total	202	19	8	8	26	1	1	3

The only player to have represented England at five different international levels. Arrived at The Bridge as a 15-year old in 1958-59 to develop into an outstanding midfield player, strong in the tackle and a brilliant passer of the ball. He was in the 1962–63 Second Division promotion side and in the teams which then went on to finish 5th, 3rd and 5th, again, in the first three seasons back in the top class. After his playing career ended he managed Crystal Palace, Queens Park Rangers and Barcelona.

TERRY VENABLES

COLIN VILJOEN   ANDREW M. WALKER

VILJOEN, Colin (1980–1982) Midfield

Born Johannesburg (South Africa) 20.6.48. Height 5ft 9in, Weight 11st 8lb
Career South African football, Ipswich Town, Manchester City, Chelsea (March 1980, £60,000), Contract cancelled May 1982
Honours England (2 caps), Second Division Championship medal 1968
Chelsea details Debut 15.3.80 22(1) Appearances

	Appearances			Goals		
	FL	FAC	LC	FL	FAC	LC
1979–80	4	–	–	–	–	–
1980–81	6(1)	–	1	–	–	–
1981–82	9	–	2	–	–	–
Total	19(1)	–	3	–	–	–

South African player who adopted British nationality in 1971. After a distinguished career he arrived at Chelsea, aged 31, but never fitted into the scheme of things and seemed not to possess the necessary motivation. As a result his appearances were isolated and his place never assured.

WALKER, Andrew M. (1913–1920) Half-back

Born Dalkeith. Height 5ft 10½st, Weight 12st 7lb
Career Dundee, Chelsea (May 1913), Newport County
Honours F.A. Cup Final losers' medal 1915
Chelsea details Debut 13.9.13 23 Appearances 2 Goals

	Appearances		Goals	
	FL	FAC	FL	FAC
1913–14	3	–	2	–
1914–15	12	5	–	–
1919–20	3	–	–	–
Total	18	5	2	–

Something of a utility player, he played in a variety of positions from centre-forward, where he made his debut after the team had been stricken with a mystery illness en route to their away fixture at Oldham, to full-back. Never a regular first teamer, his career was interrupted by World War I when he might have had a chance of establishing himself. His main claim to fame was playing at left-half for Chelsea in the 1915 F.A. Cup final.

WALDRON, Colin (1967) Centre-half

Born Bristol 22.6.48. Height 6f6, Weight 12st 8lb
Career Bury, Chelsea (June 1967, £25,000), Burnley (October 1967, £30,000), Manchester United, Sunderland, Rochdale
Chelsea details Debut 19.8.67 10 Appearances

	Appearances			Goals		
	FL	FAC	LC	FL	FAC	LC
1967–68	9	–	1	–	–	–
Total	9	–	1	–	–	–

This tall fair-haired centre-half spent an unhappy four months at Stamford Bridge, failing to find his form and not settling in London. Moving to Burnley he went on to play more than 300 League games for the Lancastrians in a nine-year stay with the club.

WALKER, Clive (1975–1984) Winger

Born Oxford 26.5.57. Height 5ft 8½, Weight 11st 4lb
Career Chelsea (March 1975), Sunderland (July 1984, £75,000), Queens Park Rangers
Honours: England Schoolboy International
Chelsea details Debut 19.4.77 191(33) Appearances 65 Goals

	Appearances			Goals		
	FL	FAC	LC	FL	FAC	LC
1976–77	0(1)	–	–	–	–	–
1977–78	21(2)	4	–	7	3	–
1978–79	23(7)	1	1	4	–	–
1979–80	29(7)	1	1	13	–	–
1980–81	35(2)	1	1(1)	11	–	–
1981–82	31(5)	7	2	16	–	1
1982–83	23(6)	0(2)	2	6	–	–
1983–84	6	–	2	3	–	1
Total	168(30)	14(2)	9(1)	60	3	2

A speedy striker down either flank, or in the centre of the attack, his flair for scoring spectacular goals made him an exciting player. Particularly remembered was his long-range effort at Bolton which staved off relegation to the Third Division at the end of the 1982–83 season. At times an unpredictable and erratic performer, he was playing the most consistently good football of his career when injury caused him to drop out of the first-team and, unable to regain his place, he was soon transferred, while still in his prime.

COLIN WALDRON

CLIVE WALKER

JOSEPH WALTON

WALKER, Thomas (1946–1948) Inside-forward
Born Livingstone Station 26.5.15. Height 5ft 9in, Weight 11st 7lb
Career Berryburn Rangers, Livingstone Violet, Broxburn Rangers, Heart of Midlothian, Chelsea (September 1946 £6,000), Heart of Midlothian (December 1948, Player/Assistant Manager)
Honours Scotland (20 caps), Scottish League XI (5 appearances), Scottish Schoolboy International.
Chelsea details Debut 9.9.46 104 Appearances 24 Goals

	Appearances		Goals	
	FL	FAC	FL	FAC
1946–47	39	5	9	1
1947–48	37	2	7	–
1948–49	21	–	7	–
Total	97	7	23	1

One of the most famous players ever to wear the Chelsea shirt. Known as one of soccer's gentlemen, he had "guested" for the club during World War II and his permanent signing, albeit in the autumn of his career, was a great coup. During his two and a half seasons at Stamford Bridge he delighted crowds with his marvellous skills and ball control – his dribbling being one of his greatest assets. At one time destined for a career in the church he attached himself to a London Boys' Club and won great respected and affection during his time in London. He later became manager of Hearts, Dunfermline Athletic and Raith Rovers before joining the Board of Directors with his first professional club, Heart of Midlothian.

WALTON, Joseph (1906–1911) Full-back
Career New Brompton, Chelsea (August 1906) Not retained May 1911, Swansea Town
Chelsea details Debut 1.9.06 53 Appearances

	Appearances		Goals	
	FL	FAC	FL	FAC
1906–07	35	–	–	–
1907–08	1	–	–	–
1908–09	12	–	–	–
1909–10	5	–	–	–
Total	53	–	–	–

Playing only one season as undisputed first choice, he was a calm, unruffled defender, respected as a strong tackler and a most reliable player. After suffering an injury in the opening fixture of 1907–08 he lost his place to Jock Cameron and was subsequently unable to regain it on a regular basis.

WARD, Joseph (1920–1922) Half-back

Born Co. Tyrone
Career St. Johnstone, Chelsea (May 1920), Swansea Town (Summer 1922)
Chelsea details Debut 16.10.20 16 Appearances

	Appearances		Goals	
	FL	FAC	FL	FAC
1920–21	12	2	–	–
1921–22	2	–	–	–
Total	14	2	–	–

Having been signed as a centre-half he played most of his football at Stamford Bridge in the wing-half positions. Not the most fortunate of players, injury robbed him of an Irish international cap (v Wales in April 1921) and he was never selected again.

WARREN, Ben (1908–1914) Wing-half

Born Newhall (Derbyshire) Died 1914. Height 5ft 8½in, Weight 12st 8lb
Career Derby County, Chelsea (July 1908–14)
Honours England (22 caps), Football League XI (1 appearance), F.A. Cup losers' medal 1903
Chelsea details Debut 1.9.08 101 Appearances 5 Goals

	Appearances		Goals	
	FL	FAC	FL	FAC
1908–09	34	3	3	1
1909–10	17	–	–	–
1910–11	31	6	1	–
1911–12	10	–	–	–
Total	92	9	4	1

An outstanding right-half whose total of 22 international caps is testimony to his ability, at a time when far fewer games were played at this level, and who died in tragic circumstances when he was still at the height of his career. He was renowned for his fitness and enthusiasm for the game, as well as for his scrupulously fair play. A Benefit Match was played at Stamford Bridge for his dependents in April 1914, between North and South.

JOSEPH WARD

BEN WARREN

ROBERT E. WARREN

IAN WATSON

WARREN, Robert E. (1948–1951) Centre-half

Born Plymouth 8.1.27. Height 6ft, Weight 11st 10lb
Career Plymouth United, Plymouth Argyle, Chelsea (July 1948), Torquay United (August 1951)
Chelsea details Debut 9.4.49 1 Appearance

	Appearances		Goals	
	FL	FAC	FL	FAC
1948–49	1	–	–	–
Total	1	–	–	–

Spent three seasons at Stamford Bridge, playing almost entirely in the reserve and "A" teams, as understudy to John Harris.

WATSON, Ian (1962–1965) Full-back

Born Hammersmith 7.1.44. Height 5ft 11in, Weight 11st 11lb
Career Chelsea (February 1962), Queens Park Rangers (July 1965, £10,000)
Chelsea details Debut 30.1.63 9 Appearances 1 Goal

	Appearances			Goals		
	FL	FAC	LC	FL	FAC	LC
1962–63	1	1	–	–	–	–
1963–64	2	–	–	1	–	–
1964–65	2	–	3	–	–	–
Total	5	1	3	1	–	–

Signed professional after two years as a Chelsea Junior. A well-built full-back who was discovered by Wilf Chitty, the former Chelsea player. Never achieved a permanent place in the first-team but played some 200 senior games after moving to Queens Park Rangers.

WATSON, James (1905–1906) Inside-forward

Born Inverness. Career Sunderland, Chelsea (September 1905), Brentford (Summer 1906)
Chelsea details Debut 9.9.05. 14 Appearances

	Appearances		Goals	
	FL	FAC	FL	FAC
1905–06	13	1	–	–
Total	13	1	–	–

Signed before the start of Chelsea's first season, "Dougal" provided "cover" for Player-Manager Jackie Robertson, and in fact was called upon to play in almost half the games.

WEAVER, Reginald (1929–1932) Centre-forward

Born Radstock (Somerset). Career Newport County, Wolverhampton Wanderers, Chelsea (March 1929), Bradford City (June 1932)
Chelsea details Debut 13.3.29. 20 Appearances 8 Goals

	Appearances		Goals	
	FL	FAC	FL	FAC
1928–29	11	–	4	–
1929–30	8	–	4	–
1931–32	1	–	–	–
Total	20	–	8	–

Noted for his speed (he was a Powderhall sprinter), he had been top goalscorer with the Wolves in 1928–29 and, in his restricted opportunities, found the net with regularity at Stamford Bridge. But with George Mills already on the staff, and the signing of Hughie Gallacher shortly after his arrival, he was allowed to move on after two full seasons.

JAMES WATSON

REGINALD WEAVER

| SAMUEL WEAVER | DAVID WEBB |

WEAVER, Samuel (1936–1945) Wing-half

Born Pilsley (Derbyshire) 8.2.09 Died 15.4.85. Height 5ft 9in, Weight 11st 7lb. Career Pilsley, Sutton Town, Hull City, Newcastle United, Chelsea (August 1936, £,6000), Stockport County (December 1945)
Honours England (3 caps), F.A. Cup winners' medal 1932
Chelsea details Debut 29.8.36. 125 Appearances 4 Goals

	Appearances		Goals	
	FL	FAC	FL	FAC
1936–37	38	2	3	–
1937–38	39	1	1	–
1938–39	39	6	–	–
Total	116	9	4	–

He was the automatic choice for the left-half position in the three seasons immediately before World War II, and was first-team captain in 1938–39. He was a stylish player and the first to develop the tactical use of the long throw (once measured to be 35 yards), now fairly commonplace in the game. After the war had virtually ehded his playing career he was a coach with both Leeds United and Millwall before being associated with Mansfield Town as Coach, Manager, Trainer and Scout. In addition he was Masseur to Derbyshire C.C.C. for many years, having played two matches for Somerset as a left-hand batsman in 1939.

WEBB, David (1968–1974) Defender

Born Stratford 9.4.46. Height 6ft, Weight 12st 13lb. Career West Ham United (amateur), Leyton Orient, Southampton, Chelsea (February 1968, £40,000/part exchange Joe Kirkup), Queens Park Rangers (May 1974, £100,000), Leicester City, Derby County, A.F.C Bournemouth (Player-Manager).
Honours F.A. Cup winners' medal 1970, European Cup Winners Cup winners' medal 1971, Football League Cup losers' medal 1972
Chelsea details Debut 2.3.68 299 Appearances 33 Goals

	Appearances					Goals				
	FL	FAC	LC	FC	ECWC	FL	FAC	LC	FC	ECWC
1967–68	13	–	–	–	–	–	–	–	–	–
1968–69	42	5	3	4	–	6	2	–	–	–
1969–70	35	8	3	–	–	4	3	–	–	–
1970–71	34	3	4	–	10	4	–	1	–	1
1971–72	41	3	9	–	4	4	1	1	–	2
1972–73	26	2	7	–	–	2	–	1	–	–
1973–74	39	2	1	–	–	1	–	–	–	–
Total	230	23	27	4	14	21	6	3	–	3

(Appearances also include 1 F.A. Charity Shield, 1970–71)

Wrote his name into the Chelsea F.C. history book by scoring the winning goal against Leeds United in the F.A. Cup final replay in April 1970. A strong defensive player whose enthusiasm for the game was a spur and morale-booster to those playing around him, his versatility saw him wearing every shirt on the field, with the exception of number 11. His emergency appearance as goalkeeper, v Ipswich Town on Boxing Day 1971 (when he kept a clean sheet), typified his value to the club.. After his playing career ended he managed A.F.C. Bournemouth, Torquay United and Southend United.

WEGERLE, Roy (1986–   )

Born: Johannesburg (South Africa) 19.3.64
Career Tampa Bay Rowdies, Chelsea (July 1986, £75,000)
Chelsea details Debut 8.11.86 9(5) Appearances 2 Goals

	Appearances			Goals		
	FL	FAC	FMC	FMC	FL	FAC
1986–87	7(5)	1	1	2	–	–
Total	7(5)	1	1	2	–	–

Brought up in South Africa in a rugby football environment, he joined a local soccer club where he was coached by Roy Bailey, the former Ipswich Town 'keeper. After a brief flirtation with Manchester United he went to U.S.A. to begin a university career and became a professional footballer. Came to Stamford Bridge for two months early in the 1985–86 season, returning to sign professional forms the following summer. A fine natural athlete of great potential as an attacker, both down the flanks or through the middle, he possesses considerable skill and pace – as well as being a strong finisher.

ROY WEGERLE

KEITH WELLER   COLIN WEST

WELLER, Keith (1970-1971) Forward

Born Islington 11.6.46 Height 5ft 10in, Weight 12st 1lb.
Career Tottenham Hotspur, Millwall, Chelsea (May 1970, £100,000) Leicester City (September 1971, £100,000)
Honours England (4 caps), Football League XI, European Cup Winners' Cup winners' medal
Chelsea details Debut 15.8.70 49(5) Appearances 15 Goals

	Appearances				Goals			
	FL	FAC	LC	ECWC	FL	FAC	LC	ECWC
1970–71	32(4)	3	3	8(1)	13	–	1	–
1971–72	2	–	–	–	1	–	–	–
Total	34(4)	3	3	8(1)	14	–	1	–

Appearances also include 1 F.A. Charity Shield, 1971–72.
Having played mainly as a central striker before his arrival at Chelsea he was utilised as an attacker down the right flank, where his speed and strong shooting power were considerable assets. After eight seasons with Leicester City he continued his career in the N.A.S.L.

WEST, Colin (1985–) Striker

Born Middlesbrough 19.9.67 Height 5ft 7in Weight 11st
Career: Chelsea (September 1985)
Honours: England Youth International
Chelsea details Debut 7.3.87 5(2) Appearances 1 Goal

	Appearances		Goals	
	FL	FAC	FL	FAC
1986-87	5(2)	–	1	–
Total	5(2)	–	1	–

Speedy front-runner and regular goalscorer who made a dramatic entry when, after seven months on loan to Partick Thistle in the Scottish First Division, he scored within five minutes of his first-team debut against Arsenal at Stamford Bridge. First arrived at Stamford Bridge as an Apprentice in August 1983.

WHIFFEN, Kingsley (1966–1967)

Born Welshpool 3.12.50
Career Chelsea (1966–67, Apprentice), Plymouth Argyle (1967, Trialist)
Chelsea details Debut 9.6.67 1 Appearance

	Appearances		Goals	
	FL	FAC	FL	FAC
1966–67	1	–	–	–
Total	1	–	–	–

Never signed professional forms, this Welsh junior 'keeper was at Stamford Bridge, for one season only, playing almost entirely for the Juniors. He made no further appearances in the Football League after leaving Chelsea.

WHITE, Alexander (1937-1948) Full-back

Born Armadale (West Lothian) 28.1.16 Height 5ft 7in Weight 11st 10lb.
Career Bonnyrigg Rose, Chelsea (February 1937), Swindon Town (July 1948), Southport
Chelsea details Debut 14.9.46 18 Appearances

	Appearances		Goals	
	FL	FAC	FL	FAC
1946–47	13	1	–	–
1947–48	4	–	–	–
Total	17	1	–	–

One of the many players whose career was disrupted by the Second World War. A solid defender, he made two appearances for Scotland v England in Army internationals during the hostilities, in which he served as a Sergeant-Instructor.

KINGSLEY WHIFFEN

ALEXANDER WHITE

| BEN WHITEHOUSE | ROBERT WHITING |

WHITEHOUSE, Ben (1906–1908) Inside-forward

Career Bilston, Chelsea (November 1906), Stockport County (Sumer 1908)
Chelsea details Debut 12.1.07 13 Appearances 2 Goals

	Appearances		Goals	
	FL	FAC	FL	FAC
1906–07	–	2	–	1
1907–08	10	1	1	–
Total	10	3	1	1

Began and ended his football career in the Birmingham League, his chief claim to fame in his time at Chelsea was to score the fastest-ever recorded goal by the club – in 13 seconds, against Blackburn Rovers on December 2nd 1907.

WHITING, Robert (1906–1908) Goalkeeper

Born West Ham Height 5ft 11in, Weight 13st 12lb
Career Tunbridge Wells Rangers, Chelsea (Summer 1906), Brighton & Hove Albion (Summer 1908)
Chelsea details Debut 28.4.06 54 Appearances

	Appearances		Goals	
	FL	FAC	FL	FAC
1905–06	1	–	–	–
1906–07	36	2	–	–
1907–08	15	–	–	–
Total	52	2	–	–

Saddled with the unenviable task of taking over from Willie Foulke, Bob (or "Pom Pom" as he was affectionately known) played a sterling part in the club's first promotion season of 1906–07. Noted for the enormous length of his kicking, he lost his place to Jack Whitley at Christmas 1907 and never played for the first-team again. He then played regularly for Brighton & Hove Albion, in the Southern League, for the seven seasons leading up to the outbreak of World War I.

WHITLEY, Jack (1907–1914) Goalkeeper

Career Darwen, Aston Villa, Everton, Stoke City, Leeds City, Lincoln City, Chelsea (Summer 1907), Retired 1914.
Chelsea details Debut 23.9.07 138 Appearances

	Appearances		Goals	
	FL	FAC	FL	FAC
1907–08	23	2	–	–
1908–09	36	3	–	–
1909–10	35	2	–	–
1910–11	1	2	–	–
1911–12	26	2	–	–
1912–13	3	–	–	–
1913–14	3	–	–	–
Total	127	11	–	–

As player and trainer he was a part of the Chelsea scene for 32 years. He was a sound and competent goalkeeper who shared the custodian's duties with Jim Molyneux for most of that time, his best season being the promotion year of 1911–12. However, it is perhaps as Head Trainer that he is best remembered. A father figure to generations of Chelsea players, he retained that post from 1914 to May 1939 and his energetic dashes on to the field, bald-headed and coat-tails flapping, were very much part of the Chelsea scene during the inter-war years.

WHITTAKER, Richard (1952–1960) Full-back

Born Dublin 10.10.34 Height 5ft 9in, Weight 11st.
Career: St Mary's B.C. (Dublin), Chelsea (May 1952), Peterborough United (July 1960), Queens Park Rangers
Honours Republic of Ireland (1 cap), Republic of Ireland Under-23 (1 cap), Irish Schoolboy International
Chelsea details Debut 28.4.56 51 Appearances

JACK WHITLEY

RICHARD WHITTAKER

ROBERT WHITTINGHAM

	Appearances			Goals		
	FL	FAC	FC	FL	FAC	FC
1955–56	1	–	–	–	–	–
1956–57	11	1	–	–	–	–
1957–58	12	–	–	–	–	–
1958–59	16	–	2	–	–	–
1959–60	8	–	–	–	–	–
Total	48	1	2	–	–	–

Signed professional after joining the Chelsea groundstaff. This compactly-built full-back remained on the fringe of a regular first-team place for five seasons, usually coming in as deputy for one of the Sillett brothers, before seeking his fortunes in the lower divisions.

WHITTINGHAM, Robert (1909–1919) Inside/Centre-forward

Born Goldenhill Died 1919. Height 5ft 8in, Weight 12st 1lb.
Career Blackpool, Bradford City, Chelsea (April 1909, £1,300), Stoke City (September 1919)
Chelsea details Debut 16.4.10 129 Appearances 80 Goals.

	Appearances		Goals	
	FL	FAC	FL	FAC
1909–10	3	–	1	–
1910–11	38	5	30	4
1911–12	32	2	26	–
1912–13	20	3	7	5
1913–14	20	–	6	–
1919–20	6	–	1	–
Total	119	10	71	9

This bustling, vigorous, well-built forward was renowned for his powerful shooting and he became a scourge of goalkeepers – "I'd rather face his Satanic Majesty than Whittingham", one was said to have remarked. Many of his goals came from long-range efforts, and he delighted in picking up loose balls in midfield and setting off on lightning dashes towards goal. He played in one "victory" international for England against Scotland in 1919 and died soon after his transfer to Stoke City, later that year.

WHITTON, William A. (1923–1926) Centre-forward

Born Aldershot Height 5ft 8½in, Weight 10st 10lb
Career Tottenham Hotspur, Chelsea (March 1923), Contract Cancelled (April 1926)
Chelsea details Debut 17.3.23 39 Appearances 19 Goals.

	Appearances		Goals	
	FL	FAC	FL	FAC
1922–23	6	–	2	–
1923–24	10	–	1	–
1924–25	22	1	16	–
Total	38	1	19	–

One of several players brought to Stamford Bridge in an attempt to solve the goalscoring "famine", and keep the club in the First Division. Having failed to do either of these things, he scored regularly in Division II in the first part of the 1924–25 season before losing his form and deciding to give up the game and take up a business career.

WICKS, M. Stanley (1954–56) Centre-half

Born Reading 11.7.28 Died February 1983. Height 6ft 2½in, Weight 13st 3lb.
Career Reading, Chelsea (January 1954, £10,500), Retired through injury (1956)
Honours England "B" (1 cap), Football League XI (1 Appearance), Football League Championship medal
Chelsea details Debut 6.11.54 81 Appearances 1 Goal

	Appearances		Goals	
	FL	FAC	FL	FAC
1954–55	21	3	1	–
1955–56	42	6	–	–
1956–57	8	–	–	–
Total	71	9	1	–

Appearances also include 1 F.A. Charity Shield, 1955–56.
This tall, dominating centre-half followed manager Ted Drake to Stamford Bridge from Reading, having already played nearly 200 first-team games for the Berkshire club in Division III (South). Making the transition to the higher class of football with ease, he took over the centre-half spot from Ron Greenwood in the second half of the League Championship season, won representative honours and just when, even at the age of 28, a full England cap seemed within his reach he was cruelly struck down by a knee injury and never played football again.

WILLIAM A. WHITTON

STANLEY M. WICKS

STEPHEN J. WICKS

WICKS, Stephen J. (1974–1979 & 1986–   ) Centre-half

Born Reading 3.10.56 Height 6ft 2in, Weight 13st 2lb
Career Chelsea (May 1974), Derby County (January 1979, £275,000), Queens Park Rangers, Chelsea (July 1986, £450,000)
Honours England Under-21 International (1 cap), England Youth International, Second Division Championship medal 1983, Football League Cup losers' medal 1986
Chelsea details Debuts 31.3.75 & 23.8.86 144(1) Appearances 8 Goals

	Appearances			Goals		
	FL	FAC	LC	FL	FAC	LC
1974–75	1	–	–	–	–	–
1975–76	18(1)	4	–	–	1	–
1976–77	34	–	2	4	–	–
1977–78	41	2	–	–	1	–
1978–79	23	–	1	1	–	–
1986–87	15	2	1	1	–	–
Total	132(1)	8	4	6	2	–

Like his namesake, Stan, a giant and powerful centre-half from the same place of birth. Graduated to professional from the ranks of the Juniors and was a first-team regular at the age of 19. Dominant in the air and firm in the tackle, with a strong left foot, he was a member of the 1976–77 Second Division promotion team, moving, briefly, to the Midlands with Derby County the following year. Returned to Stamford Bridge over seven years later – at a new record fee for a player signed by Chelsea F.C.

WILDING, Harry T. (1914–1928) Centre-forward/Centre-half

Born Wolverhampton Height 6ft 1in, Weight 12st 12lb.
Career Chelsea (April 1914), Tottenham Hotspur (November 1928), Bristol Rovers
Chelsea details Debut 20.8.19 265 Appearances 25 Goals

	Appearances		Goals	
	FL	FAC	FL	FAC
1919–20	35	4	4	1
1920–21	40	8	3	1
1921–22	29	1	–	–
1922–23	29	2	3	–
1923–24	39	2	4	–
1924–25	17	–	1	–
1925–26	19	2	2	–
1926–27	16	5	1	1
1927–28	17	–	4	–
Total	241	24	22	3

His career was interrupted by the outbreak of World War I before he had played in the first team. But having won the Military Medal whilst serving with the Coldstream Guards, he returned to become a pillar of the side in the immediate post-war period. First at centre, or inside, forward, but more permanently at centre-half he was a dominating figure, possessing clever ball skills as well as being a fine header of the ball. Greatly respected by his fellow professionals, he was noted for his consistency and strength in the tackle.

WILEMAN, Arthur (1909–1911) Inside-forward

Born Newhall (Derbyshire) Killed in Action 1916. Height 5ft 7in, Weight 10st 9lb
Career Burton United, Chelsea (Summer 1909), Luton Town (1911), Millwall
Chelsea details Debut 25.9.09 14 Appearances 5 Goals

	Appearances		Goals	
	FL	FAC	FL	FAC
1909–10	14	–	5	–
Total	14	–	5	–

Was signed, together with his brother, and was soon making an impression in the League side with his clever footwork and ball skills. However, apart from two spells in a season ending with relegation from Division I, he never fulfilled his early promise and the signing of Bob Whittingham finally ended his Chelsea first-team career.

HARRY T. WILDING

ARTHUR WILEMAN

GRAHAM WILKINS	RAYMOND C. WILKINS

WILKINS, Graham C. (1972–1982) Full-back

Born Hillingdon 28.6.55. Height 5ft 6½in, Weight 10st 2lb
Career Chelsea (July 1972), Brentford (Summer 1982, free-transfer)
Chelsea details Debut 26.12.72 148(1) Appearances 1 Goal

	Appearances			Goals		
	FL	FAC	LC	FL	FAC	LC
1972–73	1	–	–	–	–	–
1973–74	4	–	–	–	–	–
1974–75	1	–	–	–	–	–
1975–76	13	–	–	–	–	–
1976–77	26	–	3	–	–	–
1977–78	21	3	–	–	–	–
1978–79	28	1	–	1	–	–
1979–80	18	–	1	–	–	–
1980–81	14	–	2	–	–	–
1981–82	10(1)	1	1	–	–	–
Total	136(1)	5	7	1	–	–

Son of former Brentford player, George Wilkins, he signed professional from the apprentice ranks. A stylish, lightweight, full-back he was rarely assured of his place in the first-team at a time of many comings and goings in the club, and he lacked the consistency, and physique, to become a top class defender.

WILKINS, Raymond C. (1973–1979) Midfield

Born: Hillingdon 14.9.56. Height 5ft 7in, Weight 10st 10lb
Career Chelsea (October 1973), Manchester United (August 1979, £875,000), A.C. Milan
Honours England (84 caps), England Under-23 (2 caps), England Under-21 (1 cap), Football League XI (1 appearance), England Youth International, F.A. Cup winners' medal 1983
Chelsea details Debut 26.10.73 193(5) Appearances 34 Goals

	Appearances			Goals		
	FL	FAC	LC	FL	FAC	LC
1973–74	4(2)	0(1)	–	–	–	–
1974–75	20(1)	2	0(1)	2	–	–
1975–76	42	4	1	11	1	–
1976–77	42	2	3	7	–	2
1977–78	33	3	1	7	1	–
1978–79	35	–	1	3	–	–
Total	176(3)	11(1)	6(1)	30	2	2

Younger brother of Graham, he graduated to full professional status after beginning his Stamford Bridge career as an apprentice in October 1973 and made his senior debut the same month. Immensely gifted central midfield player whose accuracy and range of passing the ball was his trademark. He was Chelsea's youngest-ever captain when appointed in April 1975, aged 18.

WILLEMSE, Stanley B. (1949–1956) Full-back

Born Brighton 23.8.24. Height 5ft 10½in, Weight 11st 9lb
Career Brighton & Hove Albion, Chelsea (July 1949, £6,500), Leyton Orient (June 1956 £4,500)
Honours England "B" (1 cap), Football League XI (1 appearance), England Schoolboy International, Football League Championship medal 1955
Chelsea details Debut 31.8.49 221 Appearances 2 Goals

	Appearances		Goals	
	FL	FAC	FL	FAC
1949–50	18	–	–	–
1950–51	15	–	1	–
1951–52	11	4	–	–
1952–53	39	7	–	–
1953–54	41	1	–	–
1954–55	36	3	1	–
1955–56	38	7	–	–
Total	198	22	2	–

STANLEY B. WILLEMSE

> **WANTED**
> If anyone has a photograph of **ERNEST** It would be appreciated if you would allow us to copy it. Please forward it to Ron at 36 Lockier Walk, Wembley, Middx. It will be returned safely

ERNEST W. WILLIAMS

PAUL WILLIAMS

Appearances also include 1 F.A. Charity Shield, 1955–56
Rugged, fearless, hard-tackling full-back (and useful emergency striker), this one-time Royal Marine was signed to take over from Welsh International Billy Hughes. For seven seasons his whole-hearted enthusiasm endeared him to supporters and he was a vital member of the 1954–55 League Championship side.

WILLIAMS, Ernest W. (1909–1910) Outside-left

Born Ryde (I.o.W.)
Career Chelsea (1909–1910, Amateur), Portsmouth (Amateur)
Chelsea details Debut 18.12.09 8 Appearances 1 Goal

	Appearances		Goals	
	FL	FAC	FL	FAC
1909–10	6	2	–	1
Total	6	2	–	1

This amateur wingman signed forms at the same time as Vivian Woodward, then went straight into the first team, in which he held his place until the middle of February, after which he never played for Chelsea again. He was noted for his speed and direct approach to goal.

WILLIAMS, Paul (1980–1983) Centre-half

Born: Lambeth. Height 6ft, Weight 11st 7lb
Career Chelsea (July 1980), Free transfer May 1983, Leatherhead
Chelsea details Debut 9.4.83 1 Appearance

	Appearances		Goals	
	FL	FAC	FL	FAC
1982–83	1	–	–	–
Total	1	–	–	–

Signed apprentice forms in July 1979 and then spent three years on the staff as a full professional, playing in the junior and reserve teams.

WILLIAMS, Reginald F. (1945–1951) Wing-half/Inside-forward

Born Watford 28.1.22. Height 5ft 11in, Weight 12st 3lb
Career Watford (amateur), Chelsea (October 1945), Retired October 1951
Chelsea details Debut 5.1.46 74 Appearances 17 Goals

	Appearances		Goals	
	FL	FAC	FL	FAC
1945–46	–	6	–	1
1946–47	9	1	2	1
1948–49	13	3	3	1
1949–50	21	4	5	–
1950–51	13	2	3	1
1951–52	2	–	–	–
Total	58	16	13	4

A most talented player whose career was later to be mirrored by Ken Shellito. For much of his six years on the staff he was in hospital, or on the treatment table, fighting a series of injuries which ultimately caused his premature retirement from the game. Well-built and of graceful movement, he was a skilful, yet forceful player either in defence or attack. Called up for the England International squad for the matches against France and Switzerland in 1946, he was destined never to play a full season and his promising career, already retarded by the outbreak of World War II, petered out sadly.

WILLIAMS, William Dennis (1927–1928) Inside-forward

Born Leytonstone. Height 5ft 8in, Weight 11st 6lb
Career Australian Tourists (1925), West Ham United, Chelsea (June 1927), Not retained (May 1928)
Honours England Schoolboy International
Chelsea details Debut 26.12.27. 2 Appearances

	Appearances		Goals	
	FL	FAC	FL	FAC
1927–28	2	–	–	–
Total	2	–	–	–

Apart from deputising for Albert Thain in two games his Chelsea career, limited to one season, consisted of playing in the reserve team.

REGINALD F. WILLIAMS

WILLIAM DENNIS WILLIAMS

ANDREW N. WILSON

WILSON, Andrew N. (1923–1931) Centre/Inside-forward

Born Newmains (Lanarskshire) 14.2.96 Died October 1973. Height 5ft 6½in, Weight 12st 5lb
Career Cambuslang Rangers, Heart of Midlothian, Dunfermline Athletic, Middlesbrough, Chelsea (November 1923, £6,500), Queens Park Rangers (October 1931), Nimes
Honours: Scotland (12 caps)
Chelsea details Debut 1.12.23 253 Appearances, 62 Goals

	Appearances		Goals	
	FL	FAC	FL	FAC
1923–24	19	2	5	1
1924–25	36	1	10	–
1925–26	23	–	7	–
1926–27	24	5	3	2
1927–28	38	1	11	–
1928–29	21	–	9	–
1929–30	39	1	10	–
1930–31	34	5	4	–
1931–32	4	–	–	–
Total	238	15	59	3

One of the most loyal and popular players to have worn the Chelsea shirt. He had already won his 12 Scottish caps before moving to London and it was, indeed, strange that the selectors never recognised him again. At Stamford Bridge he was converted to inside-forward (having previously played almost entirely as leader of the attack), in a "W" formation evolved largely as a result of the change of the offside law. A fine dribbler and passer of the ball, he was a true artist and overcome the handicap of almost totally losing the use of his right arm as a result of an accident in the First World War. Despite this disability he was a fine golfer, billiards and bowls player. After ending his English career with Queens Park Rangers, he moved, briefly, into French football before returning to become Manager of Walsall for a spell. Then he retired to live in London where he was a familiar figure at Stamford Bridge almost up until his death. His son, Jimmy, was on the Chelsea professional staff in the 1950s.

WINDRIDGE, James E. (1905–1911) Inside-forward
Born Sparkbrook (Birmingham) 21.10.82, Died 23.9.39. Height 5ft 7½in, Weight 11st 3lb
Career Small Heath, Chelsea (August 1905, £190), Middlesbrough (November 1911)
Honours England (8 caps)
Chelsea details Debut 2.9.05 152 Appearances 58 Goals

	Appearances		Goals	
	FL	FAC	FL	FAC
1905–06	20	2	16	2
1906–07	31	–	16	–
1907–08	29	2	9	2
1908–09	34	3	6	–
1909–10	23	2	6	–
1910–11	4	–	1	–
1911–12	2	–	–	–
Total	143	9	54	4

Played at inside-left in Chelsea first-ever League fixture and, indeed, outlasted all his colleagues in the team that day by remaining at Stamford Bridge for more than six seasons. Renowned as a "scientific close dribbler", the ball was seemingly glued to his boot, and he was also a good distributor of the ball and a powerful marksman. He was also a county cricketer with Warwickshire C.C.C., playing seven matches between 1909 and 1913, as an all-rounder.

WINTER, Daniel T. (1945–1951) Full-back
Born Tonypandy 14.6.18. Height 5ft 8½in, Weight 11st 1½lb
Career Bolton Wanderers, Chelsea (December 1945, £5,000), Worcester City (Summer 1951)
Chelsea details Debut 5.1.46 155 Appearances

	Appearances		Goals	
	FL	FAC	FL	FAC
1945–46	–	6	–	–
1946–47	41	4	–	–
1947–48	28	2	–	–
1948–49	25	3	–	–
1949–50	32	7	–	–
1950–51	5	2	–	–
Total	131	24	–	–

JAMES E. WINDRIDGE

DANIEL T. WINTER

FRANK WOLFF

DARREN WOOD

Welsh war-time International who had made his League debut for Bolton Wanderers in the 1937–38 season, he first made his mark at Chelsea, as a Bombadier serving in the Army in 1944, going on to play 57 games in war-time "regional" football. He then proved himself a bargain signing, becoming a fixture as a skilful and reliable right-back in the first four post-war seasons. He was one whose League career was disrupted by the war and it is most likely this prevented him having a fruitful international career as well. Played for Chelsea in the 1944–45 Football League (South) Cup Final at Wembley.

WOLFF, Frank (1905–1096) Centre-half

Career Chelsea (August 1905), Not retained (May 1906)
Chelsea details Debut 18.11.05 1 Appearance

	Appearances		Goals	
	FL	FAC	FL	FAC
1905–06	–	1	–	–
Total	–	1	–	–

A member of the Chelsea professional staff during the club's first season. A regular in the reserve team he made only one senior appearance, in an F.A. Cup tie on a day when the recognised first-team were fulfilling a League fixture.

WOOD, Darren (1984 –   ) Full-back

Born Scarborough 9.6.64. Height 5ft 10in, Weight 11st
Career Middlesbrough, Chelsea (September 1984, £50,000)
Honours England Schoolboy International, Full Members' Cup winners' medal 1986
Chelsea details Debut 27.10.84 101(10) Appearances 1 Goal

	Appearances				Goals			
	FL	FAC	LC	FMC	FL	FAC	LC	FMC
1984–85	17(2)	3	–	–	1	–	–	–
1985–86	28	–	6	6	–	–	–	–
1986–87	34(7)	3	3	1(1)	–	–	–	–
Total	79(9)	6	9	7(1)	1	–	–	–

After more than 200 games for Middlesbrough, by the age of 20, he rejoined his former manager at Ayresome Park, Mr John Neal. Immediately winning his place in the first-team, he showed himself to be a competent full-back, or occasional midfield player. Speedy and strong in the tackle, he is a long kicker of the ball and good auxiliary attacker.

WOODLEY, Victor R. (1931–1945) Goalkeeper

Born Cippenham (Bucks) 26.2.11 Died October 1978. Height 6ft, Weight 12st 4lb.
Career Windsor & Eton, Chelsea (Summer 1931), Bath City (December 1945), Derby County, Bath City
Honours England (19 caps), Football League (4 appearances), F.A. Cup winners' medal 1946

Chelsea details Debut 29.8.31 272 Appearances

	Appearances		Goals	
	FL	FAC	FL	FAC
1931–32	7	–	–	–
1932–33	42	1	–	–
1933–34	36	5	–	–
1934–35	15	–	–	–
1935–36	32	5	–	–
1936–37	41	2	–	–
1937–38	40	1	–	–
1938–39	39	6	–	–
Total	252	20	–	–

One of Chelsea's greatest goalkeepers whose sequence of 19 England caps in succession was only terminated by the outbreak of World War II. Pitchforked into the First Division from amateur football within weeks of his arrival at Stamford Bridge, he became a permanent fixture between the posts for the next fifteen years, despite competition from Johnny Jackson, Scotland's international 'keeper – also on the club's staff. Indeed, it was his wonderful consistency and sure handling which kept Chelsea in the First Division in some difficult seasons for most of the 1930s. He played a further 109 unofficial "regional" games during the hostilities before, apparently, moving out to grass with Bath City, and then being summoned to play for Derby County in the early months of 1946. Within weeks he had crowned his long career by keeping goal for them against Charlton Athletic in the 1946 F.A. Cup final, a fairy tale ending to his football days.

VICTOR WOODLEY

| VIVIAN J. WOODWARD | MAX WOOSNAM |

WOODWARD, Vivian J. (1919–1915) Inside/Centre-forward
Born Kennington. Height 5ft 11in, Weight 11st. Died 6.2.54.
Career Corinthians, Tottenham Hotspur (Amateur), Chelsea (Amateur, 1909)
Honours England (23 caps), England Amateur International (43 caps), Football League XI (2 Appearances).
Chelsea details Debut 27.11.09 116 Appearances 34 Goals

	Appearances		Goals	
	FL	FAC	FL	FAC
1909–10	13	2	5	–
1910–11	19	3	6	3
1911–12	14	–	2	–
1912–13	27	3	10	1
1913–14	27	2	4	–
1914–15	6	–	3	–
Total	106	10	30	4

The greatest amateur centre-forward of his time and one of the famous Corinthians. Often described as the "perfect attacker", he was noted for his solo dribbling, besides being a fine distributor of the ball. Equally impressive was his heading and powers of shooting. "A human chain of lightning; the footballer with magic in his boots." Having obtained special leave from the Army to play in the 1915 F.A. Cup final, he sportingly stood down at the last minute to allow Bob Thomson (who had appeared in the earlier rounds of the competition) to take his place. In fact, he never played for Chelsea again as the war ended his brilliant career. Later, he was a Director of Chelsea F.C., from 1922–1930.

WOOSNAM, Max (1914) Centre-half
Born Liverpool 6.9.92 Died 14.7.65
Career Cambridge University, Corinthians, Chelsea (Amateur 1913–14), Manchester City (Amateur)
Honours England (1 cap), England Amateur International
Chelsea details Debut 21.3.14 3 Appearances

	Appearances		Goals	
	FL	FAC	FL	FAC
1913–14	3	–	–	–
Total	3	–	–	–

Played three games in the latter part of the 1913–14 season. A centre-half very much in the old-style amateur tradition, he was a six-footer renowned for his ferocious shoulder-charging, but he also possessed high skills and artistry. He won 4 "blues" at Cambridge and played Davis Cup tennis for Great Britain. A broken leg ended his football career shortly after playing his only full international for England v Wales in 1922.

WOSAHLO, Roger F. (1964–1967) Winger

Born Cambridge 11.9.47. Height 5ft 7½in, Weight 10st 4lb
Career Chelsea (December 1964), Ipswich Town (April 1967), Peterborough United, Ipswich Town
Honours England Schoolboy International
Chelsea details Debut 22.4.67 0(1) Appearances

	Appearances		Goals	
	FL	FAC	FL	FAC
1966–67	0(1)	–	–	–
Total	0(1)	–	–	–

Former apprentice who signed professional forms after being leading goalscorer in Juniors. He was a regular member of the reserve team in 1966–67 but was never able to break through into the senior side.

YOUNG, Allan R. (1961–1969) Centre-half

Born Hornsey 20.1.41 Height 6ft, Weight 12st 10lb
Career Arsenal, Chelsea (November 1961, £6,000), Torquay United (January 1969, £8,000)
Chelsea details Debut 23.12.61 26 Appearances 1 Goal

	Appearances				Goals			
	FL	FAC	LC	FC	FL	FAC	LC	FC
1961–62	6	1	–	–	–	–	–	–
1964–65	–	–	1	–	–	–	–	–
1965–66	13	–	–	3	–	–	–	–
1966–67	1	1	–	–	–	1	–	–
Total	20	2	1	3	–	1	–	–

This tall centre-half gave loyal service to the club for more than seven years, usually in the reserve team, but proving a dependable deputy whenever called up to play in the senior side.

ROGER F. WOSAHLO

ALLAN R. YOUNG